The Roots of Amerta Movement

The Roots of Amerta Movement

An introduction to the movement improvisation of Suprapto Suryodarmo

Lise Lavelle

To

Martin and Thomas

Published in this first edition in 2021 by:
Triarchy Press
Axminster, England

info@triarchypress.net
www.triarchypress.net

A catalogue record for this book is available from the British Library

ISBN: 978-1-911193-53-1
eBook ISBN: 978-1-911193-54-8

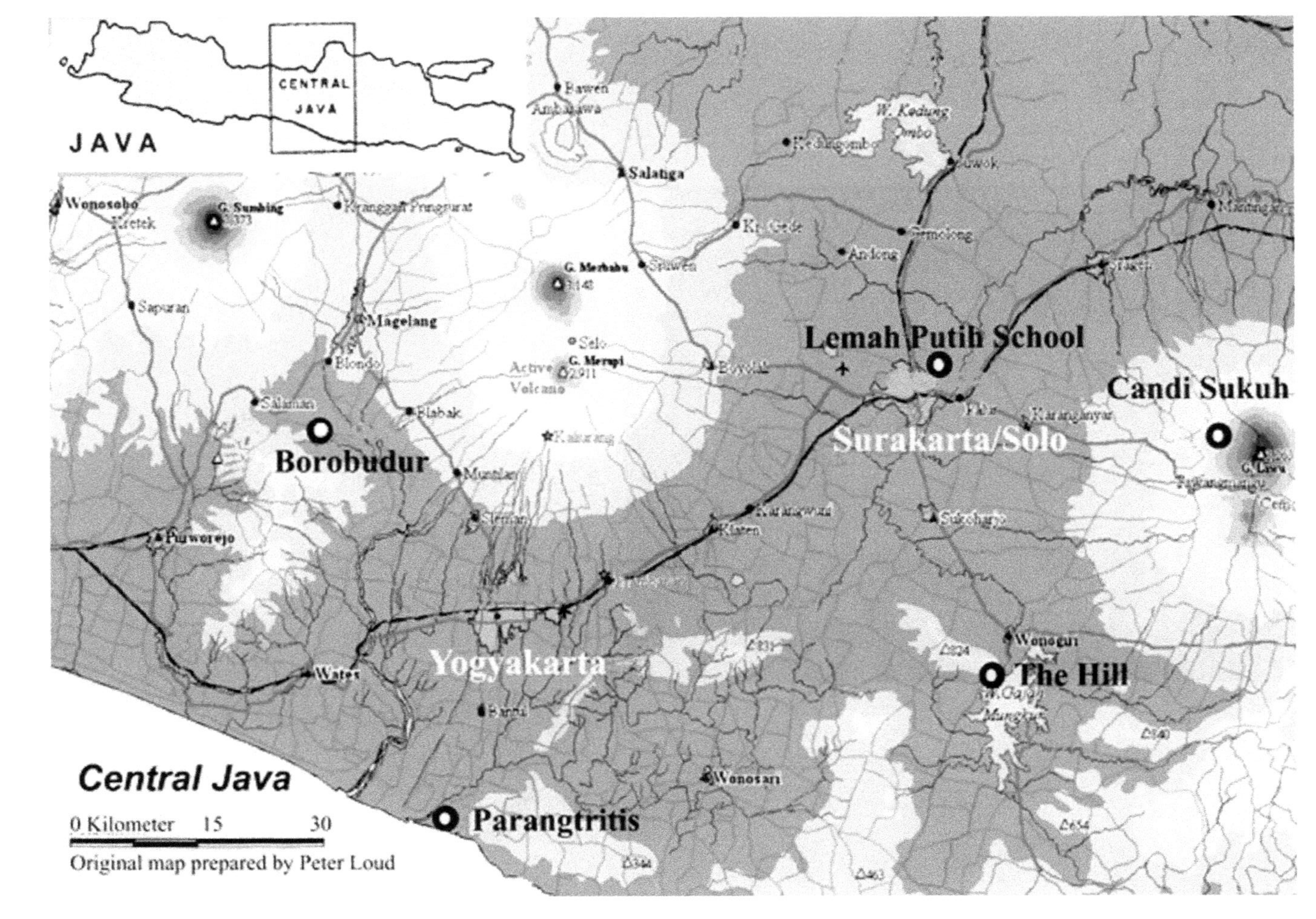
JAVA
CENTRAL JAVA
Lemah Putih School
Candi Sukuh
Surakarta/Solo
Borobudur
The Hill
Yogyakarta
Central Java
Parangtritis
0 Kilometer   15   30
Original map prepared by Peter Loud
Wonosobo
G. Sumbing
Kranggan Pringsurat
Bawen
Ambarawa
Salatiga
Kaloran
Andong
G. Merbabu
Saparan
Magelang
Selo
G. Merapi
Active Volcano
Boyolali
Salaman
Borobudur
Blabak
Muntilan
Sleman
Purworejo
Klaten
Wates
Banul
Wonosari
Wonogiri
Mangku

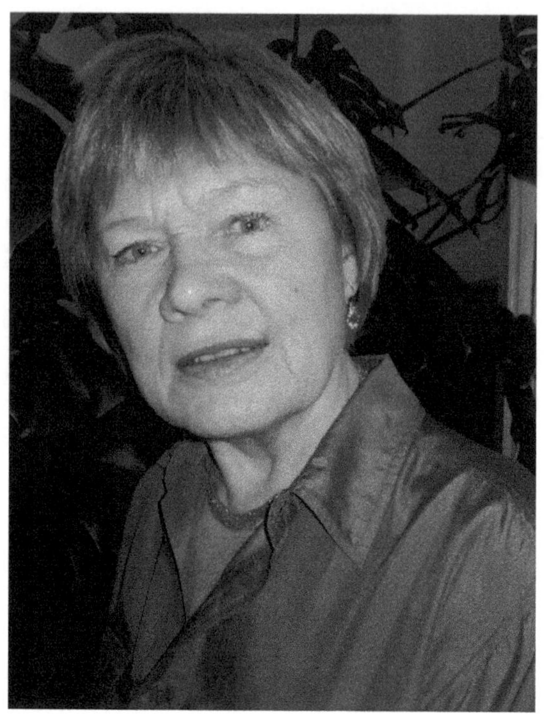

The author

Contents

List of Illustrations

Unless otherwise attributed, all images are taken from *Amerta Movement of Java 1986-1997* (Lavelle, 2006).

List of Tables

Personal names

A note on personal names in Indonesia might be helpful, especially for reading the References.

Indonesians and Javanese people generally have personal names only. This is in contrast to the Western convention of people having a personal name and a family name.

In Indonesia, personal names are cited as they stand. These personal names may consist of one or two names. Examples (related to this book) include: Suprapto Suryodarmo, Bagong Kussudiardjo, Dijah Endraningsih, Jodjana and Koentjaraningrat. In these cases, Endraningsih, Kussudiardjo and Suryodarmo are not family names, but part of the respective person's personal name. In the case of Suprapto Suryodarmo, 'Suprapto' (abbr. Prapto) is his personal name (meaning 'good coming'), given at his birth, and, 'Suryodarmo' (Suryadarma in Javanese writing) is the name he was given when, as an adult, he became a Buddhist. This name means 'the learning' or 'the art of clarity'. Finally, sometimes, there is an initial at the beginning of an Indonesian/Javanese name, for example, F. Hari Mulyatno.

In this book, Indonesian names are rendered as such: thus I will write 'Suprapto Suryodarmo' or the shorter version: 'Prapto'.

In the spoken language of Java, the name Prapto is preceded by a title of respect addressed to an older man, such as 'Pak' (Pak Prapto) or by the Javanese title of address to an older man, a grandfather or leader 'Mbah' (Mbah Prapto).

In the book's references, I follow Western convention when listing Indonesian/Javanese names. Spelling of names follows the latest version used or preferred by that person.

Abbreviations

a.k.a.	Also known as
Indo	Indonesian
ISI	Indonesia's National Arts Institute in Solo (Institut Seni Indonesia, Surakarta), a government, tertiary-level academy (a.k.a. STSI and ASKI Surakarta), started in 1965
Jav	Javanese
Lat	Latin
MAM	Movement Art Meetings, held by Sharing Movement (Amerta Movement practitioners) in Europe from 1999 onwards
MATS	Movement Art Teachers' Society
Old Jav	Old Javanese
PLP	Padepokan Lemah Putih (The Lemah Putih School in Java)
Skr	Sanskrit
TBS	Taman Budaya Surakarta; Central Javanese Art Centre in Solo/Surakarta
UNS	Universitas Sebelas Maret (The University of 11th March), Surakarta; Indonesian State University, Solo

Foreword

It was with great sadness that we heard from Lise's family of her death just as this book was being sent to press.

Lise herself had already had to come to terms with the death of Prapto a year earlier, after the joy of his visit to Denmark in 2019.

Encouraged by Lise's family to continue with publication, we therefore have the unhappy honour of offering *The Roots of Amerta Movement* in loving memory of Lise and her teacher, Prapto.

Rahayu.

Triarchy Press
April 2021

Preface

The Roots of Amerta Movement

This book looks at the early period of Suprapto Suryodarmo's (Prapto's) Amerta Movement in Java, i.e. the period from 1986 to 1997, starting from the establishment of the Amerta Movement School, the Padepokan Lemah Putih.

For this reason, it focuses on Prapto's first approach to Amerta Movement which he called *'Pribadi Art'* or 'Individual Art' or the 'Reality' approach, for personal development and expression. It focuses on what Prapto calls 'nature in the body', i.e. on our relationship to the natural world inside us and outside us, taking its point of departure in the concrete, physical world, as the term 'Reality' approach suggests. This book also briefly presents the second approach to Amerta Movement, 'Messenger Art' or the 'Dream World' approach, aimed at the performing arts and at message-giving beyond the individual mover's personal life.

A long journey

A long journey has led me to write this book and I would like to share a little of that process, to explain some of the book's background, its time horizon and my focus on Amerta Movement rather than on Prapto himself.

The 1980s and 1990s was the period when Prapto established his school in Java. That I came to practise and study Amerta Movement from 1987 on in Java has, first of all, to do with my relationship to Indonesia and the Indonesian people. In 1959, at the age of 17, I sailed to New York from Rotterdam with a bunch of other young kids on a ship with an Indonesian crew to go to school in the USA. The 10-day crossing became quite dramatic because of a violent storm over the Atlantic, a situation which was markedly aggravated for me by acute illness needing surgery. In this connection, the Indonesian crew showed exceptional help and kindness. I will never forget it and I decided to visit their country sometime in the future if at all possible.

It took nearly twenty years before this happened: in 1977-1978 I was on leave from my job as a lecturer in French Language and Literature at teachers' college in Denmark – the Danish government having decided to close down French as a subject at teachers' college as a cost-cutting measure. Hence, when I came to Indonesia in 1977, I was also looking for new ways of making a living. I was ready to change the centre of my life from the head and academic studies, to the physical body and somatic practice. I wanted to return to the bodily, athletic skills, or the creative and musical activities, which had filled my youth. I wanted training like that of a physiotherapist, so as to be able to get a job with which I could travel, having an urge to see the world. I was, moreover, especially interested in living rituals and in religions, not least in Buddhism.

My journey to South-East Asia in 1977 started in Thailand, at the Wat Kiriwong Buddhist temple, where I practised Vipassana meditation, mindfulness and walking meditation with the nuns there and also alone. I really liked the walking meditation, especially practising at night in the huge temple, which never slept. There was only a hard floor to rest on, day and night. This was all part of how I learnt about the way of the Buddha.

After some time, this journey took me to Indonesia, across Sumatra to Java, where I settled in the inland town of Solo/Surakarta. I continued my meditation studies, now practising a Javanese form of 'relaxed meditation' called Sumarah. This Javanese style of meditation, based on relaxation of the whole body, was unlike the focus on the breathing that I had practised in Thailand. I met Prapto at a number of meditation meetings guided by the Sino-Javanese meditation teacher Sudarno Ong.

The background to my settling down in Solo for some time in 1977 was that, when I arrived, I felt that I had 'come home'. This was strange in that the smiling, light-brown Javanese people, Solo's green fertility, the burning sun and expressive language sounds, did not seem to have anything in common with me and Denmark. Also Java, at this time, was under President Suharto's New Order, and not a particularly peaceful place to live or study. On the contrary, this was a politically turbulent time in Indonesia, where the need for change was obvious.

The New Order in Indonesia

While I was pondering all this, at the beginning of 1978, my Indonesian visa ran out and I had to go to Singapore to renew it. On my return to Jakarta, a city of ca. 5 million, a taxi took me from the airport to the centre of town. It was only then that I fully realised the seriousness of the political situation in Indonesia and the huge country's desperate need for a change of government: traffic in Jakarta is normally chaotic and overwhelming, but on this day the streets were empty. Only tanks on 'lions' feet' with soldiers armed with machine guns rolled through the empty streets. The students of Central Java, especially from the university town of Yogyakarta (which is some 60km from Solo, the home town of the Padepokan Lemah Putih) were in revolt against the regime and so were the workers as well as the people at large, accusing their leaders of corruption, nepotism and human rights abuses.

It was nevertheless going to take some 20 years until the situation started to change for the better in Indonesia.

Change

The change I was looking for personally and professionally began when, during the early 1980s in Denmark, I completed a 3-year physical training as a certified teacher of relaxation and movement. I studied at the school of Ingrid Prahm, a former royal ballet dancer and one of the pioneers of 'classical relaxation pedagogy and movement' in Denmark.

Having finished my relaxation and movement education, I started teaching courses of bodily relaxation and movement in adult education as well as giving somatic treatments. I did not see myself as a therapist, but as a healer, defining therapy as a more interventional technique than healing, one where the person treated is seen from a pathological view, i.e. as a patient, a sick person, and where the sickness is in focus. By contrast, being a healer, to me, meant centring on the whole person and helping restore wholeness and the natural life force in the body of the person under treatment through physical touch. This corresponded to the ideas of Ingrid Prahm, as I understood them. Prapto called this kind of process, 'blossoming', seeing it in terms of nature, or 'nature in the body' as he called our relationship to our bodily instincts, reflexes and sensations, especially those not under the control of the willed nervous system.

My training as a relaxation and movement teacher became an important basis for starting the courses in Amerta Movement with Prapto in Java from 1987 on. Being interested in Javanese performing arts, especially in Classical Javanese Dance, in 1986 I started taking private dance lessons from Prapto's daughter, Melati Suryodarmo, a practice I continued after Melati left Java, with teachers from the Indonesian National Arts Institute in Solo. As a result, I later discovered rules within Amerta Movement which I believe have a background in Javanese dance: for example, the Amerta practitioner, when moving in and through a space, has to look at the moving part of her/his body, and not focus vaguely out into space. In saying this, I do not mean to suggest that Amerta Movement is not a unique and personal creation pioneered by Prapto.

Amerta Movement practice with Prapto and continued political unrest

By 1998, with unrest and uproar because of the financial crisis in Asia, I had just managed to open negotiations with people in Bonoroto, the neighbouring village to Prapto's Plesungan Mojosongo village, to form an NGO. My aim was to create an exchange between the Danish Folk High Schools and a traditional Javanese village art project, called the Bonoroto Project. The Bonoroto Project had been started by the Javanese artists, F. Hari Mulyatno and Sri Setyo Asih, dancers and lecturers at Indonesia's National Arts Institute in Solo (ISI) and used art as a tool to help rice-growing peasants who had lost their land to be trained in a new skill. But because of the political situation, the exchange with the Danish Folk High Schools had to be abandoned. Things were turbulent in Java during 1997 and 1998, not least because of fierce, carnival-like election campaigns with crowds of young people, dressed in colourful clothes, rushing on their motor bikes in great numbers through the streets of Solo.

The tense situation came to a climax on 14-15 May with the arson and looting of Solo, where much of the town burnt down and many people were injured or killed.

President Suharto resigned on 21st May, 1998, which meant that 31 years of the 'New Order' in Indonesia had come to an end. Today, the former mayor of Solo known as Jokowi, President of Indonesia since 2014, is a trustworthy, non-corrupt, popular president, at the head of the world's third biggest democracy. With Jokowi, for the first time, a civilian president was installed in Indonesia.

From programmed to free, non-stylised, improvisational movement

Having changed from the academic to the somatic field of bodily movement I retrieved my right element, connecting with the physical and athletic activities – as well as with the creative skills – of my childhood and youth. Prapto's courses, moreover, were a true gift, bringing me into complete harmony with my natural urge for movement expression, starting me not only on the road of movement in all its aspects, but – and this is the point – these courses started me on free, non-stylised improvisational movement, on somatic movement art and performance. They started me onto a free, creative process crucial to the kind of person I am. My creativity is dependent on freedom from preconceived rules and demands. When exploring unknown 'lands' movement-wise, I need to be free to create my own personal movement expression or movement-dance. In this way, I was free, and so were my co-practitioners in the sense that a child is free to move and to play. Until then my movement, as learnt at my school in Denmark, mostly consisted of choreographed series of movements, inspired and even based physically on Western dance traditions like ballet or modern dance, and intended to be aesthetically pleasing.

Nevertheless, I also continued to take private lessons in classical Javanese dance, which gave me form and tradition, an opposite pole or a complement to the non-stylised improvisational freedom of Amerta Movement. I was also involved in several projects in Java apart from Amerta Movement, including the Bonoroto project.

Ritual

To participate in Prapto's courses during that period felt to me like being part of a large, ongoing ritual* or *rite de passage*, helping me to pass from one situation or one development state to another. This also felt like being inside a living story or a big book, which was 'telling me': the practice and natural environment gave me a feeling of complete fullness and of being alive in every cell of my body.

Moving in the natural environment of Java, my condition of body-mind-spirit was slightly dilated, a state well-known from another bodily movement approach: the work of Eugenio Barba, director of Odin Teatret in Holstebro, Denmark. In spite of this slightly dilated condition of body-mind-spirit, I was, nevertheless, solidly grounded in my physical body with a felt contact to the practice area, to other practitioners and to the whole environment.

Practising with Prapto, we also learnt about Javanese culture in a way that few foreigners do. Prapto would sometimes take us to performances, for example, at the Central Javanese Art Centre (TBS) or the neighbouring campus of Solo's ISI where a performance was almost always taking place. He might also take us, in our free time, to cultural events, like a wedding or local concert, or to an art gallery, etc.

Becoming a performing artist

In short, through practising Amerta Movement with Prapto in Java, I became an artist. This marked a positive step on top of, or beyond, my training as a Danish relaxation and movement teacher. During this period in Java, I quickly developed into being an actively performing artist and choreographer. My artistic activities were all based on Amerta Movement improvisation and on the so-called crystallisation-performances that concluded the courses. Very soon, learning from these crystallisation-performances, I began creating my own independent projects:

At first, I 'performed myself', i.e. my being in this life, so to speak, in a movement project where I was accompanied by a Javanese puppeteer singing and playing the flute. This performance took place in a green valley still used by the local village people among other things for taking their animals to the river. This valley was situated at the easternmost part of the Padepokan Lemah Putih. Practising alone in the valley for months in a row, as I did, with the

---

* Many specialised or unfamiliar terms (marked with an asterisk the first time they appear) are explained in more detail later in the book. For a quick definition, see the Glossary.

Javanese village people, their children and animals, including the big white cows grazing there, as my only companions day in and day out, was really an act of fieldwork and an everlasting positive experience.

My solo performance in the valley, called 'A Woman gets her Face', was about learning to face the world as one is, i.e. based on one's 'true being', as Prapto would say, or on one's true self. This performance is described in the book *Embodied Lives*. Very soon I also engaged in collaborating and performing with Javanese dance- and theatre-artists in other performances.

Healing Theatre and Tari Sari

Working with Prapto and in the multi-religious, multi-cultural and multi-artistic atmosphere of Solo of that time was utterly fulfilling. Moreover, Amerta practice with Prapto in Java is also how I came to co-found a Healing Theatre.

In 1988, while taking a communication course with Prapto, I formed a 'group' with a German actor. We made our crystallisation-performance at the end of the course at the huge stage of the TBS, and gave it the title, 'Can I speak to you?'. It was a collaboration between me as a healer by profession, and the German as an actor by profession. Back in Europe at the end of 1988 we co-founded, with others, the Healing Theatre of Cologne – a vision based on a synthesis of healing, i.e. the idea of wholeness and theatrical art, dance and free movement.

A few years later, our ways parted and the Healing Theatre of Cologne continued for many years before it gave way to 'Schule der Bewegung' (The Movement School), largely based on Prapto's Amerta Movement. In Denmark, I continued my own movement work and classes with the title 'The Dance of Life and Healing Theatre', which later became 'Embodyment: Dance of Release and Transformation'. This was a synthesis of Amerta Movement, of healing according to classical Danish relaxation* pedagogy and movement, of Asian movement forms like Chinese Qi Gong and Tai Chi and, finally, a Jungian approach to personal development and creativity, drawing on my 5 years study of Jungian psychology in my youth. In 1997, I opened a private school of movement in Copenhagen with the Indonesian name Tari Sari (The Essence of Dance). It centred on my personal concept and practice of Amerta Movement, which I taught at the Tari Sari School.

Returning to academia

After some time teaching day-school classes of Amerta Movement, at the turn of the century, I went back to university. This time it was to Lund University in Sweden, which housed the expertise I needed with the largest Indonesian language faculty outside The Netherlands at the time. I wanted to try to better understand Prapto's work with Amerta Movement by studying in a systematic manner the civilisation from where he and Amerta Movement come.

Although already an experienced academic in French, I started all over again in Asian studies, the end being a PhD. Before this I studied the Indonesian language and literature, specialising in Javanese for my dissertation. These studies, together with my earlier meetings with the Indonesian people and culture, may explain my focus in this book on Amerta Movement and Java, rather than on the person of Prapto, the creator of Amerta Movement, but himself also a product of Java. Finally, the process leading to my PhD in 2006 took me to Java for several years of fieldwork.

Prapto in Denmark

In 1992 and 1993 I arranged two workshops for Prapto in Denmark. The first was held in June 1992 for three days at the 'Dramaskolen' (The Drama School), Copenhagen. The second took place over ten days in 1993 and was co-sponsored by the Danish Foreign Ministry Department DANIDA. It received an official visit by the cultural attaché from the Indonesian Embassy in Denmark. After the course Prapto was officially received by the Indonesian ambassador to Denmark.

In 2019 I had the joy of witnessing Prapto's return to Denmark after 26 years for two programmes. For the first, in June 2019, Prapto taught workshops on the island of Fyn starting, the first day, at Præstens Skov (the 'Forest of the Priest'), situated on the sea near the town of Svendborg. On the second day his class took place at the megalithic sites of Lindeskov, Gl. Hestehave, also near Svendborg, where there are dolmens dating back to ca. 3,500 BCE. On the third day, the group went back to Præstens Skov.

One of the ideas of practising at those sites was to participate in the worldwide celebration of megalithic sites, held on 5 July, 2019. The Svendborg and Hestehave, Lindeskov workshops were set up by Jacob Rubinovitz, a long-term student of Prapto in Java, and a teacher of Messenger Art (the second approach to Amerta Movement).

Prapto's second programme in Denmark in July 2019 took place in Aarhus, Jutland, the second biggest town in Denmark, where he performed in an intercultural performance hosted by the Danish Contemporary Art Museum, ARoS and by the Danish musician, Jonas Stampe, who also participated in the performance, as did Pauline Lumholt, an Inuit drum dancer/performer from Greenland and Hans Oldau Krull, a visual artist from Denmark.

Post scriptum

Amerta Movement is a living, ever-changing, ever-developing movement and style of life, not least because its founder Prapto, who died in December 2019, was an ever-changing, endlessly creative person. That is why the Amerta Movement we experience today seems to be or really is very different from the early period between 1986 and 1997, treated here.

With this book, covering the 1986-1997 Amerta Movement period in Java, my intention is to try to clarify the rationale of what we Amerta Movers, at the end of the 20th century, were doing in Java moving with Prapto, what his thinking was and how things progressed from one course to another. I hope that this book will be helpful to read in that sense. I also hope that readers who have previously studied with Prapto in Java, will be transported back to Indonesia. And if you are a 'new' practitioner, studying with one of Prapto's teachers, that you will see Amerta Movement anew. Through a new 'regard' on Amerta Movement based on you as a human being in combination with your profession or hobby, you may create new movement arts – because life goes on.

Happy reading!

Lise Lavelle
Copenhagen, September 2020

PART I: The Movement

Chapter 1

Introduction to Amerta Movement

Amerta Movement is a contemporary, non-stylised form of free movement improvisation based on our movements in everyday life: for example, the way we move when doing our daily chores or the way children move when they're playing. Throughout the book, whenever I talk about 'movement', or 'movement improvisation', I am referring to this kind of non-stylised, free movement.

Amerta Movement originates in Indonesia, where it was created by the Central Javanese performance artist, movement instructor, philosopher and Theravada* Buddhist, Suprapto Suryodarmo (1945-2019), usually referred to by his short name, Prapto. Amerta Movement is practised by a wide range of people, around the world, from all walks of life.

This book deals with the early period, the roots, of Amerta Movement in Java covering the years from the mid-1980s to the end of 1997. Many of the ideas and practices described here have subsequently evolved or been expressed differently by Prapto, but the descriptions here are very closely based on Prapto's teaching at that time. That is the period when Prapto created his own movement school in Java, the Padepokan Lemah Putih, also referred to as the Lemah Putih School or the Lemah Putih Garden, in the northern outskirts of the Central Javanese city of Solo (also known as Surakarta). There, in the mid-1980s, he started to publish a yearly programme in English and to receive students, mostly from abroad, on his movement courses.

This book focuses particularly on the approach to Amerta Movement called *Pribadi Art** or Individual Art. *Pribadi Art* is based on personal development and was the first approach taken by Prapto. It also introduces the approach developed later by Prapto, which he called Messenger Art*. Messenger Art, unlike *Pribadi Art*, uses movement improvisation as a language for performance art, installations and new ritual art*.

Amerta Movement is both a theoretical approach and a movement practice designed to help us engage in 'a dialogue with life'* through our physical

---

* Many specialised or unfamiliar terms (marked with an asterisk the first time they appear) are explained in more detail later in the book. For a quick definition, see the Glossary.

movement. The intention is to facilitate our development as individuals and for practitioners to gain understanding, to develop their potential and resources and to build a movement vocabulary and a movement language comparable to our spoken language.

In *Pribadi Art*, the physical body is used as an instrument for exploring our identity, our inner and outer nature, self-expression, relationships, communication, the spiritual or sacred dimension of life, as well as for exploring our potential for artistic expression.

The name Amerta means, in old Javanese and deriving from Sanskrit *amrit*, 'the nectar of life' (in the sense of an elixir of life or of immortality). It refers to the widespread Javanese belief that human life has a spiritual origin, that it comes from – and returns to – an everlasting living essence. 'Movement' refers to dance or physical or bodily movement, specifically as in free, non-stylised, improvisational movement.

For the individual practising Amerta Movement, this approach to life involves asking questions such as: 'Who am I?' 'Where do I come from?' and 'Where am I going?' In Prapto's terms, Amerta Movement "is not only a language for communication, but also an expression of being"; that is to say, it is an expression of one's self and of one's existence in the world. Both aspects – beingness and expressive communication through bodily movement – are involved at the same time when practising Amerta Movement, i.e. the attention is turned both towards the inner world and towards the world outside. There has to be a balance between the attention given to these inner and outer worlds.

A feature of Amerta Movement is that it combines a dynamic physical movement practice with awareness and the cultivation of 'attitudes'; that is to say with a training of the mind, feelings and body as in meditation or in mindfulness training. It does so through the application of a consciousness technique called 'reading'* which is specific to Amerta Movement, and which is covered in Chapter 4. As a result of the way that it combines these different approaches, the practice of Amerta Movement is both an art and a training for life.

Site-specific and person-specific movement

Amerta Movement is a somatic practice. It has to be felt in one's body. As a non-stylised approach to movement, it embraces free, spontaneous, improvised movements without a fixed form or choreography – movements such as walking, sitting, standing, running, stopping, breathing, sensing, feeling, seeing, hearing, touching and so on, as well as one's more subtle, inner sense of awareness. It is person-specific and site-specific: it is rooted in what emerges from within each of us, (person-specific) and it is intended to be practised in a well-defined space in nature (site-specific). The movement originates in our individual dialogue (exchange of input and impulses) with the site of practice, as well as with co-practitioners and our whole environment. Person-specific also refers to the fact that the movement's physical expressions or gestures are shaped individually by each practitioner. Hence, Amerta Movement is a personal 'language through movement', based on our personal perception of our condition and of our surroundings. There is very little structure in the practice: the practitioner may begin for example by lying down on the ground in order to rest and to feel their body and breathing. This position allows us to 'let go' and to 'listen' to our body (the whole being). We do this through an inner feeling or rasa*. Rasa is a non-intellectual phenomenon comparable to the way we listen to music. More precisely, it is a tool whereby we receive or experience all aspects of life including those beyond our conscious mind and five senses. In this way, our whole nervous system wakes up. This allows us to acquire awareness and a heightened sensitivity to our own body.

Human, Sacred and Nature

The individual student's practice is always seen not only in relation to their whole being but also in relation to the wholeness of life and society, as expressed in the three fields: Human, Sacred and Nature.

Each field is connected to an overall theme: Human is connected to the overall theme of Physical/Bodily expression; Sacred is connected to the theme of Prayer; and Nature is connected to the theme of Purification*. This means that the practice can be carried out in three ways: based on the physicality of the body as a cultural expression (Human); based on an attitude of prayer, bowing to life as a divine power (Sacred); or based on purification (Nature).

1. **Human.** This field represents the human being, based on human values in a modern sense, where the human being is seen as a creature in its own right, with its own characteristics. This is distinct from the traditional Javanese outlook on life, still found at the end of the 20th century, where the human being was not generally seen, in traditional Java, as a creature in its own right, but as half animal and half god. There was no such thing as a society or a culture based on humanistic values, never mind democratic values. Within Amerta Movement, 'Human' is expressed as physical/bodily movement in the present moment based on an attitude of human creativity or on an attitude of social and political engagement and activity.

2. **Sacred**. This field represents the human being seen as part of the divine. It is expressed through physical/bodily movement based on an attitude of prayer. (Especially in the early years, Prapto used the term 'Temple'. I shall use 'Sacred' where possible, as Amerta Movement is practised by people from all over the world with different religious beliefs).

3. **Nature**. This field represents the human being as part of nature, part of organic, animal life, and is expressed through physical/bodily movement based on an attitude of purification. In Amerta Movement, purification is seen both in terms of natural bodily functions, as when our body is cleaned by the blood circulating through it, and also refers to how one may clear one's body, one's mind or one's nature through an enhanced awareness, as in meditation. In this way, we become aware of the condition of our body, as well as of thoughts, feelings and emotions, and we become aware of our perceptions of our surroundings. What are these like? Are they 'biased'? Through 'the light', the clarity of the awareness process, practitioners may purify themselves, purify their nature, their spontaneous way of looking at things and dealing with things and other people. They may discover misunderstandings in and about their perceptions and become aware of prejudices as well as of bodily and psychic tensions that hinder a non-attached outlook on life, during their movement practice. Purification, like healing, is not a goal in itself in Amerta Movement. Practitioners need purification, not because they are bad, but because they have accumulated, in the course of their lives, many attitudes that may not be needed any more. They can release this accumulated material, purify themselves, learn the lessons contained within these experiences and thereby hopefully find a better and a clearer quality of being in the present moment.

Square, Circle and Oval

Each of the three fields of Human, Sacred and Nature was also linked to a specific physical space, reflecting actual spaces in the Lemah Putih School's garden landscape when this was first constructed in the 1980s and 1990s.

Human is related to the square (a space with a square or rectangular form), which facilitates 'creation in reflection', according to Prapto.

Sacred is related to the circle, which facilitates 'bowing in praying'.

Nature is related to the oval, which facilitates 'purification in circulation'.

Square

Practice in the square space relates to physicality and facilitates the movement quality of 'creation in reflection' – i.e. it facilitates a creative movement piece based on the physicality of the body forming a kind of a 'movement dance' or a 'dance by movement'. This is based on reflective movement, i.e. on my looking inwards, finding myself in the inner world and then translating that inner world, those inner stirrings, into movement in the outside world, while at the same time also paying attention to impressions and input received from outside.

Circle

Practice in the circle space relates to spirituality, the sacred, to ritual and prayer and it facilitates the movement quality of 'bowing in praying' – i.e. practising movement with an attitude of respect for life, an attitude of prayer and of bowing to life as a divine power or 'bowing to god'. It involves a spiritual attitude to life in which new rituals are created. These may include creating a vocabulary or special movement language expressing or embodying the sacred.

Oval

Practice in the oval space relates to purification and facilitates the movement quality of 'purification in circulation'. It does so through my being aware of nature's circulation inside me, as well as in nature outside.

Field	Human	Sacred	Nature
Overall theme	Physical/Bodily Expression	Prayer. The spiritual, god, the source of life.	Purification through awareness of inside/outside
Specific space	Square	Circle	Oval
Movement quality	Creation in Reflection	Bowing in Praying	Purification in Circulation

The Fields: Human, Sacred and Nature

Application

As a physical/bodily technique comparable to verbal communication, Amerta Movement can be applied in many ways.

Movement in the Human field may be applied to movement teaching and movement art, including installations, as well as to performance art, drama, music, singing and acting. It may also be applied to the creation of a vocabulary or movement language for communication and for different cultural, social and political purposes including street art, social campaigns and petitions (for example, petitions for clean drinking water).

Movement in the Sacred field may be applied to the area of spiritual expression, including the creation of new rituals. It can also take the form of performances and prayers for the preservation of temples and shrines, as well to help the victims of attacks and disasters, refugees and so on.

Movement in the Nature field may be applied to health, healing, bodywork, psychoanalysis and psychotherapy. It uses processes of purification of one's body and is based on awareness of one's body and being.

The Roots of Amerta Movement

Asian influences are evident in Amerta Movement through Prapto's background as an Indonesian who grew up in the ancient cultural centre of Solo, Central Java, influenced by *kejawen**, the traditional Javanese outlook on life, (sometimes called Javanism), and the Central Javanese multi-ethnic, multi-spiritual/religious and multi-cultural society with its meditation practices and highly-developed arts. Prapto was much influenced by *kejawen* spirituality and mystical thinking, not least as his father would take him, as a child, to meditate in natural environments, temples and other sacred places. Through Prapto, Amerta Movement has also been influenced by Theravada Buddhism as this has developed in Java, especially by *Vipassana,* a form of Theravada Buddhist insight meditation (mindfulness).

I will first look at *kejawen,* the traditional Javanese outlook on life. According to the Dutch anthropologist Niels Mulder, *kejawen* harks back to the Hindu-Buddhist period* of Javanese history. It constitutes "a cosmology and a mythology, a set of essentially mystical conceptions that give rise to a Javanese anthropology" (Mulder, 1994). Furthermore, "*kejawen* is a philosophy, a system of thought complete in itself with principles for the conduct of life" (*ibid*).

According to Mulder, god in Java has two aspects: one is god as understood in the more transcendental conceptions of the modern monotheistic religions such as Islam and Christianity (*Allah* or *Tuhan* in Indonesian). The second is god as a non-personal, immanent and omnipresent part of nature, who can be felt in one's inner being, in one's heart and who is referred to in numerous ways, such as, 'god who is all in one', 'life as a divine principle', 'the totality of existence', 'the 'numinous', or 'the source of life'. (Mulder, 1994: 8-9).

Traditionally, Central Java abounds in mystical movements and in different styles of meditation practice. People in Central Java would traditionally, irrespective of their religion, also belong to a meditation group or a mystical group (Mulder, 1994: 2,3). They might practise both a modern religion like Islam and Christianity as well as traditional Javanese mysticism.

Dancers traditionally meditate in Central Java, or are in a state of enhanced awareness and sensitivity while dancing. They express this by placing their hand on their heart, saying, "I dance with feeling (*rasa*)" meaning that they dance in a state of inner meditative awareness and sensitivity, i.e. with an open heart.

As an adult, Prapto joined the Sumarah* meditation movement which is still a living practice in Java. In Sumarah, people of different religions meditate together. Sumarah meditation practice was considered more modern than many other mystical groups in Java, mainly because Sumarah allows the meditator, at least potentially, to connect directly to the highest being/god, without necessarily having to pass through the guide (*pamong*)*, or through a hierarchy of *devas** or spirits, as is seen in other forms of meditation in Java.

To be relaxed is a central point in Sumarah meditation. The meditator normally sits on a chair while meditating or in any way that is comfortable and reduces tension. It is essential not only to relax the body, but also the mind and feelings. This relaxed attitude to meditation within Sumarah as well as in Amerta Movement when practising free moment, contrasts in Java with 'concentration meditation', where the meditator focuses or concentrates on a specific point inside or outside themselves or on a specific part of or point in their body, such as on a *chakra**.

In Sumarah, concentration during meditation is thought to lead to the meditator being tense, whereas a relaxed attitude of body, mind and spirit allows the meditator to be aware of their whole body simultaneously in a relaxed way – we can say that the whole body forms the *mantra* of the meditation. The Sumarah meditator is said, moreover, to 'surrender to life', i.e. to accept life and also to accept the meditation process – as these processes unfold – in the sense of acknowledging what is happening in their lives and acknowledging what is happening inside themselves during the meditation: what kind of sensations, feelings and thoughts arise? Can they let go and just be aware? Whether the process is 'nice or not nice' is not important: what matters is to be aware. Prapto often referred to the practice and guidance he received from his Sumarah meditation teacher (*pamong*), Sudarno Ong*, who, unlike most Sumarah members and pamongs, was a Theravada Buddhist and a vegetarian. Sudarno Ong was also much sought out by Westerners in Java for his systematic style of guiding meditation and for his stories used as a teaching method illustrating the meditation process, as well as for his simple style.

The Walking Buddha

A key idea for Prapto was that the Buddha walked for much of his life, even though he is usually portrayed in a sitting position. Prapto used the walking Buddha to show the importance of walking. He saw walking both in a physical sense as movement and in a symbolic sense as representing change. Hence moving in Amerta Movement, as well as meaning physical movement, also refers to the primacy of movement in life. It indicates that movement, not a static condition, and movement in the sense of a willingness to change and develop, underlies everything in life. Life is flux. Prapto's use of the word 'walking' also refers to the fact that the Buddha did more than walk in a physical sense. His wanderings were also journeys full of lessons and insights. So Prapto was also referring to traditional Javanese

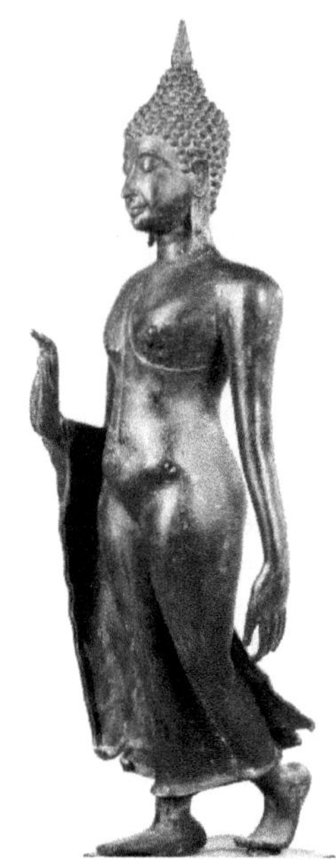

Sukhothai Walking Buddha

'walking retreats' (*laku*)*, where people walk in the mountains, go on pilgrimages to holy sites, as well as meditating and performing ascetic exercises (*tapa*) to improve themselves and their attitudes to life. This double meaning of 'walking', comprising a physical sense and a symbolic sense, is part of traditional Javanese spiritual and mystic practices. Walking is also an important element of Amerta Movement, but Amerta Movement has no ascetic exercises.

Suprapto Suryodarmo

Beginning in 1970, Prapto explored and developed non-stylised, free, improvised, bodily movement in a wide range of conditions. He practised in temples, in the mountains, the forest, by the ocean, at the marketplace and in the studio, exploring movements like walking, crawling, sitting, lying, rolling, jumping, running, breathing and stopping to feel one's condition or to check one's position and, one's environment. In developing Amerta Movement, he combined the naturalness of everyday movements, as described above, with awareness, i.e. with a heightened consciousness or a heightened sensitivity and with a cultivation of our attitudes to life, i.e. our attitude to self, to the environment and to other practitioners. The latter may be described as processes of sensitising the body, mind and feelings or the whole body of the individual student through the movement practice. Prapto tried to create a bridge between the practitioner's inner self and the outer, visible self, between the traditional and the modern, between the village and the wider world, between the parochial and the cosmopolitan, between Javanese and Indonesian/Asian, and between Indonesia and the West. In so doing, he tried not to lose contact with traditional Javanese values based on life in an agricultural environment where respect for nature and one's ancestors prevails. This society is characterised by cultural, ethnic and religious plurality. Because Prapto was inspired by *kejawen*, he maintained that life originates in a spiritual source to which it returns and he talked about the 'wheel' of life and about life as flux. He also said that there is an inseparable connection between humans, nature and god/the spiritual or sacred dimension of life. Moreover, through Amerta Movement, Prapto tried to lift the process of modern daily life from a prosaic material level to a spiritual one, as expressed in traditional Javanese philosophy on the origin and destination of life. (Ramelan, 1995: 76)

Prapto's inspiration also came from the Javanese martial arts, *pencak silat*, and from the classical forms of Javanese dance and performing arts. However, the influence did *not* come from the physical forms/positions of classical Javanese dance and performing arts, especially since Amerta Movement, in contrast to Javanese dance with its highly stylised positions, originates in daily life, non-stylised and so-called natural movement. The influence has come in the form of the spiritual, religious and ritual qualities, which formerly characterised these movement arts in Java, as well as from the rituals formerly inherent in the Javanese lifestyle.

Human Spirituality/the Sacred and Nature

To understand Amerta Movement, it is essential to understand Prapto's view of the three fields of Human, the Sacred and Nature in more detail.

Human: In Amerta Movement human beings are seen as beings in their own right. Nevertheless, according to Prapto the human being is also part of nature, as well as part of god/the sacred, and part of society.

Also, according to Prapto, the human being is not placed above nature, as is often seen in the West, because of Christian influence and the dualism between body and mind still prominent in Christian thinking.

According to Amerta Movement, the human condition is not static for the individual. Instead, it is a striving for a dynamic cultural and ecological balance between an individual and their society, the spiritual dimension of their life in the form of the Sacred and their Nature, inside and outside.

Hence, our process of growth and blossoming as human beings has to be seen in the context of the whole of life, since the individual is part of the natural world, the spiritual/sacred world, and part of society. This process of growth and blossoming has to proceed in a way that respects and benefits the natural and the spiritual world and society. Prapto sought to show that the position of the human being within creation, according to Amerta Movement, is 'a being among others' rather than being placed above nature, which, according to Prapto, cuts the human being off from a closeness with nature.

Sacred: Prapto was a Theravada Buddhist. In that tradition, there is no god. As a Javanese, however, Prapto also seemed to believe in the 'totality of existence' as something sacred and in 'life as a divine principle'. He believed in a concept of god that seems to comprise 'nature', life, 'reality', 'being' and 'inner being'.

Prapto's view was ambivalent: he saw nature as sacred, as animated by divine forces in the more traditional Javanese sense, as well as stressing that he saw god as a power that comes to nature from above and illuminates nature. Hence, according to Prapto, god is above nature.[3] (This is one of several areas where Prapto's view became less 'hierarchical' subsequently, but this accurately represents his views in the 1980s and 90s.)

Nature: The concept of nature in Amerta Movement has been inspired by *kejawen*, according to which, nature's elements represent qualities, attitudes or potentials that are present in every human being. Hence, elements that exist in nature/the universe (macrocosm) also exist in human beings (microcosm) (Mulder, 1994: 20). Human beings are driven by the same forces as the elements of nature. Prapto used this idea not as a religious instruction but as a pedagogical device to inspire or help students to understand their process and to develop; he also used it to describe our ways of relating to life, to society and to each other. He talked, for example, about sky and earth as representing the mind and the body respectively and as metaphors for feelings and for describing what takes place inside each of us when we practise movement. He maintained that we can grow as human beings by becoming more aware not only of each other and of society, but also of nature and of the spiritual/sacred dimension of life. He encouraged students to observe the natural elements, suggesting that we can study how to grow an attitude like that of the moon, for

---

[3] Unless otherwise attributed, all the claims I make about Prapto's ideas and beliefs and all statements of his that I quote are taken from the field notes I made in Java during the period in question whilst studying with Prapto and during the research for my PhD. The notes cover his teaching to different groups and interviews I conducted with him.

example, by observing the moon, and the attitude of the water by observing the element of water, and so on.

In summary, our process of growth in Amerta Movement must always be seen in the context of the whole of life. We need to strive for a dynamic balance between an individual, society, nature and the spiritual/the sacred. Practitioners of Amerta Movement, however, are free to believe in god or not, and to cultivate or not, nature, life, reality and their 'being' or 'inner being' as divine creations.

Java and the West

While Amerta Movement is rooted in the Javanese soil and outlook on life, during the early period of Amerta Movement, i.e. during the 1980s and 1990s, people who studied with Prapto in Java at the Padepokan Lemah Putih mostly came from outside Indonesia. They would often share a modern, global mindset, which was not so common in Central Java at that time.

During this early period, many locals in Java resented Prapto's ideas of development and modernisation, seeing him apparently making money from an approach that was inspired by the traditional arts and mystic practices which belonged, as they saw it, to the collective heritage and not to an individual. And the general opinion was that the traditional arts are sacred – they should not be touched or changed by an individual on his own initiative. Nevertheless, especially since the turn of the century, as modernity and globalisation have been felt very clearly in Central Java, this attitude has changed. As a result, the early resentment towards Prapto and Amerta Movement has been replaced by a more enthusiastic response to his initiatives and creations. A sense of pride and vital interest started to emerge among younger people towards Prapto's work, his non-stylised movement and his new performing arts initiatives, which, though being a renewal and representing a constantly developing work, were rooted in traditional values. People in Java are now usually impressed by Prapto's success in teaching people from overseas, often highly educated ones.

Given that the majority of students and practitioners of Amerta Movement, both then and now, are not Indonesian, a cultural dialogue between Java and other parts of the world is almost built into Amerta Movement. This intercultural dialogue is a hallmark and strength of Amerta Movement.

The Javanese society in which Prapto grew up and created the Padepokan Lemah Putih is characterised by the cultivation of feeling, intuition and instinct, as well by an attitude of patience and acceptance. It is also a society where communal life is given priority over the life of the autonomous individual. Furthermore, in Java, harmony and balance are felt to be essential.

Harmony, in the sense of keeping one's balance and proper place in life, is crucial. This is true in relation to society, family and one's personal life. Everything and everyone has their place in society and in the family, both of which are hierarchically ordered. Not upsetting this order is important – the traditional culture being geared more towards preventing than resolving conflict. Hence, being too emotional or expressing oneself too directly is not advised; even too much thinking may seem strange to the Javanese.

Finally, Javanese culture, like Amerta Movement, is characterised by a holistic and ecological approach. There is no dichotomy between mind and body or soul and body. At the level of the practice, this means that movement starts from the whole person. Moreover, our inner and outer worlds are seen as a continuum. Thus, the practitioner and the movements expressed are part of the environment and vice versa.

In summary, in Amerta Movement, mind and body cannot be separated; in other words, movement, as well as dance, 'dance-movement' and 'movement-dance' cannot be separated from thinking, from ethics* or from cognition; nor can they be separated from our physical surroundings. I am seen as part of the environment, which also means that I am part of the group of people moving with me and part of the site where I am moving, just as they are part of me. I am understood to be interconnected not only with the surrounding society but also with nature and the spiritual/the sacred world, and so are my movements. My movements are influenced in their form and content by my surroundings, i.e. by the whole environment, including the practice site and by my co-practitioners, by their being there, as well as by their way of moving. In the same way, my co-practitioners and my surroundings are influenced by me as, for example, when I step on the ground – "maybe the grass needs exactly that pressure", Prapto used to say – or when I touch a fellow being, engage in a movement dialogue, a movement exchange with a co-practitioner, or when I 'construct the space' with my movements and make it come alive. I am a part of it all and it all is part of me.

Because attitudes, approaches and perceptions differ from one culture to another, they can be difficult to 'translate'. In Amerta Movement our attitude and approach to, and perception of, for example, gender and bodywork is crucial, because Amerta Movement is a personally founded bodily movement. So communication, 'translation' and discussion of different cultural approaches, attitudes and perceptions often take place as part of the practice.

When, for example, Central Javanese concepts are translated into Western ones, the boundaries tend not to match exactly. This is clearly seen in the case of the traditionally trained Javanese dance theatre artist, who is both a skilled dancer and actor. Similarly, art is not a discipline in its own right in Central

Java and often forms part of broader, traditional religious ceremonies and social festivities. Likewise, many Central Javanese, irrespective of profession, are quite skilled in the practice of an art without considering themselves professional or even amateur artists.

Amerta Movement's method of improvisation is different from that familiar in the West. It is not based on acting out feelings and thoughts directly or on releasing emotions directly, as is found in some Western body disciplines including body therapy, where clients may 'unfold like a flower' or are sometimes encouraged to focus on their feelings (like anger) and express them directly. In Amerta Movement, this is not encouraged. It is thought of as being like 'blowing on a fire' and not a procedure that will reduce anger or tension, because it is not a true release of the anger or the tension at their source. Such a release can only happen through transformation via a purification process, taking place in the practitioner, leading to an awareness of what is really going on, or simply by the practitioner letting go of the anger or tension. The attitude to healing in Amerta Movement is one of letting the natural healing process take its own course, like a wound healing by itself.

So Amerta Movement is the result of Prapto's own personal research and practice. It has been also nurtured by Prapto's local network within the rich, creative and spiritual milieu of Central Java and it has been influenced by Prapto's foreign students who have contributed to its development, as well as by the Javanese artists who have collaborated in practices and public presentations in Java.

~

A reminder that this book offers an overarching view of Amerta Movement during the period 1986-1997 when the roots of Amerta Movement were formed and the Padepokan Lemah Putih School was founded. It focuses on the approach called *Pribadi Art* or Individual Art, dealing with personal development, which was the first approach used in Amerta Movement. It also introduces the later approach used in Amerta Movement, called Messenger Art, which deals with making performance art, installations and new ritual art. Although Messenger Art courses were only officially introduced in the course programme at the end of 1997, which also marks the end of this study, Prapto had earlier on, informally, started to introduce Messenger Art, sometimes in the middle of other courses. On that basis, I have included an introduction to Messenger Art in this book.

Before presenting *Pribadi Art* in detail, and introducing Messenger Art, to set the context, I will first explore various aspects of Amerta Movement.

Chapter 2

Prapto in Java

From the turn of the century, Prapto chose to call his own personal work and teaching of Amerta Movement, *Joged Amerta*. *Joged* means dance and movement in Javanese. Prapto did so in order to distinguish his own work from that of his students. Sometimes movement taught by Prapto's students in their native countries is also called 'Sharing Movement'. In this book, we are dealing with the early period, the roots, of Prapto's movement work, where it was called Amerta Movement. So this is the term I will use here.

The Padepokan Lemah Putih

Prapto's school and art institution in Central Java, the Padepokan Lemah Putih, was officially recognised as a school of art and culture by the Indonesian government in 2015. The school was also known as the Taman Lemah Putih or Lemah Putih Garden.

The Padepokan Lemah Putih was situated in the northern part of Solo in approximately two hectares of hilly land, formerly used for rice terraces. Prapto re-shaped and redesigned the land especially for Amerta practice, among other things creating practice sites of different shape and material and of different geometrical forms. In this way, Prapto created a 'landscape studio in nature', or, as he called it

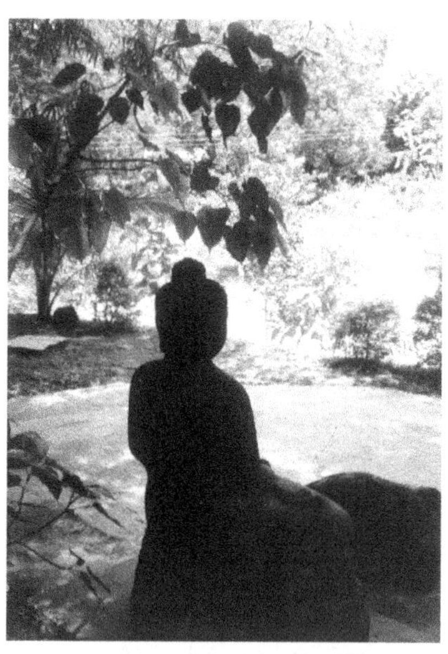

The Buddha overlooking the Padepokan Lemah Putih

colloquially, a 'school in nature,' or a 'nature garden'.

The intention was that people work not only with nature and from nature but also with human design and consciousness. They worked with a dialogue, an exchange and a mutual inspiration between nature and culture, as well as with the creativity and ideas of human mind in modern society. This dialogue, exchange and inspiration between nature and culture is a hallmark of Amerta Movement. In short, the layout of the school was seen as a human design, a cultural expression of nature, i.e. a cultured garden with culture and nature in one, forming a unity.

In this book, I focus on the different geometrical forms, especially square, circle and oval, as sites for bodily expression and human design, not only because these forms existed as physical practice sites at the school, but also because these shapes can be found anywhere and can be used for Amerta Movement practice by anyone anywhere in the world. The square, circle and oval which were physical practice sites at the school represent a conceptual framework for practising movement at the Lemah Putih School. By using the conceptual framework of these physical sites, when he started to travel widely, Prapto could teach Amerta Movement abroad as it had grown out of Java's culture and of the physical land of his school. This was possible because square, circle and oval as forms and themes in Amerta Movement were linked to the school's land and Javanese culture. Now Prapto, for teaching abroad, also linked them to the human body, i.e. to the practitioner in terms of physicality, sound and light or to 'body nature', 'body sound' and 'body light'.

The pendopo

At the Lemah Putih School, there were two traditional Javanese practice halls or pendopos, constructed for Amerta Movement – for daily practice as well as for performances. Prapto's main pendopo was near the river bordering his land on the south; it was square like a house, but open on all four sides as is usual in Java. It was covered by a vaulted roof of Javanese design, carried by sixteen pillars: twelve round the edge and four in the centre. The pendopo looked like a large, open, roofed pavilion.

According to Prapto, a pendopo represents a 'home in nature' or a 'house in nature' to the Javanese, i.e. a home or a house closer to nature than homes and houses in a city. This is connected to the themes of prayer and devotion because the home in Java is sacred in the same way that life is sacred: behind a traditional Javanese house there is a space where the Javanese pray to their ancestors.

The pillars of the main pendopo were made of rough wood – the shape of the trees from which they had been cut was still apparent. These pillars divided the pendopo into two areas, an outer one and inner one and thus made it possible to divide the space further into smaller sections of different kinds. In terms of the movement practice, the pillars served as structural points in space helping students to give structure and direction in the outer world when moving freely in and through the space. The pillars also played a fundamental role in movement exercises, as described in Part II.

Prapto distinguished between 'nature's order', which he called 'organism', and a 'human-made order', which he called 'organisation'. For example, the structure and functions of the practitioner's body are based on nature's order: hence, the body is an 'organism' in Prapto's terms. In contrast, the way a pendopo is structured and the way the pillars have been organised by the builders is a human-made order, hence a pendopo is the result of 'organisation'.

When practising movement in the main pendopo, students were at the heart of the school's 'landscape studio in nature' and had a clear view of several of the school's practice areas in the hilly, sloping, tropical scenery. In the pendopo, they were sheltered from sun and rain, as if under a huge parasol, but no doors or windows separated them from their surroundings. So, chickens from the village would often walk through the main pendopo during practice and sheep could often be seen grazing nearby. Local schoolchildren and youngsters often came to the pendopo to watch the movement practice on their way to and from their homes, sometimes quietly but at other times driving their motor bikes right up to the edge of the school's grass areas. They saw this landscape studio in nature (or garden, as Prapto also calls it) as being partly theirs, because they lived there, in simple, concrete houses directly bordering the river behind the main pendopo.

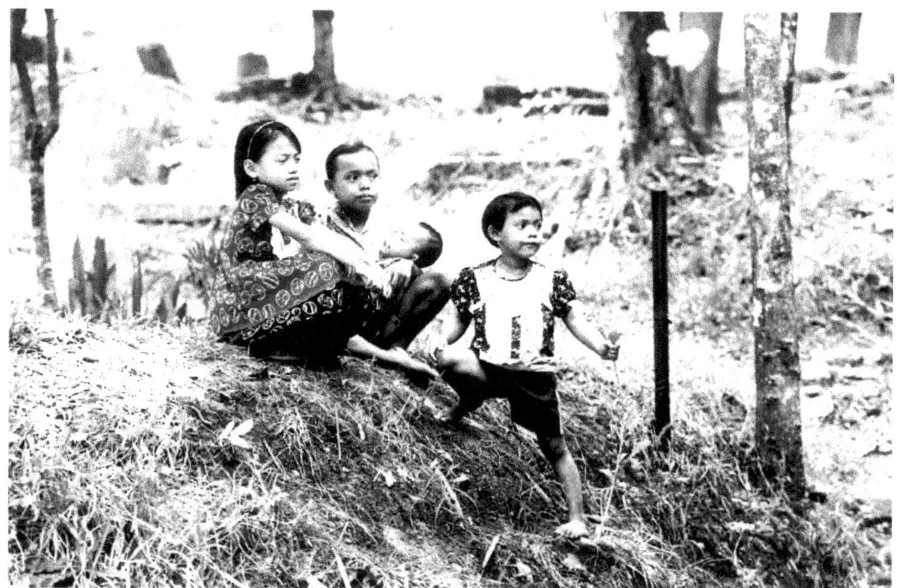

Some spectators

Next to the Lemah Putih School was another art institution mainly for traditional Javanese performance arts and eco-tourism, which also had a forge, where Javanese artefacts were produced. The sound of this forge mingled with other daily life sounds, reminding Amerta Movement practitioners of the fact that they were in the midst of a Javanese village.

The city of Solo and art

Solo is a city of historic royal power, containing two palaces with respectively a major and a minor royal dynasty. Solo is a centre of traditional Javanese culture, including the sophisticated, classical Javanese high arts of dance, music, shadow puppet theatre, operatic drama and *batik*. It is also a centre of commerce with a little more than half a million inhabitants. Solo is situated on the bank of Java's largest river and lies on a fertile plain with rice paddies surrounded by the volcanos Merapi and Merbabu in the northwest and Mount Lawu in the southeast. The majority of inhabitants are ethnic Javanese, with the rest made up of Indonesians from other parts of the archipelago, a large group of Chinese and a small group of Arabs and Indians.

Solo has several state universities, including the ISI, (Institut Seni Indonesia, Surakarta), 'the Surakarta Performing Arts Academy' with the largest dance faculty in Indonesia, which fosters much artistic activity as well as bringing students from all over the world to study there, sometimes for several years. Another important art institution and neighbour to the ISI is the TBS, (Taman Budaya Surakarta), Central Java's Art Centre in Solo. TBS has one of the largest pendopos of the arts in Central Java, as well as a small, modern, black box, indoor theatre called Teater Arena and an exhibition hall. The TBS's artistic activities include practice and performance in all the Javanese performing arts, as well as guest performances from all over Indonesia at all levels, i.e. popular village art, highly sophisticated classical Javanese performances, as well as expressions of contemporary art. The ISI and the TBS are situated so close to each other that they look like one large art city. Close by these two institutions, is the state university, UNS, (Universitas Sebelas Maret). This is worth mentioning in this context because it has a dynamic visual arts department, which is very active within the field of modern Indonesian theatre, some of which is presented at the TBS Art Centre. Moreover, the city's two royal palaces also support sophisticated, living art traditions.

Like all of Central Java, Solo is known for its tolerance of diversity, which has permitted the peaceful co-existence of people of different races, cultures and religions. In Solo, the birthdays of Mohammed and Jesus and the day commemorating Buddha's birth, passing and enlightenment, are all official public holidays. Mediaeval and modern lifestyles exist side by side, with influences from ancient agrarian societies, based on rice cultivation, ancestor and nature worship, still lingering on and an atmosphere reminiscent of Java's Hindu-Buddhist high culture with the God-King being worshipped as Buddha and Shiva in one – especially at Solo's royal palaces. Nevertheless, changes are happening in the 21st century as the majority of the population follows a modern and moderate form of Islam. It also includes quite a large group of Christians, many of whom are of Chinese origin. Central Java is developing rapidly and, after centuries of oppression by foreign powers followed by tyrannical local rulers, the Javanese are headed towards modernisation and a fully developed Asian democracy.

The Lemah Putih School was not closed off from the surrounding communities, so the school's two pendopos were used for several purposes other than Amerta Movement, as is customary in a Javanese village. These included meetings, receptions and all kinds of artistic activity: classes in Javanese dance offered to the local children, martial arts classes, meditation sessions, shadow puppet plays (*wayang kulit*) and music, be it Javanese orchestral music (*gamelan*), operatic drama (*Lesung ketoprak**), or contemporary Javanese music, including modern experiments. In the 21st century, these modern experiments have often been led by Prapto's youngest son, Galih Seno. At least once a year, international, contemporary performances, installations and seminars have also been offered by Prapto's daughter, Melati Suryodarmo, a famous installation and performance artist.

Hence, the Lemah Putih School was not only a school for Amerta Movement practice but a focus for art activities involving intercultural collaboration as well as practice- and art-based explorations and artistic research* with the aim of creating new forms, rituals and compositions that bridge traditional disciplines without losing cultural roots. As a result, Prapto's students had a unique opportunity to collaborate with Javanese artists for their crystallisation-performances and at other times.

Cultural sites in Central Java

Parts of Prapto's courses took place at temples and heritage sites, also called 'power-sites'*, including Candi Sukuh (a Hindu-Buddhist temple in the mountains), Borobudur (a World Heritage site and perhaps the world's largest Buddhist temple), and Parangtritis Beach (an ancient power-site in Central Java on the Indian Ocean).

Prapto also taught in East Java, Bali and Kalimantan, as well as running regular courses in the USA, Mexico, Australia, the Philippines and Europe – but these are outside the scope of this book.

Prapto's teaching approach

Students from abroad studying Amerta Movement with Prapto in Java entered a 'master class' process rooted in Asian culture, within which, everyday life, spirituality/the sacred, healing and personal development cannot be separated from artistic expression. Prapto characterised his teaching style as a master-apprentice approach, meaning that it is not academic. However, he encouraged others to develop an academic approach, if they wished to, for example his practitioners connected to the Dutch School for New Dance Development (SNDD) and others. Students were treated as colleagues and sparring partners, with whom Prapto carried on a dialogue, an exchange of ideas and experiences of life based on the practice, instead of lecturing to them. Prapto also spoke of Amerta Movement as 'garden art' and in that context saw himself as a 'gardener', rather than as a Javanese teacher (guru) in the conventional sense: the relationship between Prapto and his practitioners was one of equals.

A practice session might take many different forms. Normally it started with Prapto speaking on a theme, which he also demonstrated physically, giving students a framework for their free, improvised movement. Discussion with the students followed and continued 'physically', so to speak, through the practice itself, as when students, who sit on the floor of the main pendopo during the discussion, get up and enter the practice space and start to move. The physical part of the practice session also included Prapto's guiding of the students. He would do so by moving physically with them, i.e. guiding them through the mute language of the movement itself, thereby offering them some individual suggestions *through* the movement, rather than telling them in words. In this way, Prapto would aim to inspire students in a direct, physical way that makes the student's body 'wake up'. This mute dialogue between Prapto and individual practitioners might take place with or without physical contact with the student. Prapto's non-verbal instruction or his physical message to the individual student might be intended for example to draw the student's attention to a particular part of the body, so as to stimulate that part, or to give the student direction in and through the space. Physical contact between Prapto and an individual student might proceed as a mute, tactile 'conversation' or 'dialogue', which would often activate or point to the hidden potential or the so-called 'tacit knowledge' of the student's body, i.e. knowledge and memories held in the body but not yet formulated or expressed consciously by the students. Hence, the 'tacit knowledge' of the body is, among other things, related to students' 'potential', to the hidden abilities not yet realised by the individual, because they are not yet aware of possessing such abilities. This potential, when realised in the outside world – according to students talking about their experiences with being guided by Prapto – might manifest itself, for example, in the form of a new bodily activity, like whirling or jumping high, or mentally, as when discovering a new skill or capacity. Prapto, through his teaching method, offered the movement student tools and techniques rather than ready-made solutions and finished movement forms. Hence, Amerta practice is process-oriented and exploratory – it forms a journey of discovery in known and unknown landscapes.

Prapto said his teaching method was, amongst other things, designed to stimulate and inspire people: 'Being with you' is one term he used and he said that his method, if he had any, took the form of a dialogue, an exchange or an inspiration, between him and the students, rather than being a teaching method in a traditional sense, where the teacher instructs and the student receives.

> *My job is to stimulate that you grow, that you are inspired so that you can see what happened before and what is happening now so that you can create your own mirror, your own echo, your own sculpture.*

> *The stimulation is very important because in fact this [Amerta Movement] is more the dialogue of inspiration than teaching.*

> *…stimulate Westerners so that they can find their own material.*

> *Students have to find their own way on Java, their own expression or own personal story.*

Prapto added that he could only solve 10% of the problems people bring to the practice. By asking others to solve our problems, according to Prapto, we lose the opportunity to grow through solving them ourselves. Moreover, we may need to wait for an answer to our questions. As he said,

> *If you have a problem, keep your problem, the fire of life will deal with it. If you put your problem to me and make me find the solution, you develop me, not you….*

In summary, Prapto would encourage people to learn for themselves, exploring their own identity, expressions, forms, steps and gestures, because we have to discover our own way for ourselves. He would expect students to be motivated and curious to know what the practice is all about when they arrived and he would also expect students to discuss among themselves how they felt and thought about the practice, outside the hours of practice. Students could only learn by being curious and by asking questions.

Chapter 3

Fundamentals

This chapter looks in more detail at the broad, underlying approach of Amerta Movement and the assumptions that underpin it.

Prapto's ideas and philosophy

According to Prapto, life is a gift and each of us has a special purpose or task in life. Moreover, in Prapto's view, as a human being, it is advised that I get to know myself before I enter into a relationship with another person, whether this be for a friendship or an intimate relationship. The same is true when I enter into collaboration in movement practice with another practitioner. In these cases, I must try to feel my own condition before expressing myself or before interacting with other people or interacting with the environment. So Prapto as a Javanese, and possibly because he was especially influenced by his Javanese meditation practice, attached great importance to preparing oneself to enter into relationships with other human beings and this is perhaps one of the biggest lessons of Amerta Movement. Prapto's ideas and attitudes usually initiate much discussion among students and encourage them to think about themselves, as well as about their own culture or civilisation, in a new way.

His ideas also apply directly to the physical practice itself, as when he would ask people to start from their own 'being'* (or self in Western terms), and to try to 'stand on their own legs'. At the same time, he would stress that movement in and across a space starts from the feet and the legs, because they are the main support for the physical body.

As we have already seen, according to Prapto, life itself is movement and movement is the basis of life – just as an alphabet is the basis of a language. Amerta Movement, moreover, is a multi-level approach that can engage with people from many different backgrounds and languages simultaneously. Through movement, we enter a common platform for expression, development, relationship and communication; one, where we can meet what Prapto called our 'genuine being' or our 'true self'. Amerta Movement is designed to integrate embodied movement into all aspects of life via a non-verbal form of bodily expression that is true to our genuine being or true self.

Prapto, as we have also seen, stressed the importance of seeing physical/bodily movement not only as 'a language for communication but also as an expression of being'. This means that he was less engaged in aesthetics than in the human condition. Being genuine or true to oneself is crucial in Amerta Movement, as well as movement being a 'language of liberation', as Prapto termed it. In other words, form is less important than the quality of the movements released, and less important than the practitioner touching upon inner potentials and resources, as well as the honesty and the attitude with which the movement is expressed. This does not mean, however, that Prapto was not interested in aesthetics, but only that the emphasis in the movement practice – at least during the early period of Amerta Movement treated in this book, – was placed on retrieving lost aspects of ourselves, on a 're-membering', as Prapto termed it, rather than on what the movement looks like. Emphasis was also placed on becoming whole, body, mind and spirit, on blossoming via expression of self, i.e. expression of one's whole being in embodied movement, receiving the inner and outer worlds and the subsequent expression of self through embodied movement. Hence, emphasis was placed on 'becoming', i.e. on the discovery and realisation of our inner potentials and of resources ready to manifest themselves in the outer world through new bodily forms and manners, new styles, gaits and gestures. In summary, for the individual practitioner, the emphasis is on entering into new 'landscapes' of oneself and of physical, expressive art.

Liberation

Liberation, in Prapto's terms, means adaptation to change by identifying less with our material life and appearance. On a practical level this means being flexible, maybe with a less strong ego in some situations, as is favoured in Central Java, thereby facilitating an open and aware attitude in the practitioner, adapting oneself to reality, accepting it, moving with it, responding to it physically and mentally, changing when life changes instead of reacting in an automatic, non-conscious, insensitive or unaware manner.

Liberation, in this practice, may also mean identifying less with our physical expressions (i.e. with our movements in the outside world), and with our emotions, feelings and thoughts as these emerge during the movement practice – by being aware and conscious. It may also mean that our inner material (sensations, emotions, feelings and thoughts) *transform* into movement, i.e. into another quality in the outside world. By being transformed into physical movement, the material finds an outlet. It is 'liberated' in Prapto's terms. The same is true of inner physical sensations. If these inner stirrings take place only in my inner world, they remain inside me, 'under the skin' according to Prapto. In contrast, it is a positive development, an act of liberation, as Prapto termed it, when this inner material of emotions, feelings and thoughts transforms into a new value, i.e. into movement expression or a movement dance in the outside world. That's why these stirrings are said to be 'liberated'.

Dialogue with life

What is essential, especially before doing anything, is to enter 'a dialogue with life', by which Prapto meant paying attention not only to our own condition and feelings but also to what is going on in other people around us, to what is going on in the wider environment and in life in general. On a practical level, for example, we need to pay attention to the others in the practice space, in order simply not to bump into each other, just as we also need to be sensitive to the form, material and atmosphere of a place. This is because the movement is improvised in the here and now and anything can happen. Furthermore, I need to see my own movement as taking place within the frame of life in general, not just in terms of my personal life but also in that of others, because we are all interconnected. This is what is meant by moving in dialogue with life.

A learning process takes place through the physical practice; it comprises the practitioner's whole being (body, mind and spirit) including cultural background, conditioning and physical surroundings. Through the practice, we learn to inhabit the physical body in a state of heightened awareness and sensitivity and, through the practice, we learn to respond to life physically, not just through words – and we also learn to build a somatic movement vocabulary.

Rebirth

Human growth is attained by the practitioner being 'reborn' into their true identity, thereby meeting their 'genuine being' in Prapto's terms, or their true self. This aim is achieved through the expression of self in physical movement and consists of building a movement vocabulary or a physical 'language by movement', as we saw earlier. This physical language by movement has the potential of being applied not only to our daily life activities and to the daily movement process; it may also be applied to art (including performance art), to installations, improvisations and movement teaching, to spirituality (including the sacred and new rituals) and to health (including healing, becoming whole, therapy and psychoanalysis).

This 'rebirth' should not be seen in a religious sense, but rather in the modern sense of a search for identity. It is a process that starts during 'Basic'

Amerta Movement courses, continues during the subsequent courses and later evolves on still deeper levels. This 'rebirth', this meeting ourselves, is a 'door' being opened to a wider reality than the one we have known hitherto. A process of purification takes place. It does so in the sense that we become newly aware of certain sensations, feelings, emotions and thoughts, of attitudes to self and to life, all processes that might make us change our previous attitudes to ourselves and to life. Hence, Amerta Movement aims to broaden our perspective on life by encouraging us to enter into a dialogue with our surroundings and cultural heritage, i.e. to be open to our surroundings and take them into consideration, rather than being closed off and focused exclusively inwards, only using the surroundings as a backdrop. This openness enables us to broaden our outlook on life and to get a more spacious perspective. In this way, we become more awake in the present, more aware and sensitive to what is going on both inside us and outside us. We also come to integrate more of our unconscious/subconscious world into our conscious mind and enter into a more flexible, spacious, creative and spiritual/sacred dimension. Ordinary, everyday life may become a sacred adventure where high and low, holy and profane go hand in hand.

For the individual practitioner, this rebirth means that I must find or learn my own mode of 'being' through the practice, i.e. learn to stand on my own two feet, to express myself based on my genuine being, my true self, according to my own identity as a human being who is part of nature and of the spiritual/sacred world, as well as being part of society. From there, when I am moving, I may start to become aware of the fact that my body 'speaks' through movement, a fact I may have been unaware of before.

Feelings, emotions, thoughts and attitude

Feelings, emotions and thoughts are brought to the surface by the movement practice. They are, however, not dwelt upon, investigated for their content or directly expressed. What is essential is for us to be aware of our attitude to our feelings, emotions and thoughts. Do we accept or reject them? The recommended attitude within Amerta Movement is not to repress them and also not to focus on them, but to receive them, in the sense of acknowledging them, and move with them. In this way we can allow feelings, emotions and thoughts to be transformed into physical movement in the outside world – to be embodied in the outside world, and to be liberated, in Prapto's terms, thereby creating a bridge between our inner and outer worlds. Alternatively, students can just let go of feelings, emotions and thoughts. By accepting them without acting on them and without judging them, we allow different, even controversial, feelings, emotions and thoughts to co-exist, without our having to suppress 'undesirable' ones.

If we start to analyse our thoughts or become absorbed in our emotions while practising, our awareness is pulled away from the present moment. At such moments, it is important to shift our attention back to feeling the body's physicality in the present moment and to postpone any scrutiny of feelings, emotions and thoughts until after the movement practice session.

Balance and neutrality/non-attachment

Balance and neutrality or non-attachment are essential in our attitude to our inner universe of sensations, feelings, emotions and thoughts. From a perspective of wholeness, each aspect of our inner self receives equal attention; the same is true of our movements: each movement is granted the same value.

Just as we are asked to practise facing our limitations, we can also work on accepting our potential and inner resources without false modesty or pride. For example, this may mean accepting that I am tired or upset and do not want to practise, or conversely, that I love to move, love my natural movement in and across the space, love to be looked at by others and to take the lead. All that is fine. Whether the experience is pleasant or unpleasant, the most important thing is – while moving – to be conscious and to live life with eyes open to ourselves and to our environment. Or, as Javanese mystics put it: 'Be grateful for having been given remembrance', i.e. be grateful for having been given the ability to reflect on an inner world, on our life through a process of consciousness.

Prapto would recommend that students start their movement practice with a neutral attitude to sensations, feelings, emotions and thoughts. 'Neutral' means entering the movement practice with a relaxed body, a relaxed style of breathing and a calm mind. The term 'non-attachment' might also be helpful in this context, since he also referred to the act of 'not catching' or 'being caught' by emotions (two well-known Amerta Movement expressions). Where the term seems the most appropriate, I will use it. This means not reacting in an automatic way to our emotions, but calmly being aware of our emotions and moving with them in a non-attached way, as far as possible. If I am emotionally upset, my mind will be like a rough sea where the waters are disturbed by strong waves. This causes me to perceive both the inner and outer world in a distorted manner, as an upset mind is a mind out of balance. Prapto acknowledged, however, that it is easier to adopt a neutral or non-attached attitude at the end of a practice session than at the start. As he said:

> *We try to realise moving now, starting from neutral, starting*
> *from breathing without catching and also without being caught.*

Moreover, in Amerta practice, movements are carried out in a relaxed, comfortable and 'natural' way, insofar as 'natural' movement exists. This, in turn, implies using the body without wasting muscle energy. The simplicity of the movements brings us back to fundamental life skills, whether physical, emotional, mental or social.

Purification

In Amerta Movement, I learn to experience my body in a new way with heightened sensitivity, thereby becoming aware of my learnt patterns of movement. Emotions can surface and a process of purification via 'de-coding' or 'de-programming' my body and myself of learnt patterns can take place (see next section). In this way, I can shed what is not genuine and start to discover inner resources and a hidden potential, which will gradually unfold. I can enter a process of growth and personal development. Prapto, who related the human being and movement to what happens in nature, called this process of growth and personal development, 'blossoming'*. Finally, I meet my being, my true being, to use Prapto's term. In other words, I meet my own self, my true self.

Here a note on natural movement may be helpful. So-called 'natural' movements are culturally influenced and differ from culture to culture. Hence, Amerta movement looks quite different depending on whether it is a Westerner or a Javanese moving. The latter's movement generally shows clearly the influence of Javanese body language in a way that is easy for a Western observer to detect. There may be more vivid and undulating movements of hands, fingers and arms than we are used to in Western daily life movements, with more frequent bending at the knees, for example. It is more difficult for people to see their own culture clearly and to realise that our 'natural' daily life movements are culturally shaped.

Programming*

Sometimes our 'natural' movement is obscured by learnt patterns of movement, as we have seen. These start to run as an automatic program, so to speak, when we set out to move freely. This is because these 'programs' can stem from bodily positions, which are now on 'automatic pilot' in our bodies, so that we do not pay attention to them and are not aware of reproducing them. Examples of such postures are the sitting posture in *tai chi,* or in martial arts, where practitioners tend to move with legs bent as if sitting on the edge of a chair. Some even walk in the sitting position while lifting their knees high. *Karate* and Western classical ballet have their own postures and programming. These can all be released by the process of 'de-coding' or 'de-programming' oneself through awareness.

Awakening body and mind

As a practice for human growth in terms of awakening body and mind, Prapto compared Amerta Movement to the stages of child development. Both are bodily processes taking place in time and space. The child's journey from conception to birth is a journey from darkness to light. At the moment of birth, the baby yawns and stretches, signalling life. In Amerta Movement, especially in the *Pribadi Art* approach, stretching is the 'starter', the moment we 'come to life' and become aware of the self in the body. This journey from darkness to light, or from not being conscious to being conscious, takes place within the whole physical body, not just on a mental level. Human development, whether the sensorimotor development of the physical body or the development of mind and spirit, takes place within the physical space of the body. It is through the movement of my physical body that I can exist. I cannot breathe, sense, feel, think, rest, walk, act, express, communicate, change, develop or be spiritual except through the dynamics of my body in movement in the present moment. Life would otherwise be relegated to fantasy or imagination, to the speculative world of thoughts and dreams never realised.

When we practise movement intensely in a state of heightened sensitivity, alert to ourselves and our environment, we may also discover new aspects of ourselves from beyond our personal story. In this way I may, in the midst of moving and exploring my private self, also open up beyond this personal self, to the more archaic, collective field of human development and consciousness, and maybe experience how we humans as part of our evolution share some rudimentary physical characteristics with fish and other simple creatures.

Human in the human body

In Amerta Movement, everyday life goes hand-in-hand with the divine. This is an expression of how the Javanese, including Prapto, view spirituality/the sacred as a natural part of a human being's daily life in the family or at work. Prapto stressed that we are ordinary human beings with good and bad sides. He also referred to this as being 'human in the human body'.

Furthermore, being 'human in the human body' means accepting and acknowledging myself, the way I am and my ordinary everyday life, as part of the practice. Hence, the practice always takes as its starting point the individual practitioner: "Let me see what you have", Prapto would say when inviting a new practitioner to enter the space and move. This is by no means an audition or a test, but a kind invitation arising out of sincere curiosity to see an individual's movement. From the outset, Prapto would accept people as they are.

Body: physical body, heart and head

Prapto's concept of body in Amerta Movement reflects the traditional Javanese view that body, mind and spirit form a whole. Moreover, in movement practice, the mover is also seen as interconnected with society and life around. Prapto also spoke about how elements that are found in nature are also in the human body. The body with its form and functions is also seen as an instrument, a tool, for development and expression with three parts, qualities or sources: physical body, heart and head – the physical, the emotional and the mental. Each part has its own law, 'intelligence' or 'being', as Prapto terms it. Together they form an integrated whole.

According to *kejawen,* the body is seen as a focal point where the vertical and horizontal axes of life meet. The vertical axis consists of our relationship to earth and heaven (i.e. to the material world and to the spiritual/the sacred world, god and cosmos), and may also be seen in terms of microcosm and macrocosm in the sense that the human being is seen as a little universe in itself, part of the phenomenological world, part of microcosm which in turn is a reflection, a shadow of a higher truth, a higher order, a big universe, i.e. part of macrocosm. Together microcosm and macrocosm form the unity of existence (Mulder, 1994: 5-6). 'As above so below', as the saying goes. The vertical axis can also be seen as encompassing three worlds – the underworld, the middle world, (the world of human life on earth), and the higher world – and three kinds of consciousness: sub-consciousness, consciousness and higher consciousness.

The horizontal axis is the worldly, material axis, the phenomenal world, which includes the practitioner's daily life, relations to and communications with the environment and fellow human beings.

Communication in movement practice – whether between two people moving or between the mover and the spectator – never goes directly between two people but always via the vertical axis, i.e. via my inner nature and the spiritual/sacred dimension. This helps me not to react 'in automatic' but to become aware of my own condition and of the higher dimension of life before engaging with my environment or fellow human beings.

According to Prapto, it is important that we inhabit our body with an awareness of all four sides when moving through a space. This means being aware of the body in three dimensions: not only the front of the body but also the sides, the back, from the top of the head to the soles of the feet. Westerners, according to Prapto at that time, as a rule, had little or no awareness of their backs when starting the practice. Their awareness is often centred in front of the body and they tend to move straight ahead without being aware of the back of their body. This corresponds to an attitude of always being headed somewhere without much thought given to the process or to our inner being or surroundings. I need to keep in mind that basic movement includes expression of my being and that this occurs not in a vacuum but in relation to my surroundings. In other words, my movements show an awareness of my surroundings (i.e. of co-practitioners and practice-site) and attention paid to them. This is what Prapto called moving 'in dialogue with the surroundings'. Even when moving forward, it is important not to forget my back and what is behind me. Symbolically, according to Prapto, the back represents our past and our subconscious. He also maintained that the Javanese generally are more 'in their bodies' when they move than his Western students. Central Javanese do not so much move through a space with the sense of reaching a goal as move with a sense of the process of getting there. They pay attention to space in all four directions simultaneously. So, the Javanese, more than his Western students according to Prapto, inhabit the body with awareness and heightened sensitivity. Of course, in cities like Jakarta, this could be very different and people there could be more like city people elsewhere in the world.

Body in motion

Prapto saw our movement as our 'parents' in the sense that we learn from our movement, provided we are moving in a state of heightened awareness or sensitivity. As the child learns from its parents and uses them as role models or mirrors, when we move in a state of heightened awareness of body, feelings and thoughts we are guided by the movement itself, by the body itself in movement, using the body in movement as a mirror for what to do next. This means that we are being guided by our own body in our practice as well as in our development process and journey through life. Among other things, the movement process itself helps us to make choices and to cope with changes, thereby allowing us to grow as human beings, physically, emotionally and mentally. In Javanese culture, this traditional way of learning is called 'learning by doing' or learning from the experience of one's own body. In the West we might call it learning from 'practice-based' and 'art-based' research and knowledge, or simply, learning from 'artistic research'.

Three sources for movement

In the 1990s, Prapto talked about three sources or body qualities for initiating movement, or three different ways of perceiving the body, namely from physicality, from sound and from light or thought. This was different in the 1980s, when movement was seen to be initiated from the body's physicality only and there were no practice areas with special themes, such as the square, circle and oval. Practice mainly took place in the school's pendopo. In the 1990s, movement was still bodily based, but the material for the transformation process was now seen to come from the three different sources or body qualities. These related respectively to the body's physicality, the heart and the head, i.e. to the body as nature; the body as sound; and the body as light. In the 1980s Prapto also called these Body-nature, Body-sound and Body-light. These three body qualities are associated with the spaces of square, circle and oval:

1. *Body-nature*, also called 'body-body', is the body perceived in terms of physicality. It is connected to instinct, reflexes, muscles, sensations and the five senses and includes paying attention to 'texture' and sculpturing in the outside world. It is associated with the square space.

2. *Body-sound* is connected to hearing, including echo, resonance and inner dimensions of vibration, inner feeling, feeling of heart/intuition, inner resonance, the emotional. Inner feeling may also mean scanning for input at the level of the heart. Body-sound includes paying attention to colour and painting in the outside world. Body-sound is associated with the circle space.

3. *Body-light* is the body perceived in terms of light and the mind. It includes paying attention to light/shadow and calligraphy. Body-light is connected to eyesight, to the perception of seeing, to thought, clarity and creativity. It is also understood as insight in the sense of a higher visionary aspect, including higher consciousness and inner dimensions of vision and aura, being possibly related to the Javanese concept of receiving divine revelation or blessing. Body-light is associated with the oval space.

Movement initiated from the body as	Amerta Movement category	Shape	Connected to
Physicality	Body-nature	Square	Instincts. Reflexes. Sensations. Five senses.
Sound	Body-sound	Circle	Hearing. Echo. Resonance. Feeling of heart. Intuition. Vibration.
Light	Body-light	Oval	Eyesight. Clarity. Thought. Creativity. Vision. Aura. Divine revelation.

The three sources for movement

Each quality has two aspects. One is the material dimension of outer perception, the other is an inner, non-material, subtler spiritual dimension as used in meditation, inner consciousness and purification processes involving enhanced awareness and sensitivity. These two aspects have fluid borders and can be seen as a continuum within the wholeness of the practitioner's body-mind-spirit.

Finally, each space of square, circle and oval connected to body-nature, body-sound and body-light, facilitates a specific movement quality: square facilitates 'creation in reflection', circle facilitates 'bowing in praying' and oval facilitates 'purification in circulation'.

Garden Art, Daily Life Movement and General Practice

Especially from the 1990s when Prapto started to travel and teach abroad a lot, he talked about Amerta Movement in terms of Garden Art, and about the practice areas at the Lemah Putih School, such as the square, circle and oval as fields or themes for general practice and for performance. This change of square, circle and oval from primarily being a physical practice site at the Lemah Putih School, to being linked to the practitioner's body, provided a framework for people coming to Java from abroad to practise Amerta Movement from square, circle and oval at home in their own countries, independently of the school's physical practice areas.

We may ask what is the garden for Prapto and what is its significance in Amerta Movement? According to Prapto, it is a mixture of nature and human design or culture. It is a place for meeting and socialising. Lemah Putih embodies this concept. Prapto, moreover, said about the term 'garden':

> *I use the realm of garden as a source for the creativity of art …*
> *There is the quality of diversity, but we can still feel unity in the*
> *garden… Garden has a quality of religiosity: Paradise, Zen*
> *Gardens, temple gardens.* (Suryodarmo, 1998)

So, Garden Art, as it emerged in the mid-1990s, is not only a form of movement art; it is also a movement practice related to the sacred, spiritual world. We have a spiritual attitude while practising Garden Art, aware of life beyond the human dimension and also aware of the creativity of the movement's expression. Garden Art is, furthermore, connected to movement as part of daily life. So it includes general practice. Garden Art is process and practice in the present moment, carried out without any intentions of goal or application beyond the present moment. Maybe for that reason, the Garden Art approach was sometimes called 'garden joy and freshness' by Prapto. Alongside Garden Art students can practise from one of the three approaches of square, circle or oval.

Garden Art comprises general practice in Amerta Movement, or 'daily life movement', also just called 'The Movement Process'. These ways of practising have always been part of Amerta Movement, from its very beginning referred to as 'process'. The term 'daily life movement' refers not only to general practice in Amerta Movement, and Amerta Movement as process, but also to movement/Amerta Movement as part of one's daily life activities in the home, at work, outdoors and indoors – i.e. movement as part of life in general. In Amerta Movement, 'daily life movement' has always been as important as the special approaches of square, circle and oval.

Applicant programme

During the 1990s, Prapto introduced an applicant programme in Java: an initiative he had already tried out in his courses in Europe. He preferred the term 'applicant' to apprentice and used it in the sense of applying oneself to something. Being an applicant was for people who had already studied Amerta Movement with Prapto. It provided an opportunity to combine one's professional skill with Amerta practice under Prapto's supervision. Applicants did not train in Amerta Movement in order to reproduce Prapto's technique and manner. Rather, the aim was that they bring their own professional field to studying with Prapto, thus creating their own personal movement practice.

Prapto taught process, the applicant provided an application. This could be in combining movement with voice, for example, or with an event, like poetry reading, or with environmental art. Or it might involve health or therapy as when, on one occasion, a therapist among the practitioners moved with a wheelchair as a dialogue partner. In this way, applicants showed how they had applied their own professional field to the Amerta practice language or merely how they had applied the Amerta practice language to a specific end. They would choose to present their interpretation of Amerta Movement in relation to their own professional background but within the fields or themes of: square (creativity), circle (religiosity/the sacred), or oval (purification). Other examples of how Amerta students have applied their practice of Amerta Movement can be found in the book *Embodied Lives*.

Crystallisation

In Amerta Movement, emphasis is placed both on process and on outcome in the form of a public presentation through improvised movement at the end of a course: a so-called 'crystallisation-performance' or just crystallisation. There is in principle no difference in terms of movement between the process of everyday practice and the crystallisation. Both are improvisations based on the non-stylised, free movement approach of Amerta Movement. Both also take place within a given framework, i.e. at a specific site and in relation to a specific theme, story or myth. However, the movement's form, steps and gestures are free and improvised within that framework. At times, individuals or groups of students collaborate with local artists for their crystallisations. Those who emphasise the spiritual aspect might collaborate with a Buddhist monk, a Christian nun, a Muslim poet or philosopher, or a shaman. Those giving priority to art might collaborate with a Javanese dancer or performer. This means there is no common, pre-conceived standard, form, steps or gestures, and no common, pre-conceived choreography to be shared by practitioners or studied by observers. The movement is site-specific and person-specific and makes sense in terms of the site of practice (its form, material and atmosphere), and in relation to my physical form, gait and gestures (expressions), as well as to the attitude or energy with which movements are expressed in the present moment. But, for the crystallisations, a 'score' or outline is sometimes prepared beforehand: i.e., some places where the movement will take place, or a particular scenario.

Choreography is not normally involved, at least not in a traditional sense, unless I am using the crystallisation as a springboard to help in creating a professional performance. Otherwise, in a crystallisation, I often initiate my movements in the same way as in general practice, i.e. by responding to my inner being, to the site, and to co-practitioners as well as to the environment as a whole in the present moment. The spectator is seen as part of the environment. The site, in turn, influences my postures, manner of moving and attitude, through its physical form, material, themes and stories, while I 'construct the space' through and with my particular movement.

As an example of how an area's physical form stimulates the practitioner's physical movement, we can compare a circular practice space with a rectangular one. In a circular space, I may feel encouraged to move in circles or to rotate around my own vertical axis and even to whirl like a Sufi dancer. I might also be inspired to make circular movements with my arms and hands. If I want to, I can easily keep running non-stop in a circular space. In a rectangular practice space, I can of course also run in circles and make circular movements, but in Amerta Movement we practise with an awareness of the space. This means that, via my movements, I enter into a dialogue, an exchange, with the area's specific form. Here, in a rectangular practice space, I am forced to stop at the edge and turn in order not to walk off the practice area or, if indoors, bump into a wall. I could also, however, continue to run, walk or crawl on the spot. The rectangular area also invites me to make straight lines with my arms and hands. One task in the practice is, via our movements, to show awareness of the physical form of the space. Another is to indicate an intended direction in and through the space with our physical movements – pointing to it with an arm or with another part of the body – not as a fixed rule, but in a way that is coherent with my movement and whole movement situation, here and now.

Likewise, the make-up of the practice area whether principally cement, rock, marble, wood, grass, gravel or sand also influences and stimulates my movement – gait, gestures, positions and rhythm – in different ways. If I am practising on an even, smooth surface, like the main pendopo's concrete floor at Lemah Putih, I will be more inclined to run than when practising in long grass or on small pebbles. The latter two stimulate awareness and I need to feel my way first by carefully probing the ground with a foot before entering it fully.

My movement themes and the atmosphere of the site also stimulate my movement practice. Take first the overall themes of Amerta Movement – physical/bodily expression, prayer/the sacred and purification. These themes stimulate my movement expressions via my attitude. For example, if I have chosen the overall theme of prayer/the sacred and a practice area related to prayer/the sacred, I will enter the space with an attitude of piety. This is very different from someone who has chosen the theme of physical/bodily expression and a practice area on the same basis. Prayer implies a sacred dimension whereas physical/bodily expression implies a worldly expression or creation based on human values. A comparison in the West would be with creative activities carried out in a church or community centre. Of course, a temple or church has a very different atmosphere from that of a beach or a sports arena and a student practising at such places is influenced accordingly.

Crystallisations, as we have just seen, never proceed as a direct communication between the moving performer and the spectator, but always go via the vertical axis. The quality of a crystallisation depends not only on the practitioner but also on the spectators who are also responsible for what they see and experience, as 'beauty is in the eye of the beholder'.

~

In summary, our process of growth must always be seen in the context of the whole of life. According to the theory of Amerta Movement, the individual is part of the natural world, part of the spiritual/sacred world, and part of society. This means that our process of growth and blossoming has to proceed in a way that respects and benefits all three. A human being is part of life, not the centre of it and not above it. Hence, we need to strive for a dynamic, cultural and ecological balance between an individual, society, nature and the spiritual/sacred dimension of life.

Chapter 4

The Movement Practice

Practice

The movement practice has to be felt by and in our own bodies. It is rooted in our perceptions of our inner world and of the world outside, the practice-site and the whole, wider environment. This means that the practice is based on what emerges from within us in the present moment, as well as on our conscious intention and choices, and on input from the surroundings through our perceptions of those surroundings and interactions with them. This input from inside and outside is expressed or translated into ordinary daily movements like walking, sitting, standing, running, jumping, sensing, feeling, seeing, hearing, touching, stopping to take a breath or to feel one's condition, and so on. Practice is often not accompanied by music. However, in Java – where movement practice usually takes place out of doors – sounds from everyday life, whether from daily life activities or from rituals and celebrations going on in nearby villages, provide 'music' or atmosphere. When there *is* music during movement practice, it is live and generally takes second place to the movement. The movement and the music are seen as two different things, and so can relate to each other in different ways according to the situation. Music, in Amerta Movement, normally accompanies those moving – supporting their movements rather than being imposed on them. Of course, music can also be an inspiration or a background to provide atmosphere. Sometimes practitioners accompany their own, or each other's, practice with spontaneously made sounds or song, by playing an instrument or by beating two rocks or sticks together. Prapto would sometimes use a drum, the conga or sing songs from the *wayang kulit* (Javanese shadow puppet theatre).

In another pattern of practice, Prapto would take students through the three stages of 'walking-crawling-lying' or 'lying-crawling-walking' with variations for each movement. However, as a rule, there are no pre-determined forms, steps or gestures, and no pre-determined choreography in Amerta Movement.

Beginning a workshop

From the very first day, participants in an Amerta Movement workshop are immersed in practice, learning directly from the primacy of movement. [For immediacy, I usually write in the present tense. But these descriptions all still relate specifically to workshops run in the 1980s and 90s.] This takes place in the school's tropical green garden, where practice often starts in one of the two pendopos (practice halls), and later may end at one of the specifically created sites in the school's open landscape.

Participants practise starting from the physical body, 'from gravity' as Prapto says, and entering the pendopo with an open attitude – that is, an attitude of not knowing beforehand what is going to happen. Often they start to move freely in and through the pendopo without any warm-up, encouraged by the pleasant feeling of the warm tropical air on their body. They may start by working alone in the midst of the whole group, expressing themselves physically, until they eventually make contact spontaneously with others in the space. Their focus is both turned inside to themselves as well as at the same time turned outside to the practice hall and to co-practitioners. Movement is free. It takes the form of an embodied improvisation on what is arising inside and outside the individual in the present moment. But there are also some who start by lying down on the cool concrete floor and 'warm up' through Western style body and relaxation exercises or yoga. This might include breathing out loudly and releasing tension, moving part of the body this way or that to let the body 'wake up' and 'speak'. Alternatively, I may just feel the floor with the palms of my hands and start to roll across the floor while twisting my torso like a caterpillar and, at the same time, looking around – sensing and feeling to prepare myself for what may happen and to be aware of the others in the space.

While movements are mostly fluid and graceful, they are not necessarily so. They can also be staccato and expressive or even wild and ecstatic. This is all rather like children playing except that participants work at being aware whilst practising. An example might be training in becoming aware of my back. Here I might walk attentively backwards sensing the space with my back. Others might be working on space and the awareness of space. Here, for example, before entering the space, I might look at it from outside, observing it neutrally in order to form an intention as to my direction and end goal in space. Whilst moving freely in and through the space, people will also meet and interact with each other, in silence, as well as with laughter, sometimes with sounds and song.

Consciousness of body, attitudes and space

The physical practice centres on consciousness of body, attitudes and space, as well as on expression of self, relationship and communication with the environment, including with others moving in the space. Through the practice, we become aware of our bodies in the physical sense (body-conscious), as we make contact with the space, aware of thoughts, feelings and emotions (attitude-conscious), and also aware of the form, dimensions, material, quality and atmosphere of the space, i.e. aware of the practice-site (space-conscious).

Movements are based on my whole being, i.e. body, mind and feelings. Practice starts from the body physically, i.e. from a sense of weight and gravity and movement reading*, through which I become aware of my body and the environment. Ideally, movements are expressed through the whole body from top to bottom, radiating through all the cells of the skin, like a light from inside, shining evenly through the whole surface. Movement in and across space makes the whole body come alive. Movement also takes place at each person's particular level and speed. There is no pressure to perform and no specific or well-defined levels to be reached within certain time limits. Hence, people from all levels and backgrounds can practise and express themselves together since each of us moves at our own pace and in our own style.

We start by allowing the body's sensations, instincts, reflexes, impulses, sounds, rhythms and tempo to appear. We let the body's pre-verbal language and stirrings rise and transform in the body into movement in the outside world, helped by the ego/conscious mind. Unlike, for example, in yoga with its chakras we do not focus on one centre. The aim is a unity between body, mind, and feelings, whereby movements are initiated from the individual's wholeness. This is necessary also in order to start a developmental process where mind and body are not separated.

In the practice, it is essential to be aware with the whole body. If we cannot sense ourselves from inside or sense our physical contact with the practice site, and be aware of our thoughts, feelings and emotions, i.e. our attitudes, then we cannot make the many choices inherent in a free improvisational practice, both in terms of physical movement or of our attitudes. These choices relate to posture, gaits, proportions, levels, rhythm, speed, placement, timing and direction in space, pausing and change of direction. They also include decisions about whether or not to enter into connection, relation and communication with other people and objects in the space.

The practice is generally joyful and rewarding, sometimes with an atmosphere of myth and fairy tale and sometimes also demanding and challenging. However, this also constitutes a unique opportunity to develop, to create our own movement style and for each of us to be accommodated as a unique being into a practice shared with others. To do all this and to deal with the improvisational practice of Amerta Movement, we need individuality, described as the capacity to 'stand on one's own two legs' or 'to find one's own mode of being', as much as we need maturity.

Creating an attitude of dialogue

An essential theme in Amerta Movement practice is that 'everything is movement inside and outside'. Prapto would suggest that we make a bridge between inside and outside, thereby creating a dialogue, an exchange, between the two while practising movement. This idea provides a framework without any pre-determined form or choreography for our bodily practice. Prapto uses his attitudes and reactions as examples. Sitting in the main pendopo with a group of students, he looks out at the land and says:

> *Everything is movement inside and outside.*

> *When I feel like moving I go out there on the land and move. I imagine that this land has no movement, no life and no activity. I try to realise that when I am staying in one spot then I am also in movement and moving.*

> *The outer world, the land out there, is moving. People we know are moving. They are not standing still. They are always changing.*

> *I do not want to see this – that the world outside of me is moving. In my imagination and in my thoughts my father and mother are always staying in the same place. They are like eternity, always there and always taking care of me. (Prapto laughs heartily at his own words).*

> *But, when I see that the world outside of me is moving, the question then is: How can I become active and move with/in the outside world, which itself is already moving and changing?*

Prapto then speaks of the inner world:

> *It is the task of the soul or the spirit to look after oneself in one's inner world.*

> *I think it is good to realise that the spirit inside is also in movement moving, otherwise you are lying or not conscious.*

> *By not recognising that our inside is also moving, we want to avoid suffering. One feels insecure. But this is better than lying or not being conscious, because then we can deal with it. We can develop in a more clear way by understanding that we are all in movement. Our inside and our outside are moving and changing all the time.*

*When I have recognised that, then it is easier for me to make
solutions in life without duality.*

Prapto then suggests how to cope with the fact that inside and outside are
moving during our movement practice:

*…the main thing is how we can find an attitude to bridge
between inside and outside. That way inside and outside can
dialogue so that what is good inside is also good outside.*

Prapto then asks people to keep the following question in mind in a relaxed
way while moving in and across the space in comfortable positions.

How to find an attitude to bridge inside and outside?

*How to position oneself in a relaxed way, comfortable enough
to move and at the same time create a bridge while walking,
sitting, crawling, stopping, and so on?*

Prapto here uses the image of a bridge because Amerta Movement is about
transformation, for example transformation of inner stirrings and sensations
into physical movement, as well as transformation from one stage of
development to another. A new attitude can facilitate our passing from the old
land or old being to a new one, or simply to taking 'a new step in life'.

Landing and taking off

Alongside this, to help students to ground themselves in body and space,
Prapto suggests they find a movement exercise that involves 'landing' and
'taking off'. They are asked to do so while being aware of their own body in
terms of its physical proportions and form: they are asked to be aware of the
different bodily positions they are adopting while moving in a free and
improvised manner with their attention on landing and taking off.

~ Practising landing and taking off

The whole group walks onto the floor of the pendopo and starts practising 'how
to find – in a physical way – an attitude to bridge inside and outside?' and 'how
to land and to take off?' Prapto puts his instructions in this order so that
students first have to practise landing in the body and on the ground, before
they can set off on a genuine inner impulse.

There is no music, only the sounds of nature and village life. Prapto watches
his students move in silence from outside. The practice continues for several
sessions, some with the whole group on the floor, others with just a few people

moving. The themes he has just been teaching are practised in different ways and old themes are repeated – like moving with a neutral attitude, not getting caught up in one's inner universe of thoughts and emotions – 'not catching or being caught'. After a while, Prapto starts giving instructions like:

Crawl on the earth, crawl on the air!

Crawling, not catching.

Yes! No! Right!

Long step!

(Long silence)

Then suddenly he may start singing in response to people's movements. His singing is reminiscent of the shadow puppet theatre. Prapto then goes on the floor and joins different groups, guiding them through movement.

During the many sessions that follow, moments of stillness spontaneously arise – moments of such fullness that they have a meditative or healing effect. This kind of movement quality, by its depth and serenity, helps people to sense themselves, even to 'retrieve awareness of (lost) parts of themselves', through a 're-membering' process of enhanced awareness and sensitivity. This can also lead to episodes of performance spontaneously arising during the practice.

Movement tasks like these are designed to create a framework within which people can rediscover themselves, body and psyche. The rediscovered body will then work with the newly discovered consciousness and sensitivity.

Preparing, staying, walking

There are three phases to every practice session – Preparing, Staying and Walking. At least these three phases formed a characteristic framework within Amerta Movement practice during the 1980s and 1990s, as well as in the *Pribadi Art* approach which will be treated in Part II. These three phases need to be seen as a whole. They are not static or separate points but form a continuum with fluid boundaries and with no abrupt gaps between them.

'Preparing', for Prapto, is based on seeing my body as my 'home' or 'house' and is described as 'opening the door' [of my home in the body]; 'Staying' is described as 'being at home in the body'; 'Walking' is 'going out from one's home'. The Preparing phase in a general way indicates transitions while Staying and Walking refer to two different ways of practising free movement in and across a space. Staying refers to organic unfolding/expression of being, of self, and beingness, while Walking refers to free movement improvisation seen as a journey in and across a space.

~ Preparing

Preparing or 'opening the door' has four parts:

1. **Starting up**

    This includes arriving at the practice site and adapting to it: warming up by tuning in to the site's atmosphere, story or myth, its physical form and materials, as well as by tuning ourselves like a musical instrument for practising movement. We open all of our senses so as to be in a state of heightened sensitivity.

2. **Transitions**

    This includes transitions between Staying and Walking, i.e. between expression of being/self and free movement in and across a space.

3. **Winding down**

    This covers finishing the practice, 'digesting' the practice, leaving the site and making the transition to going home.

4. **Intention**

    This covers our intended direction or end goal in space, which we choose by looking at the site from outside before entering it.

~ Staying

Staying or 'being at home in the body' has three parts:

1. **Awareness/sensitivity and exploration of being/self**

    This means practising movement in a state of heightened awareness/ sensitivity of the whole body (including mind and feeling) and of the space; being physically grounded in body and space in three dimensions whilst being in felt, physical contact with the site and the density of the air. I meet myself through a process of awareness and sensitivity and express my being/self from inside out as an organic unfolding – "like a bonsai tree", Prapto once said.

2. **Pausing**

    This means pausing in movement, being still and 'taking a rest' or 'taking a breath' to feel the condition of the body, position and breathing. It includes checking the environment by observing or reading it, in a neutral way. Prapto's idea is that stopping is a part of movement. There is no separation between moving and stopping, so stopping becomes a naturally felt action. He talks about "developing the nature of stopping and of receiving one's inner condition, as well as that of the environment." 'The nature of stopping' relates to the kind of stopping which comes about by itself as a natural need of the organic body when a task or effort comes to an end and one is tired. This kind of stopping is commanded by the organic body, by the felt sense, in contrast to situations where the mind commands the body to stop. This kind of stopping can be, for example, because 'time is up', even though the body does not need stopping. (There are two other ways of stopping or pausing in Amerta Movement: first, we might stop during our movement because we 'catch' something, as Prapto terms it, and get distracted by, for example a falling leaf, a rock or a person. Secondly, experienced students also work with a 'sense of pause' while moving, i.e. with a so-called 'moving balance'.)

3. **Home**
   Finally, Staying, in a symbolic or spiritual sense, refers to the body as the home of my being/self or soul.

~ Walking

Walking or going out from one's home has five parts:

1. **Awareness**
   Walking or 'going out from one's home' refers to moving freely in and across a space in any chosen position, in active dialogue – active exchange – with the site and others moving there, whilst being grounded in body and space and in a state of a heightened awareness/ sensitivity of my whole body and of the space, with my eyes open, seeing, feeling and sensing what is in front and around me. Walking involves exploring an awareness of space by probing it in a physical manner through all kinds of positions. It also means that looking at the space from outside is not enough; I must actually move through the space with my body in order to understand it.

2. **Choices**
   Walking also includes making choices about which direction to take when coming to a 'crossroads', as well as choices about positions, gaits, gestures, levels, proportions, balance, speed, tempo, timing and rhythm while moving.

3. **Communication**
   We can add choices about entering into communication with other people, with the site and with objects. The latter may mean practising with materials like a bamboo stick, a rock, a cloth and so on.

4. **Journey**

   In a symbolic sense, walking in and across a space is compared to a journey and the way each of us does it suggests something about the way we travel through life. Walking, in a symbolic sense, is also related to development, to the unfolding of potential, of resources, to change and to the taking of a 'new step' in life.

5. **Time, space, expression, relating**

   Walking also deals with practising movement in terms of time, space, expression and relating – skills developed individually by each practitioner. The challenge is to keep an ongoing balance between inside and outside. On one hand, this implies not getting absorbed in feelings or analysing our movements as they take place; on the other, it means not being pulled away from our being-ness and physical grounding by what is happening in the outside world.

   Walking, in terms of moving in and across a space and pausing (Staying phase) forms a duality. This duality is comparable to that of day and night, active and passive. It is like a melody or rhythm. One is not complete without the other.

Below we will look more closely at a number of vital themes within Amerta Movement practice: 'Time' (comprising 'Balancing time' and 'Inner and outer worlds'); Space; Expression; and 'Relating' (comprising 'Training in relating to objects and people', 'Catching and being caught' and 'Looking clear').

Time

Time refers to my being in touch or in tune with the present. It relates to how I express/compose movements spontaneously while moving. I do so by being aware of my body and my surroundings, using the reading technique explained below, with all my senses. The movements I express are not formed in reaction to anything but express my being in the present moment. Because I am aware of what is going on inside me and outside me, they are formed as a conscious, free, physical response to that reality. My movements, moreover, are not based on my imagination, associations or aesthetic values; rather they result from a process of transforming inner impulses in my body into visible movements, embodying these inner impulses in the outer world. So, in order to compose my movements, I must be open to the inside and outside worlds simultaneously instead of being absorbed, for example, by a thought, by a pre-determined outer form, a specific movement style or by what is happening outside me. There is an inner time or 'timing' for each of us and an outer one in the world.

We start by exploring time in relation to the practice space. This means listening to my own being/self, my body's rhythm and manner of expression, i.e. listening to my 'own time' in relation to the practice space or the site where I am practising. Physically this involves weighing up how much physical activity and how much passivity feels right. In terms of attitude, it includes experimenting to see how much openness and receiving and how much closedness feels right for me. It may happen that I find myself moving with someone who has a different timing, speed or rhythm from mine. I may also find a difference between my 'own time', as someone from a modern society, and the timing of an ancient site – like a temple. In this case, it can seem as if we are on two different levels: there is an inner time or 'timing' for me (my 'own time') and an outer one in the external world.

To demonstrate what he means by 'own time', Prapto guides a woman by moving with her. She has a large, rather heavy body and is moving rather slowly. Little by little, influenced by Prapto's guidance and his faster movements, her pace becomes faster and more energetic. It is as if her large, heavy body wakes up. Even though she gets out of breath to begin with, she soon catches up with the faster rhythm. The joy and liveliness radiating from her whole person indicates that this is really her rhythm. It is so obvious that the rest of the group spontaneously applauds.

~ Balancing time

Finding the right balance between myself and a practice site or another person moving has to do with time, according to Prapto. As we have seen, it may be hard to find a way to make my time/timing in movement and expression fit with the time of the practice-site and the time of another person moving. The first step is to try to adapt my 'own time' to that of the outside. This might result in a 'unity' whereby I move in tune with the outside. If I cannot be completely in tune with the surroundings, whether this be the practice space or my movement partners, I can instead engage in a dialogue or an exchange with the site or movement partner. This can take the form of what Prapto calls a 'bargaining' via movement.

~ Inner and outer worlds

In Prapto's terms, my inner world, when it concerns time, is in dialogue with the outer world. Dialogue here describes the way that, through my manner of moving, I am affected or influenced by the outer world and try to adapt to it movement-wise as well as with my whole self. I might also try to use the outer world – for example, a physical structure like the ascending spiral of Borobudur Temple or a piece of marble or some sand – as a springboard for new movements, new creative postures and compositions. So the term 'dialogue' here means 'the student is taking into consideration the outside world' whilst also listening to the inner one. I pay attention to the outer world of the practice-site by adapting to its physical form, material and atmosphere. But I am not only adapting to it; whilst moving I am also trying to contribute something new to it. This can be through my way of 'constructing' my body in the space, i.e. of placing myself in a space or by adding 'props' to the space – perhaps a flower, a pebble, even constructing a mandala in the sand or a pile of rocks chime. My dialogue involves 'negotiating' with the site to see whether something is possible. I try new ways of relating to the outer world and being inspired by it.

Space

Space also relates to the two worlds of inner and outer. Internal space is formed by my inner sensations, reflexes and instincts, as well as by the energy/material or 'substance' of feelings, emotions and thoughts. External space refers to the physical practice site in terms of physical form, material and atmosphere, story or myth. Other people moving form part of a practice space as, by their presence, they contribute to its atmosphere. An awareness of space is gradually acquired by my own body. This implies that we explore the space or practice-site and adapt to it. We do so by probing its form and materials with all our senses while moving in different physical positions and ways in and across the site. It is especially important to look at the space in a neutral way, sensing it physically and, as far as possible, trying not to be influenced by emotions or preconceived ideas.

Expression

Expression refers to my 'genuine being' as embodied in movement while conducting a dialogue with the surroundings – so, I am also paying attention to my surroundings and taking this into account in my expression. Expression happens indirectly in the sense that it arises from a process of transformation – beyond my direct control – of my formless inner world together with inputs from the outer world, into physical movement. This expression is not formed actively by my conscious mind/ego, nor is it based on my imagination or mental associations. My movements are based on input or material not only from my mind but also from my whole body (body, mind and spirit) and from the world outside. The origin of this input or material lies in the unconscious. That is why our movement expression is said to 'almost happen by itself'. More precisely, my conscious mind or ego helps in the process of forming my movement expressions in the outer world. Finally, my movement takes place according to my particular level and speed. Expression leads to communication through physical movement. It leads to making contact with the surroundings and to entering into relationships with others moving with me.

Relating

According to Prapto, relating is not to be taken lightly. If someone keeps jumping into relating with others, Prapto would sometimes stop them and make them practice with one of the pillars of the pendopo instead. If practice takes place in a studio, he might recommend that they work with a chair. The pillar or chair is used as a stand-in for another person. The aim is to become aware of my own pattern of behaviour, actions and reactions, as well as to 'have a look' at the other person and become aware of the motives behind my interest in them, before entering into relationship with them. Prapto calls entering relationships without awareness of our motives, feelings and emotions 'catching or being caught'.

~ Training in relating to objects and people

When we are moving, we relate both to objects and to other people moving with us. Training to do this takes place in various ways. One is to train our awareness by looking at the object or person of interest in a neutral way. Another is to enter the practice while keeping in mind the question: 'How can I express myself and still be with the others?'

When thoughts, feelings and emotions surface in our movement – in this case, in our encounters with other practitioners – Prapto's recommendation is to try to contain them, i.e. to accept them and move with them instead of expressing them crudely, irrespective of whether they are 'nice' or not. In this way, I allow the energy of these thoughts, feelings and emotions to flow through my whole body and to be felt by me. They thereby animate my whole being, before this energy – we might also say 'material' – is transformed into physical movements and gestures in the outer world. Hence, these thoughts, feelings and emotions take on a new value by being embodied in the outside world. They are translated, so to speak, from just being inner stirrings, or energies from an inner world's unseen chaos, into bodily movements and gestures in the outside world, where they can be seen. This process from inner energy to bodily expression in the outside world can be lost if we act directly on our impulses, thoughts, feelings and emotions. Finally, we can also just let them go.

Contact with one another during practice takes place through looking or touching while moving. Contact also occurs in more indirect ways, for example by placing a rock, a stick or a cloth as a sign of approach. Sometimes, this form of contact is a lot of fun. We can feel like children playing. Anything can be right as long as I take responsibility for my choices. It is a new experience to relate not through talking but through physical movement; an unconventional way of sharing a space. It gives a great feeling of freedom, but it can also be challenging. Genuine expression does not always come automatically. At other times, our actions might not be entirely honest and might not accurately reflect a wish. This can be due to politeness or shyness. These mechanisms also apply when we are being 'caught' by others. Occasionally, it can be difficult just to mind my own business and do what I really want perhaps because my social conditioning is strong. Conversely, encounters can also be very supportive and may have a catalysing effect in helping us manifest our potential.

~ Training in catching and being caught

When an impulse arises to approach or move with another person, this is 'catching'. If I act on this impulse, I am catching the other person and vice versa. While this seems a natural way to go about things, in Amerta Movement it is not necessarily so. Some choices or impulses seem spontaneously happy while others do not. Yet we keep making these choices. It is important to be conscious of our impulses and desires in order to avoid repeating hurtful or obstructive patterns of behaviour.

A group may practise awareness of impulses in different ways while moving freely in the space. One technique based on feeling is to try, instead of acting out the impulse (catching), to feel it in my own body first and move with it. By doing so, I can often understand what the impulse is really about. Sometimes, the impulse is related to something or someone else in my personal life rather than to the person in front of me (unless I know them already). Understanding this has a liberating effect and can help me become freer in my choices. My actions and movements in the space will then be based on my own choices currently rather than directed by something or someone outside or from the past.

~ 'Looking clear'

Another technique is based on looking or, as Prapto called it, 'looking clear', which means looking at the object or person without letting my reactions, thoughts, feelings, or emotions interfere with or influence what I see. This technique is normally applied when practising together in a space. It involves observing the person I want to 'catch' in the same way as I might photograph them or describe their appearance. For example: How tall is this person? What are their proportions? Are their eyes symmetrically placed? What clothes are they wearing? What colour are they? How far away are they? This technique, like the previous one, has a liberating effect. It helps me experience the reality of a situation as it is and not be manipulated by my imagination, prejudices, emotions, fears, likes and dislikes. I can also observe myself in the same way.

The aim of these exercises is to enable us to be fully in the present moment, grounded in body and space and to experience the present situation neutrally without projecting onto it. However, if we really want to, Prapto did not forbid 'catching', 'being caught' or expressing our feelings or impulses directly.

Other central Amerta themes, which we will consider below, are: 'Mode: Home and Road'; 'Moving House'; 'Movement meditation'; 'Guiding'; and 'Movement reading'.

Mode: Home and Road

There are two modes of initiating movement practice: Home and Road. They relate to the practice both in the physical sense and a symbolic one.

In Home mode, my movement in and across the space is approached from a fixed point, to which I return, as when, in daily life, I go out from my home to work or to go shopping, for example, and later return to it. The movement is initiated from a static view and from a static point. The aim is to 'meet myself', to be 're-born' into my genuine being, and to learn from that. Home mode is also seen in terms of a society, called 'Home-society', as when a group practises together from this mode. Home-society relates to a static society and to tradition and does not fundamentally change.

In contrast, Road mode means initiating movement from movement itself or from a linear perspective, 'from line-view' or from 'following the line of the movement', as Prapto variously described it. This means starting with the line itself in the sense of a never-ending road without a fixed point of beginning and without returning to a fixed point. In this way, I am 'on the road'. Road mode is life as a journey. It is aimed at practising movement and change as a way of development or as a spiritual way. My body-mind-spirit is in constant flux and I have to make choices all the time as to direction. Road mode is also seen in terms of a group or a society, called 'Road-society', as when a group practises together from this mode. Road-society relates to a modern type of society based on change and development, a globalised society in constant flux.

Mode as a choice in relation to practising movement is independent of the practice space or physical landscape. We choose it as an approach to movement practice and to life.

Moving House

Prapto's instructions for practice sessions concerned consciousness of body and attitude, grounding in body and space and were designed to create a framework within which we can rediscover ourselves, body and mind or body and psyche. As described earlier, among the metaphors he used are the idea of my body as my house or home and movement as my parents. This means that movement is the mirror in which we can see ourselves and through which we can seek guidance in the same way that children seek guidance from their parents or use them as a frame of reference for how to live their lives.

Students practise, alone, in pairs, in small groups or all together. There are also sessions where students can ask Prapto questions, as well as having discussions among themselves after completing a movement task.

> *We try to realise moving now, starting from neutral.*

> *Starting from breathing without catching and also without being caught.*

When we start to practise, we are 'moving out of our old house' or old body and psyche. This is because our whole body and being (physicality, inner stirrings, behaviour and attitude) start to change as a consequence of the practice being carried out in a state of heightened awareness and sensitivity. The body re-creates itself or changes into a 'new house'. It does so as we let go of accumulated physical tensions, old, useless or outdated attitudes and patterns of behaviour and movement. The 'new house' is our new body, behaviour and attitudes, transformed by movement practice.

This means that, after leaving our 'old house', we are on our own and must rely on our own body, movement and experiences. We must practise 'standing on our own legs', finding our 'own mode of being' in the present moment, and building a new frame of reference that suits our new self. This leads to the development of hidden inner resources and potential, to new bodily skills and new ways of moving. Little by little, the 'new parents' will come. As Prapto said:

> *The movement is your parents.*

> *When going out from the house, I leave behind father, mother and house.*

> *Now it is clear I have no father and no mother, but my future father and mother will come.*

The resulting changes will leave us in better physical and mental condition, with a greater sense of wholeness of body, mind and feelings and with a clearer and more spacious attitude to life, to oneself, to others and to the environment.

Movement meditation

Because Amerta Movement is carried out in a state of awareness and heightened sensitivity and is based on the whole body, as well as working with attitudes towards oneself and life, it has often been compared to meditation – rather as tai chi is sometimes seen as a movement meditation. In this case, we might say that the body as the container of the entire person within Amerta Movement constitutes the tool or the device for meditation or for entering into meditation; the entire body, not just one part of it or one centre within it, the body as a whole, may be seen as a moving mantra.

Guiding

Prapto also moved with his students both individually and as a group. This he called guiding. His guidance of students, he explained, follows a 'picture' that he received while moving with his students, using his body as a diagnostic tool* for what is going on in the student being guided. He also used anecdotes, symbols, metaphors and riddles to illustrate his teachings and would respond to students' movements not only through his own movement, but also through song, sounds, mantras and prayer. He used himself and his life experience as a role model and as a tool for teaching, doing so with an enormous sense of humour, often laughing heartily in the middle of telling a story.

Prapto moved with his students in many different ways, like a wise old man, a cowboy, a female warrior, a shy maiden, even an animal like a buffalo or a tiger. In doing so, he was not trying to portray these figures or 'perform' them; rather, he was trying to embody their energy in a spontaneous manner. Through this kind of guiding Prapto gave students a precise impulse, either stimulating or challenging them to help them grow and to unfold their creative potential. His aim, he said, was for students to find their own story, to see themselves. That way they can set themselves free and move on without being perpetually caught up in repeating the same pattern of actions and reactions in their life. Instead of reacting, they can respond to life, which means meeting life, not through automatic reactions, but with a capacity for conscious choice.

Movement reading

Movement reading is a consciousness technique through which I gain information about myself and my environment during a practice session – i.e. my body and attitude, my physical environment and other people moving in it. It is rather like going out for a walk in daily life, when I have to pay attention to myself, other people, traffic, weather conditions and so on, except that, in Amerta Movement, this 'walk' takes place within a specific framework or site of practice where I practise movement in and across a space.

Reading is based on seeing, feeling and sensing, as well as on becoming attuned to the local environment. I read using the whole body (mind and spirit) as an instrument for perception and expression: I read myself and the environment in order to ground myself physically in body and space in physical contact with the site. And I read with the aim of accepting – receiving or acknowledging – my inner condition or attitude as well as that of the external environment. In this way, I can face reality with a relaxed attitude and without judging. The input from my readings, my 'material' in Prapto's terms, is transformed into my movement, which I express in the outside world. Through reading I become aware of my body, its form and functions; of my (inner) attitude, i.e. my emotions, feelings and thoughts; and I become aware of the practice site, its form, material and atmosphere. In short, I become body-conscious, attitude-conscious and space-conscious. (Reading is sometimes called 'looking', especially true during the early years of Amerta Movement).

~ The process of reading

In Prapto's terms, reading is 'seeing from the body', 'body vision' and 'body curiosity'. Comparing reading in Amerta Movement to reading a book, we might say that reading a book is a one-way process, while movement reading is an ongoing, two-way process. It comprises all my internal reactions while reading and takes place on a conscious and subconscious level, both within and outside of my awareness. In the process, my perception is refined and works at a higher level with heightened awareness. The technique may be compared to 'reading a situation': I perceive the situation plus a number of different physical aspects related to it. In this case, I rely on eyesight but also on hearing, smell and other senses, as well as on experience, intuition and instinct. This is often true in anxious situations – for example, when assessing whether a stranger is friendly or hostile – when we rely heavily on experience, instinct and intuition.

Sight is crucial when reading the external environment but other senses are also used. For perceiving the internal environment, I must especially rely on feeling my body in terms of its physicality. This is considered the most important thing, but emotions and thoughts are also essential, although they are not analysed for their content but treated as 'materials' or energies, which are transformed in my body and expressed in my physical movement in the outside world – embodied. This process of transforming my inner life into movement in the physical world is an act of embodiment and is characteristic of Amerta Movement. Inner sensations, feelings and emotions, which are otherwise outside my awareness or invisible to me, become visible by being transformed into physical movement in the outside world. This transformation process involves my whole body, not just the conscious ego as when I express an inner feeling or emotion directly – as is often the case in Western-style movement. Through the embodied transformation process, these inner stirrings take on a different value and help to widen my outlook on life. I can say that I am responding physically to life.

When moving, my ego is awake and active; I am also in a condition of heightened awareness and sensitivity, as in a moving meditation. I am both active (i.e. moving physically through space) and passive (i.e. receiving – or being aware of – my condition and that of the environment in a relaxed way).

In summary, through movement reading, we train not only our five senses but also our inner senses connected to balance and location in space, our kinaesthetic awareness and our intuition and instincts.

~ Curiosity and reading

Curiosity is the spark that initiates movement reading. Reading, in turn, is the generator that starts the process of 'informed' or 'aware' movement. This is similar to the way that stretching is the 'starter' or waking mechanism of our being, of the self in the body and of daily life movement. During movement practice, it is the reading process that leads me to change positions. Through adopting new physical positions, I gain new experiences. A change of physical position makes me look at the outside world from a new angle or perspective; this in turn may affect my feelings, emotions and thoughts, as well as my physical body and senses. We might compare this dynamic with the art of photography. The photographer, in selecting the subject and focus, provides different perspectives on the reality we observe and thereby influences our perception of that reality. By experiencing my environment, other movement practitioners and the site from different physical positions and different rhythms, I also experience them from new perspectives. Body and mind, practitioner and site all influence one another. It is not only I who am reading, I am also being 'read' and 'processed' by the environment, i.e. influenced by the practice-site, by its physical form, material and atmosphere which affect my movement and its expression in terms of form, gestures, gaits, energy, rhythm, speed and so on. When practising within a circular form, for example, like the spiral of Borobudur temple, this form will influence my movements. I am also influenced by other people present whether they are looking or not: just by their being there and by their energy.

~ Reading and free movement

Reading most importantly gives us the input, or 'material' that is transformed into physical expression in the outside world – the basis on which I compose the form, shapes, gaits and gestures of a movement piece. Reading is also a tool for cultivating and tuning my body as an instrument for movement expression – just as I might cultivate and tune my ability to play the violin. This is what makes Amerta Movement a non-stylised, free improvisational movement practice.

~ Reading and 're-membering'

Reading, as a consciousness technique, wakes me up to life and puts me in touch with the present reality, thereby starting a physical, emotional, mental and spiritual process. This process constitutes the material or energy used for my physical expression in movement and through it I achieve body-, attitude- and space-consciousness. This leads to human growth or personal development and to episodes of movement art, to crystallisations and to performance art. An enquiry into my identity takes place. Some practitioners experience what they call 'soul retrieval', a re-integration of lost or hidden parts of themselves into a wholeness of body and mind, which Prapto called 're-membering'. Others have a feeling of 'coming home' or being reborn into their genuine being/true self. Physically, practitioners also develop hidden potential and become aware of inner resources through continued physical training. They refine the plasticity of their body skills, their ability to express themselves through the whole body and in a physical language of movement, a movement-dance or a mime in the outside world. They also train in being in relationship with others and the environment through physical movement, and in communicating. So, their movement begins to speak, conveying a 'story', like a book can. Prapto said:

> *When practitioners express through the body, because they have*
> *understood about their inside and the environment outside and*
> *have come to a conclusion by reading, then their expression and*
> *creation in the sense of movement language is like a book.*

Overall, in the context of Amerta Movement, movement reading can be seen as an act of awareness used for purification, prayer and blossoming.

~ Reading and purification

Through movement reading, I meet my own self. To become aware of my true condition and to transform blocked energy and stiffened movement habits, purification is needed. According to Prapto, we all have an inner mirror. Sometimes this mirror is obscured by emotions, attitudes and so on – and needs to be cleaned to make our outlook on life clearer. In this way, reading gives clarity. It invites us to acknowledge reality by accepting – recognising and not judging – our inner condition and that of the environment. In this way, one aim of Amerta Movement is fulfilled: to receive our condition honestly and then to practise from a neutral attitude of body and mind. Purification can be seen as a healing of our nature and a way of finding a neutral attitude and a neutral body language.

~ Reading and prayer

Movement reading can lead to prayer. We learn to read on a material and on a spiritual level: when I read the atmosphere of a site, I also read its spiritual dimension. That is to say, I read god. Traditionally, in Java, as seen in Chapter 1, god is an impersonal part of nature, felt to be everywhere, within the human being and also outside, in trees, plants, rivers, rocks, the earth and the sky. In this sense, I can read god in nature and in myself. This closeness to god may incline me to prayer or to movement based on an attitude of prayer. Prayer can also be seen in terms of spirituality/the sacred and new rituals through movement.

~ Reading and blossoming

Amerta Movement's free form aims to develop inner potential and resources of bodily expression and communication. In blossoming, having shed what is not relevant or genuinely our own, we discover inner resources and hidden potential, which can then unfold. We enter a process of growth and personal development, practising movement as a way of life and as an art form. Blossoming can be seen as a cultural expression based on human values and designs. For some this leads to professional performance art. One practitioner describes it as follows:

> *Slowly it dawned on us that reading, for Prapto, was the actual awareness of one's own state of mind in movement, of physical and emotional experiences included in simply being present. Being in a particular place, sensing how that place is affecting one and how in fact there is less and less the notion of one, in the sense of me. It's more about following the line of the movement and realising how movement is a forever changing experience of travelling through space and relating with whatever comes up.* (Morein, 1994: 27-28)

In summary, practitioners engage in movement reading for these reasons:

- to cultivate and tune the body, its form and functions to become an instrument for perception, expression, relationship and communication
- to ground themselves in body and space in the present moment
- to become aware of emotions, feelings and thoughts (i.e. attitudes)
- to get material for movement
- to meet themselves, to get clarity of mind
- to respond physically to life based on daily life movements and on a neutral attitude
- to compose while moving
- for personal development and for a way of being in the world
- for purification and healing
- for prayer, spirituality/the sacred or to develop new rituals
- for performance art
- to create new forms, steps and gestures of movement – choreography
- for cultural expression, performance art and installations in nature.

PART II: The *Pribadi Art* courses

Chapter 5

Basic

Introduction

Prapto described the *Pribadi Art* approach as follows:

> *The Pribadi Art approach is individual. It is about how one is serious about oneself, just as people in Java making* tapa brata *[a spiritual retreat] with meditation and exercises of asceticism in natural environments based on nature's elements, but not in the sense of traditional Javanese mysticism. The impact is rather on how one can see the individual person's development generally in relation to nature's life, to society, as well as in relation to religiosity* (rasa ketuhanan)*.* (Sartono, 1996)

In Part II, we will focus on the *Pribadi Art* programme, also called Individual Art, looking at the courses that were run during the 1980s and 1990s. The first is 'Basic, Born in Lemah Putih', the second 'Vocabulary, Nature and Life' and the third 'Movement in Communication, Dialogue'. These are usually referred to as 'Basic', 'Vocabulary' and 'Communication'. All three normally started and ended at the Lemah Putih School but some teaching took place at cultural sites in Central Java, such as at Candi Sukuh, Candi Borobudur, and Parangtritis Beach on the Indian Ocean and also at Prapto's private property in the mountains called 'the Hill'. These sites, apart from 'the Hill', are part of the Indonesian national heritage and are also referred to as 'power-sites' or 'retreat sites', as they are also used for spiritual retreats. A public presentation, intended as a crystallisation of the process of the courses, took place at the end of the 'Vocabulary' and 'Communication' courses and of some of the 'Basic' courses. The *Pribadi Art* programme was open to everyone.

'Basic' would last about one month with two sessions a day of about three hours each, morning and afternoon, five days a week, mostly at the Lemah Putih School with short visits to cultural sites near the school. 'Vocabulary' would last about two months, with about half the course outside the school in other cultural sites. 'Communication', covered in Chapter 8, ran for about two months and took place mainly at the Lemah Putih School.

Courses normally had 10-20 participants. In each course, a few (usually 2) so-called 'applicants' from Prapto's more advanced students would participate in the double role of assistant instructor and apprentice. The applicants got the opportunity to share their application of Amerta Movement from their background. As for the participants, there was normally a great variety of age, nationality and profession in the courses with students' professional backgrounds mainly in art and healing or therapy.

Most participants were Westerners between 20 and 70 years old with more women than men. Normally one or two Javanese participants would join off and on. Usually participants had to start from the 'Basic' course with Prapto and then progress to the 'Vocabulary' and 'Communication' courses. Before joining Prapto's courses in Java, Western students would often have practised with one of his former students in Europe especially appointed to this task, called 'dialoguers' or 'teachers'. They would help students to prepare for their encounter with Javanese culture, as well as with Prapto's course programme.

On completion of one of the courses with Prapto in Java, students were expected to continue their personal development in their home countries. They could do so by applying the lessons learnt in Java to their private or professional lives. This could involve introducing bodily movement into their daily life in a more conscious way. By finding their own way to integrate their Javanese practice experience into their professional lives, students might pioneer new developments within their profession in their home society.

First we will look at the *Pribadi Art* course, 'Basic', in detail and I will describe the course from my notes, writing in the present tense.

Being born

> *Born in square, circulation of nature (mandala), way (road),*
> *pendopo in nature, Om Ah Hum ... breathing, rest, wake up,*
> *sitting, walk, to understand.*
> (Amerta Movement in Lemah Putih 1995-96 programme)

'Basic' skills are about identity, waking up and about 'being born' or rather 'reborn' into our genuine being, our true self, by responding physically to life inside and outside ourselves. 'Basic' skills also include grounding in body and space and expression of self. Practice, moreover, covers issues such as 'who am I?' 'Where do I come from?' And 'where am I going?' All three are crucial in the traditional Javanese outlook on life, *kejawen,* discussed in Chapter 1. Practice is also about Westerners orientating themselves in Java, as well as expressing themselves, relating and communicating with the environment in Java. Finally, 'Basic' is also about individual differences within the group. In the course description shown above, Prapto uses the term 'being born' to describe what takes place during the 'Basic' course for the individual student. By adding to the course description the Buddhist mantra *Om Ah Hum,* Prapto indicates that this 'being born' refers not to a 'normal' human birth but to a spiritual one. So one of the aims of the 'Basic' phase and skills in Amerta Movement is a rebirth or a transformative development process, taking place within me so I become more in touch with my genuine being and 'meet myself'.

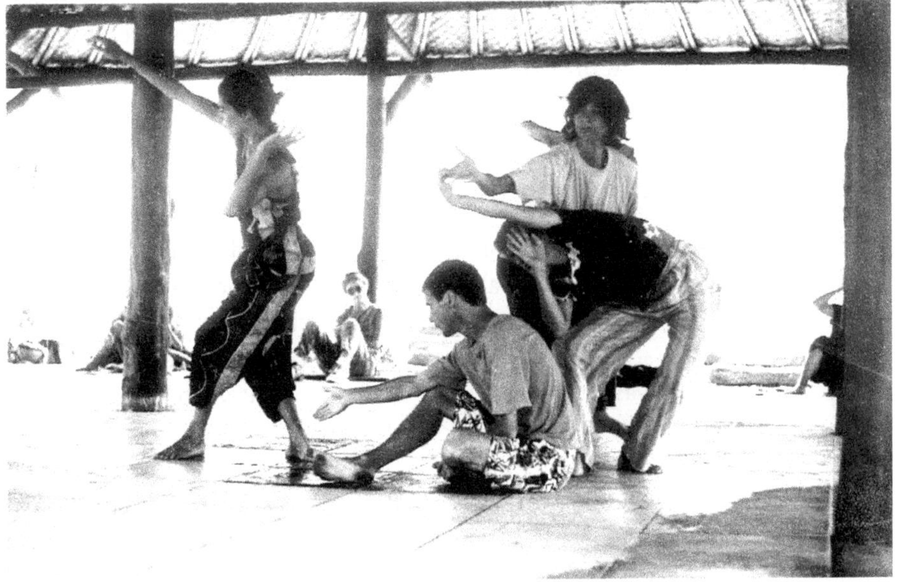

Basic 95, Practice in Pendopo

'Basic' also deals with the individual 'being born' in terms of society, nature and spirituality/the sacred, thereby stressing the importance of our conscious relationship to these dimensions. Students achieve this through ordinary physical movement, daily life movements, i.e. through the free, non-stylised improvisational movement carried out in a state of an enhanced sensitivity and awareness from one moment to the next.

Moving between earth and sky

We explore ourselves not only as social beings but also as beings of nature and spirituality. This means that we explore ourselves as creatures between earth and sky, between the material and the immaterial dimensions of life. We study how we are beings of earth and sky, of body and mind. We do so, among other things, by moving with the pillars of the pendopo. Like the pillars, which link the pendopo's floor with the roof, i.e., the earth with the sky, we human beings link together in ourselves body and mind, i.e. we link together our 'earth' with our 'sky', or our material dimension with that of the non-material world. We explore these issues through the physical practice itself while being in a state of enhanced awareness and physically grounded in body and space. We also learn to move freely whilst 'reading' ourselves, perceiving ourselves, our colleagues and the practice space with all our senses as well as responding physically to them, and training in expression of self via physical/bodily movement. Finally, students practise making decisions about direction in and through space; about how to move in terms of posture, gait, gestures, rhythm, speed, timing, levels and proportions; about entering or not into relation with others; and about communication.

A framework for the practice

At the school, students practise in one of the pendopos and in the open practice sites with their different geometrical forms described in Chapter 1. The ground at these places is also of different materials such as rock, pebbles, concrete, wood, sand or grass, each stimulating the practitioner's movement, their body and mind, in a different way. Here we will focus on the square, circle and oval. As explained earlier: Square is related to 'Physical/Bodily expression' and the field of Human; Circle is related to 'Prayer' and the field of the Sacred; Oval is related to 'Purification' and the field of 'Nature'. But the themes of 'Physical/Bodily expression', 'Prayer', and 'Purification' can be applied to movement practice at any site, anywhere.

The practice sites in the school's land, with their specific forms, physical materials and associated themes provide a conceptual framework for the movement, which, in turn, influences the form of practitioners' movement there. These sites take on a form-giving role, akin to choreography. They also help students 'warm up' as their first movement task is to adapt to the physical form and material of each space as well as to its atmosphere. They stimulate students to be awake to the present moment and to compose postures, gaits, gestures and movements on that basis. Prapto would talk about how the 'forms of the land inform', i.e. the landscape of the school gives us some information or clues about how to shape and in which spirit to express our formless inner impulses, thereby bringing inner chaos into form in the outside world.

'Basic 95'

I will use the example of the 'Basic' course in 1995 in Java: 'Basic 95'.

Participants

17 students took part (12 women and five men aged from 21 to 73 years old), including four 'applicants'. At the start of this course, there were no Javanese participants, but some joined later for short visits. Participants in 'Basic 95' had been recruited via 'dialoguers' teaching movement in Europe. Some students had also taken an interest in Amerta Movement via articles by former participants.

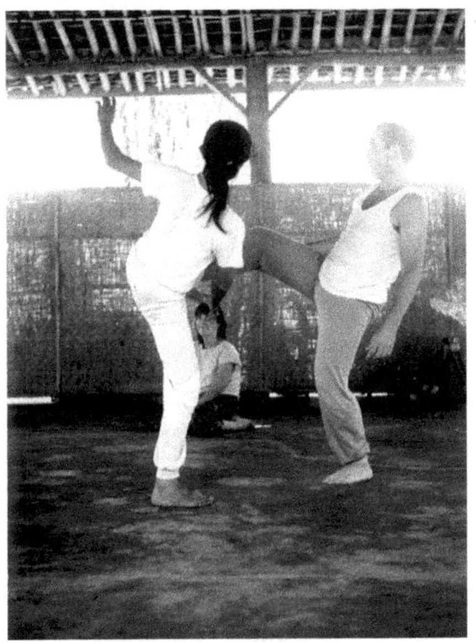

Prapto Guiding (1)

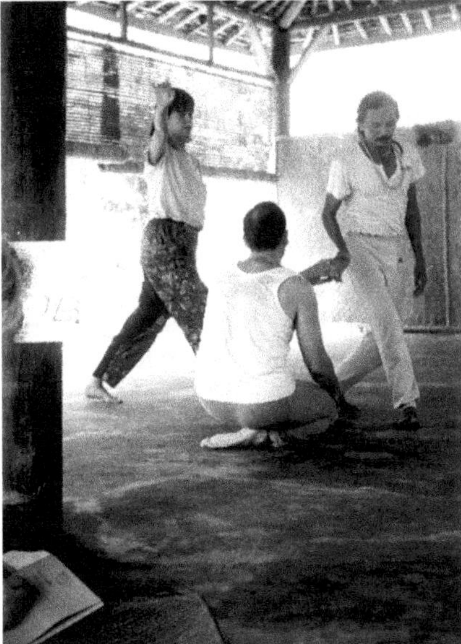

Prapto Guiding (2)

Practice background

Prapto started in the morning teaching different groups of students in relation to their choice of practice site on the school's land, such as the square, circle, oval, the *mandala* (also called nature's stage: an octagonal platform of painted concrete with a smooth surface and shaded by large trees with flame-coloured crowns) and the roads (small pathways formed between lines of different kinds of fruit-trees – the roads constituted a small grove with ditches and small earthen mounds situated directly above the main pendopo and forming a kind of labyrinth). At around 10am everyone would gather in the main pendopo. Teaching would continue until about 1pm. After lunch, we would again practise at our chosen site, partly on our own and partly assisted by the applicant assigned to our group. The applicants would mainly help by physically moving with the group. At the end of the day when tropical darkness descended, Prapto would teach the whole group in the main pendopo by torch light.

Prapto's introduction

In his introduction, Prapto talked about Amerta Movement as related and applicable to four different fields: ritual and the sacred, art, health and healing, and daily life. He also talked about the learning process and his method of teaching. Prapto then touched on the motivation of students coming to Java to study with him. Some were motivated by a deep existential wish to understand life or to try the practice with their own body. Others joined as part of a spiritual quest. Prapto also spoke about differences between himself and his Western students with regard to attitudes towards life and the body. Prapto then introduced fundamental Amerta Movement themes, as well as particular themes the group was going to work with. He demonstrated these physically in front of the students and stressed that practice starts from gravity.

> *For Basic we do around the concept of gravity. It is work from*
> *gravity view. Without gravity, we are in space.*

Basic physical skills are developed by practising walking, sitting, lying, rolling, jumping, pausing to take a rest, checking one's position, one's condition, breathing, and so on. At first, the whole group would practise together, then in smaller groups. In between talks and demonstrations, Prapto answered questions from the students.

According to Prapto we must be of open and accepting mind and attitude in order to understand life. Elaborating, he used an allegory from the natural world. Just as the valley stands under the mountain, I should put myself (the valley), under the challenges of life (the mountain). I must 'put low' my ego and listen to wisdom from my own soul, from nature or life as a divine power. The valley symbolises an open, accepting and humble attitude to ego. The mountain symbolises the challenges of life, which I try to understand and overcome in order to change my life or just in order to get on with my life. It is not advisable to jump into reactions based on my ego or emotions.

Next I will describe some specific features of Amerta Movement that were covered in the course:

The breath

The breath, according to Prapto, "like the wind blowing over the land, comes to everywhere". He means that the lungs breathing start an impulse like a wave of breathing that spreads everywhere in the body, my body being my 'land' or my 'earth'. The breath comes to all the cells of the body, at least potentially so, if I am relaxed and moving in a state of a heightened awareness and sensitivity of my whole body.

Practising breathing initiated from the body itself

Sometimes a physical exercise makes us aware of how a movement releases a 'wave' of breathing through the whole body. This kind of breathing is not initiated or controlled by the ego or conscious mind, but by the body itself. For example, we experience how stretching our arms and legs provokes yawning, which makes the whole body come alive after a period of rest. And, when for example, we work with the big muscles of the torso, we can get a sense of what is meant by 'the breath as a wave through the whole body'. We can get this kind of wave of breath experience when on all fours doing the exercise popularly known as 'the cat'.

Here, I start by arching my back like a cat, first contracting the muscles to arch the spine, then letting them extend again, so that the spine bends in the opposite direction. For the arching, I start from the pelvis, arching one vertebra at a time. At the same time, I try to sense my body from the inside, feeling how the muscles are working. Then I do the opposite movement with the spine, allowing the muscles to extend. This movement not only helps me to get into my body with my awareness and sensitivity but, and very importantly, also helps me feel how the breathing is brought about by the movement of the body. This is in contrast to when I am actively initiating the breathing.

De-programming, purification

Amerta Movement is based on 'natural movement'. Many people before starting Amerta Movement, will have practised other movement and dance forms. Some students, when practising free, non-stylised Amerta Movement, do not base their movement on their natural, everyday postures or even on their own bodily nature. Instead, without being aware of it, they base their free movement on steps and gestures that they have learnt in one of these movement disciplines. However, these movements are not genuinely their own movements, but a tacit program in the student's body, of which they need to become aware in order to move and express themselves directly from their own nature or, as Prapto says, based on their 'genuine being'. In such cases, they may have to de-program their body, directing their awareness and sensitivity to what is going on in their body when they move freely, so as to take these tacit patterns in their body of which they have been unaware, 'out of their body'. They are advised to try to feel with their whole body: what kind of movement is natural to them, to their 'genuine being'. By ceasing these 'automatic programs', held unconsciously in their body, students purify themselves of these learnt movement patterns and attitudes through an act of awareness. They de-program themselves. Then they can start moving from what Prapto calls a 'neutral body'. This de-programming does not mean that I cannot preserve and develop an individual language in movement or work on a pattern I love. It simply means that it is preferable that I become aware of my own personal movement 'language' at the outset of studying Amerta Movement so that I can purposefully move based on my own, individual organic nature, which Prapto calls 'body-nature', and create my own individual, 'person-specific' movement vocabulary and language.

'Basic' is about being re-born into my genuine, organic being, in a manner which might be experienced as a 'new self', 'new being', in Prapto's terms, as I can then consciously base my movements on my own attitudes and own body. 'Basic' is also about how to relate to this 'new self'/'new being' or 'new body' of mine, and how to express myself through it. 'Basic' is also about responding physically to the practice site, as well as to outer objects and other people in it through the tacit language of bodily movement, through my own person-specific bodily language.

Prapto jokes that this de-programming encourages each of us to become our own movement designer. He sees the old programming, still in our bodies from earlier practices, as being due to a lack of awareness and sensitivity and he suggests that we should just take it off like an inner costume.

> *Inside you have costume from Louis XIV, Steve Paxton,*
> *contact improvisation, and tai chi. Become your own designer.*
> *Make your own T-shirt!*

Quality of movement: balance, gravity and lightness

We practise with inner and outer space and with expression of self. Prapto compares the movement of any individual (based on their body, mind, spirit and personal background) to that of a tree and, in a symbolic sense, to 'the tree of life'. According to Prapto, we must express ourselves not only in terms of our roots, i.e. from deeply inside ourselves, but also based on our 'branches' and 'leaves', i.e. from our sense of playfulness, as embodied, for example, in the lightness of fluttering arms, hands and fingers or as in children's play. There must be a balance between an inside feeling and a lightness of existence. As Prapto says:

> *It is not necessary to go to your roots all the time then every*
> *time you move from one place to another one you will be*
> *uprooted, [like a tree].*

Grounding in body and space, 'being at home in the body' and expression

When navigating physically in the space we respond to our readings of self and of the space, according to our perceptions of our inner world and the outer world. To improvise and to embody the present moment, we must have body consciousness or, as Prapto says, "be at home in the body". We must be able to get through space while feeling ourselves physically from inside, grounded in body and space, i.e. in a felt physical contact with the practice site and with the air. To do this, students train in awareness and in sharpening the senses.

Students are listening to their inner body sense, the kinaesthetic sense – also called proprioception* – giving them information about placement in space, as well as using their eyesight, and they express this in their physical movement.

Grounding in body and space when moving through the space in the positions of walking, crawling, lying, standing, running and so on, comes about through being aware of body and mind as well as of the site.

Another way to train in physical grounding is to move with a question in mind. This question, which has to be relevant to the task I am practising, might be one of the following:

> *How can I put myself physically in this space?*
>
> *How can I get through this space physically?*
>
> *How can I relate to the pillars and to other people in a bodily way?*
>
> *How can I be with the others and still express myself?*

or as Prapto formulates this last one:

Still with myself but receiving the activity of the other and making my own decision.

This strategy of keeping in mind a question that relates to the intended result is used in a very relaxed way. I set out through the space with a question in mind. As the practice evolves, the question might slip from my mind. That is OK. I don't need to force myself to keep it in mind. The sentence has already served its purpose of starting my body off on a process of exploration for the desired solutions through movement.

When the whole group is on the floor, students move from pillar to pillar as if on a journey of discovery. Prapto will then at intervals instruct us to:

> *'Stop, check your position! Continue!'*
>
> or
>
> *'Stop, check your condition! Continue!'*

Then we are given the task of finding our own pillar, choosing which one to work with, by moving from pillar to pillar, sensing each one, feeling it with our body. Having each chosen a pillar, we will then practise with it. According to Prapto, the way we get to a pillar or travel from pillar to pillar says something about our ways and rhythm in life.

'Basic' training with the pillars

'Basic' skills are also trained through movement with the pillars of the main pendopo. As Prapto says:

> *When I think about pillar, I'm already in there, and I have
> lost my body.*

When practising movement in a space, as well as being open and grounded in body and space, direction is also important. We need to make choices. According to Prapto:

> *We move from pillar to pillar, training direction, always
> having to look and decide which pillar we want to go to.*

This training in moving from pillar to pillar is designed to help us make decisions about direction in space, about forming intentions of where to end our movement in space as well as about the goal of our movement. We might make this choice helped by the process, the practice itself, of moving physically (Walking phase) in and through the space from pillar to pillar. Or we might choose before entering the practice space, by looking in a neutral way (without judgment) from the outside at the practice space, and thereby coming to a choice (Preparing phase). After moving in the space for a while, I might have come to a 'crossroads', a situation

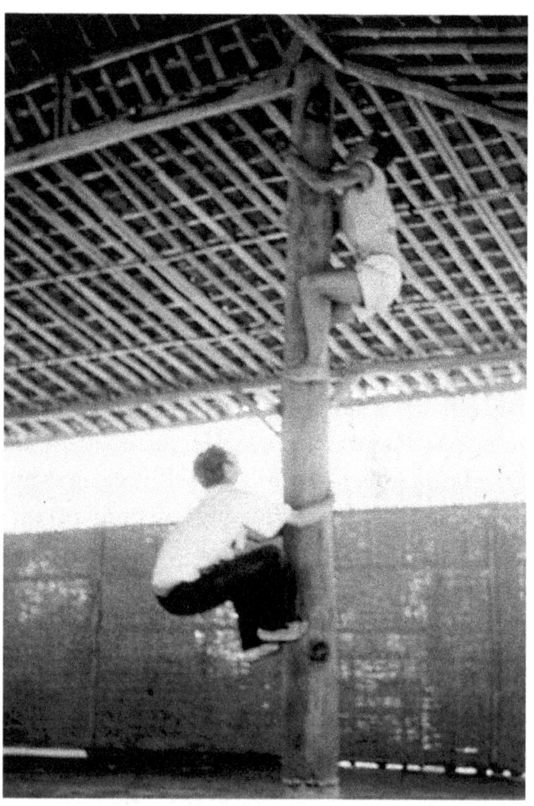

Climbing the Pillar

where making a choice is necessary, and on this basis I make my choice of pillar. I might, though, experience this choosing as overwhelming, if it presents me with too many options. These options/choices include both direction, destination or goal in space, as well as gait, gesture, posture, position, proportions, rhythm, speed, timing, level, and whether to enter into relations or not and choices as to my manner of communication. That is why, during practice, it is essential not only to move but also to give direction to my movement, i.e. to make choices. It is not enough just to 'be'. Making all these choices while practising Amerta free movement can be seen as a practice for living our life. In our daily life, we also have to make all sorts of choices that actively influence our life, as when we go out to go to work. In that situation, in order to move in traffic for example, we need to make the right choices so as not to get hurt, and so on. But the Amerta training in making decisions and in forming intentions can also be seen from an existential point of view as a way to train in the making of decisions, and choices of direction in our life.

According to Prapto, when making decisions about direction in space and about changing direction, I should try to stick to my decisions and intentions:

> *Keep the intention. Your direction is the pillar. Many things can*
> *pull you. Especially if I have a lot of not nice in my life, then I*
> *can be pulled by nice and lose my direction, which is the pillar.*

Showing my mind and responding physically to the practice space

Moving in the practice space, once I have made my decision, it is important to 'show my mind', i.e. to point my body and whole person in my intended direction. This could be by reaching out in the intended direction with an arm or a leg or it could be in a more subtle way where my intention seems to radiate from all the cells of my body from feet to head. As we saw earlier, it is important that my body and movements in some way respond to or mirror the practice space's physical form – square, circle, oval – and that they respond physically to its textures, its surfaces, materials and atmosphere. It is also vital that I touch the space physically where I am practising; and just as I touch the pillars and the ground, so I also intentionally touch the air, becoming aware not only of my whole body's contact with the air, but also of where my physical body ends and the air of the space begins. I must be aware that when I move my hands, arms, feet and legs, my whole body through the space, I can 'crawl on the air', as Prapto describes it. I must also be aware of how I touch those moving with me, if touching is an option – thus I must be using all my senses.

Through moving, we also express ourselves to a pillar and enter a relationship with it through movement as a preparation for entering into relationships with the other people who are moving with us.

The pillar has 'being'

The pillars can be used for many purposes. We train with the pillars because they give us a structure and because the pillars can be used as stand-ins for other objects and for people. According to Prapto, the pillar has 'being': it has its own characteristics, its own life and is not just there for us to use. By understanding the pillar's being and characteristics I can understand my own 'being', my own self and special or characteristic way of being. I can also express my own being or self to the pillar as I would to another person moving with me. Prapto's instructions to students working with the pillars include:

> *Find your own pillar. Crawling to understand the pillar and then yourself or yourself and the pillar. Explore in proportion when you really want to understand.*

> *I understand pillar by reading. I try to understand pillar by hearing, seeing, touching. I express my life to the material [of the pillar].*

> *We try to practise by movement and we try not to go in karmic [i.e. into an automatic reaction].*

The aim of understanding the pillar (or any other organic outer object), according to Prapto, is to get 'a sense of nature life, not just human life'. This is because, as noted earlier, Prapto thinks that human beings – especially Westerners – tend to see themselves as above nature and at the centre of things, instead of as part of nature and creation. In general, when practising with the pillars, there are two approaches, one for relating termed, 'pillar-in-relation' and the other for understanding, called, 'pillar-in-situation'.

'Pillar-in-relation'

In the 'pillar-in-relation' exercise I enter into a relationship with the pillar. Here, for example, the pillar can give me structure for my movement. However, in this exercise, I am not particularly trying to understand the pillar. I am only using the pillar as a tool and as a kind of audience for myself and my movement in and through the space.

'Pillar-in-situation'

In the 'pillar-in-situation' exercise I am trying to understand the pillar. There are two approaches for understanding the pillar, one from *identification* and the other from *dialogue.*

The *identification* approach to understanding means identifying myself with the pillar, 'becoming one' with the pillar, so to speak. As an example, this can be compared to two married people who identify themselves in terms of their union, i.e. in terms of being 'a couple', rather than as two separate individuals. One may add that in Javanese mystical practice, identification is often used to understand something or someone. The mystic simply identifies with, 'becomes one' with, the object or being they want to understand, whether a god, a spirit, an angel, a tree, a natural element or another person. In the same manner when I practise identification with the pillar in order to understand the pillar, I try to 'be one' with the pillar, i.e. to identify myself with the pillar.

The *dialogue* approach to understanding is the second way of achieving understanding in the 'pillar-in-situation' exercise. It consists of trying to understand the pillar as something separate from myself. I study or read the pillar using my whole body, observing, feeling and sensing the pillar from a distance. In this way I get to know, become aware of, the pillar's form, physicality, material and essence or 'spirit'. I study the pillar as an object or a being separate from myself while at the same time recognising how I contain within myself elements similar to those of the pillar. The benefit of this approach is that by understanding the pillar, I also can understand myself because, like the pillar, I am myself a being between earth and sky with a certain form, physicality, essence or 'spirit'.

On a practical level, the *dialogue* approach is designed to help us to practise being independent in the sense of standing on our own two feet. This helps us to experience what it means to 'be a pillar in life and in society'. It gives us a sense of a vertical dimension to life, that we are beings that exist between earth and sky, which in Java means that we are beings living between the material (worldly life on earth) and the immaterial, spiritual/ sacred world (or god), the sky. In this way, the exercise is also preparing students to leave the secure framework provided by the Lemah Putih School and work in the semi-public practice sites. It trains students so that they will not easily be pulled off balance by external influences. They will be like a 'pillar' so to speak, steadfast.

'Pillar-in-relation' versus 'Pillar-in-situation'

The difference between the two approaches becomes clearer if, instead of moving with a pillar, we move with another person. If I do so from the 'pillar-in-relation' approach, I am using the other person for my own purpose, without caring about getting to know anything about that other person. She or he is there for me.

In contrast, if I move with another person from the 'pillar-in-situation' approach, I want to understand that person, and I do so either by identifying with that person in the sense of becoming one with them, or I try to understand them by studying them from a distance with an unbiased, neutral mind.

A few of Prapto's typical suggestions are that students practise with the pillars in order to:

get 'a sense of nature life, not just human life'

get a structure in the space

understand myself

practice understanding myself as a creature between earth and sky

understand the world outside, i.e. to understand the site and the objects and people in it

express myself to the pillar.

~ Moving with pillar, with inner and outer space and the space between

As I move with the pillars for relating and for understanding, I can also use this method to relate to or to understand myself and my co-practitioners and the site. Hence, moving towards the pillar is like turning my attention to my inner self or inner space with awareness, reading my sensations, emotions, feelings, and thoughts; moving away from the pillar is like turning my attention outwards, to the space outside, to others around me, to the site, and to the environment. In this way, I understand inner and outer space.

Finally, we read the 'space between', i.e. the space between ourselves and our chosen point of focus. Whether training with the pillars or other objects I must be aware of the space between me and the pillar or between me and the person I am moving with. So, when I am moving towards them, I must also be aware of how the distance between me and them changes. Prapto says:

Space is an element like earth is an element.

When going to the pillar, see the difference of distance between you and the pillar, that's simple.

Yes I'm here and the pillar there and I still can look at something during my journey and take a breath.

The aim is to enhance my consciousness of space and my aliveness in the present moment, including my aliveness on the road to my goal (the pillar).

~ Reading the 'space between': a training in assertiveness

As well as seeing the 'space between', I must be aware of the space around and behind the other. Sometimes this exercise comes close to a kind of assertiveness training.

A female student described how this exercise helped her to stand on her own two feet when moving with a man with whom she did not feel at ease. She felt 'zoomed in on' by him so that she could not relax but was tense and uneasy and unable to behave naturally. However, by seeing the space between herself and him, she was able to relax and behave in a more natural manner. This was especially true when she gave herself the time also to see the space behind and around him. In this way she felt protected from being 'zoomed in' on and 'paralysed' by him. She was now able to include more of the space in her looking than before. That was a relief because it made her calmer, enabling her to make her own choices about her movement. Through her understanding and newly relaxed attitude, she managed to be aware not just of the man while she was moving with him, but also of herself, which before was difficult.

Looking and listening

An example of how mind and body combined in basic movement during the earliest years of Amerta Movement (mid-1980s) can be found in the perception exercises especially dealing with 'looking' and 'listening', the English terms used by Prapto at the time and before he developed the term 'movement reading', discussed in Chapter 4.

'Looking' especially relates to eyesight, to the mental function, and insights gained from there; however, one can 'look' with the whole body. That is why Amerta Movement practitioners often stress looking with the back of the body, i.e. being aware of the back of the body and of what is behind.

'Listening' is related to hearing, to feeling, as in the feeling of the heart, or listening with an 'open heart' to music, for example. Listening is about sensing my whole body as if scanning it, for how it feels and for what is going on in it. Hence, I listen from the 'felt sense' or, as the Javanese say, from 'inner feeling'. Just as I can look with my whole body, so I can also 'listen' with the whole body. Ideally, 'listening' – like 'looking' – is a neutral form of perception, one which as far as possible is without emotions or prior judgement.

The aim of 'looking' and 'listening' is to get clear about my inner and outer world. To this we can add 'looking directly', which is described below.

When 'looking' and 'listening' a neutral attitude is important, one of accepting without judging. Moreover, to accept, as it will be recalled, does not necessarily mean to agree but simply to acknowledge the state of affairs. The aim of 'looking', including 'looking clear', and of 'listening', and of 'reading' based on a neutral attitude, is to achieve clarity of mind, to facilitate grounding in body and space as well as aliveness attuned to the present moment and prepare the student for entering into relation with co-practitioners.

~ Looking clear at the pillar

'Looking clear', or 'looking directly' as it is also called, is in order not to be biased by preconceived ideas or by emotions while moving and interacting with others. Another aim of 'looking' and 'listening', just as with reading, is to get material or input or energy from inside and outside myself, which is then translated by my body into physical movement in the outer world – that is to say, embodied.

When learning to 'look' at and to 'listen' to ourselves, we may start by focusing on one part of the body, like our hands or feet. We take a 'look' at ourselves from outside in a concrete physical way, as if it were the first time we had done so. We also 'listen' to ourselves in the same way. We 'listen' to the whole body from the 'felt sense' or 'inner feeling'. We may also use other senses: we may smell our body and we may touch our body with a hand, sensing the texture and the physicality of it. That way we can 'scan' ourselves.

Basic improvising skills firstly are about sensitising the physical body, i.e. about using the senses and the instincts. This means 'opening' a specific sense, becoming aware of it and training it by using it. We might agree that senses can be trained to a certain extent, but not agree when it comes to instincts. Can instincts be trained? At least my ability to be aware of my instinctive responses can be trained by repeated exercise in trying to 'listen' to these instinctive responses. Then, little by little and with practice, we can learn to 'read' the environment and ourselves using our instincts and senses. We can get useful knowledge in that way. We might compare students to hunters. Trackers learn things about the animals and birds they are tracking that they did not know before. They learn about the whereabouts of these creatures and about the natural environment they are hunting in. They might know about this from books, but for trackers it becomes an experience felt in their own body, which is very different. Experiencing something in my own body has a much stronger impact on my behaviour and attitude to nature and to life.

Students not only move with the pillars, they also 'look clear' at the pillars. This means looking from the 'physicality of my eye' to the 'physicality of the pillar' without emotion, because emotion can create a 'fog' so that I cannot 'look clear' but get 'caught' by emotion. This is also true when looking at oneself or at other people. And that is why these exercises with the pillars form an important preparation before I enter into relation with others or form opinions about myself.

~ Practising inner and outer space from a neutral approach

When Amerta Movement was practised in Prapto's main pendopo, students alternated between looking at themselves in a neutral way and looking out at the landscape far away while being aware also of the space between the two points of focus. For Prapto, as we saw above, space is not empty and we can 'crawl on the space' or 'crawl on the air' just as we crawl on the ground. Space is an element like earth and space is an active part of movement, as Prapto says:

space has life in itself, space has its own being, its own density.

'Lying-crawling-walking with variations'

For 'Basic' movement training, Prapto often started by taking students through the series of 'lying, crawling and walking, with variations over these three postures,' encouraging them to move in a state of heightened awareness and sensitivity. This movement pattern inevitably brings to mind the three stages of a child's sensorimotor development: being born and just lying there; crawling; and standing upright to walk, trying to conquer the world on one's own.

The 'Basic' movement training following the 'lying-crawling-walking with variations' pattern may be seen as an end itself, in the same way that childhood is an end in itself, i.e. a kind of journey in movement; after this journey, we are certainly also warmed up, body and mind, and ready for free movement in and across the space. So this pattern may be seen as a preparation and an initiation, whereby I am prepared to begin with free movement. I am properly 'equipped' not only to engage in moving alone in and across a space, but also to move among other people, interconnecting with them and with the environment.

Physically 'lying-crawling-walking with variations' grounds me sufficiently in body and space and provides enough confidence and security in self and body for me to embark on free, improvised, non-stylised movement in and across a space, even without music and on my own. The atmosphere is open and accepting like that of 'happy-children-playing'. Through this training, I am in a state of openness where I listen to myself, to my own inner melody, my own genuine intentions and urges. I move from the 'felt sense' of the body. The ingredients from inner and outer inputs are all cooking in my inner melting pot, so to speak, during the practice, before being embodied into a 'movement dance' or a 'dance movement' in the outside world. Very often, this movement or dance seems almost to happen by itself.

~ Practising 'lying on the floor'

I am lying on my back, trying to sense my body physically. How does it make contact with the ground? Does it do so with the same weight all over? Is one part resting more heavily? Do I feel some parts more easily than others?

I am breathing naturally, trying to feel how the lung breathing initiates like a 'wave' through my whole body. This 'wave' or this energy may be felt in the movement of the stomach and as prickly sensations in different parts of my body. It may also be experienced as sensations of itching, of warmth or cold or it may start involuntary little jerks in the body whereby deeply held tensions are released or a natural reflex is activated. Observing this, experiencing this, helps me get body consciousness and enhances the breathing of the cells throughout my body and also enhances the blood circulation. I let go of tension in my muscles as I observe what is happening in my body.

~ Practising weight-bearing and weight-moving

Next, I practise with my body's weight-bearing and weight-moving abilities. This is to get me out of my passive, lying-on-my-back position on the ground and onto the floor to move freely. I do so through movement initiated from the weight of my muscles:

I start on my back in the lying position. To start myself into movement I have pulled one knee up to my chest. I make sure it stays there by lightly supporting my knee's position with my folded hands below the knee or with just one hand. The other leg remains stretched out on the ground. I now focus on the thigh I have pulled up, trying to relax my thigh muscles while I feel the weight of my thigh. That way I feel how my thigh becomes heavier as the muscles relax. I even try to guess how much my thigh weighs. I reach a point where I decide that I am going to let go of this weight and let it roll me over on the side. Then I do so… and land half way on my stomach. I have allowed the weight of one thigh to pull me over on my side. That was my intention. This movement has happened based on the weight-bearing and weight-moving ability of my muscles, which have been moving me, my skeleton, my bones, my whole body from being on my back to lying on my side. Prapto calls this 'movement from body-nature' in contrast to movement initiated from the mind.

Now, in order to move in and across the floor still in the lying position like a little baby, I continue to use this same technique, of moving from 'body-nature'; i.e. I focus on a part of my body, for example a leg or an arm, relaxing it so as to feel – from inside myself – the weight of it. Then I let this weight move me: a movement that is supported by my intention to start moving. I am still in the 'lying phase'. I am still a little like a baby. My movement in the space takes place without my using the palms of my hands or the soles of my feet to put any weight on the floor (or to lean against the walls, the pillars or a tree) for support or to get off the ground. I only use the muscles of my torso for moving. That way I move like a crocodile or a caterpillar or like a ball that continues to roll, when pushed. After that, I am 'aiming at' the crawling phase.

~ Crawling and walking

I also practise this crawling phase with all kinds of variations. Apart from crawling like an animal or a child, I also include the squatting position and walking in the squatting position, as the Javanese sometimes do. I do not try to stand upright yet. I am aiming at it, though.

Finally, I arrive in the standing position. Here my eyes have a freer outlook or overview of the space than before. That empowers me.

In this way, I have proceeded from the animal to the human stage of evolution so to speak, and in terms of practising Amerta Movement, I have experienced my body as a weight-bearing and weight-moving structure, and as movement from body-nature. I have prepared my body and mind for practising free movement.

Moving based on body-nature, on the body in a physical sense, has enabled me to ground myself in the body and to feel my body from inside. I am not just 'looking at my body from outside' as often happens otherwise; I am also in my body with my awareness and sensitivity. I am in an awakened state, a sensitised state where not only my mind but also my body takes the initiative. That gives me a feeling of security and confidence.

~ Walking-crawling-lying from the upright position

The same movement pattern is also often carried out in reverse. From the walking position I go down to the crawling and the lying positions on the floor and back up again – via crawling – to the upright position. The quality of the exercise, the way it is carried out, is important. I have to pay attention to my body and the space from one moment to the next, and may, for example, use different tempos and rhythms. Sometimes I will drop down very slowly so as to sense every little movement in my muscles, as well as to sense the air and the density of the air. That way the movement seems a bit like a movement meditation. Another approach is to do the whole thing in one 'wave', one breath almost, going down and getting up again quickly and dynamically. That is more like one gesture, although this 'gesture' is still carried out in a state of enhanced sensitivity. The crawling phase is neglected during the latter exercise – I just go down to the floor and back up again.

~ Just moving

It should be noted that Prapto did not normally talk about 'warming up' but about adapting oneself to the site and tuning in to it as one tunes an instrument, thus leaving 'warming up' in a Western sense to the individual student. I have often experienced the 'lying-crawling-walking with variations' movement pattern in his teaching, and thus seen this pattern as a kind of warming up, but even more often than asking students to work with 'lying-crawling-walking', Prapto would just let people start as they like. Students may start with daily life movements or movements as in children's play.

Discussions

A task for students is to discuss their experiences after a practice session. They might talk about movement in terms of consciousness: How aware am I? The aim of this is clarity, getting to know myself, getting to know the 'who am I?' It is not to judge myself, just to see what is going on.

Students may also discuss where wishes and impulses embodied in movement came from during a session. Was it from the physical body? From the feelings? The emotions? From the head, from willpower, from ego? Was it an external impulse? The important thing is to be aware of our choices, whether they are made based on feelings or on the intellect or on our body-nature or physicality. Everything is all right as long as we are aware.

We also discuss acceptance. How does it feel to accept? In some cases, I can accept with my physical body or my mind, but not with my feelings. It is also important to see what it is that we are accepting. Acceptance can be facing life, instead of collapsing in critical situations, but it can also apply to situations where it means accepting that I am in a bad mood, tired, have reached my limit or just don't want to do anything. Whether I can accept or not it is important to acknowledge the state of affairs, i.e. the reality of what is going on.

In another example of what can come up in these discussions, a man and a woman had just finished moving together. Neither had made contact with the other, but both said they had been very conscious of the presence of the other. She related how it had been a conscious choice of hers not to make contact. She simply had not felt like it at the time. He said that for him it was wonderful that the obvious had not happened – i.e. making contact – as this had given him an unexpected insight. In this way, we try to put into words what the movement is about. Sometimes also, the movement is compared to an abstract painting, which is understood in different ways by the individual spectators.

Verbalising what the practice is about is a challenge. We are moving like children playing, albeit very aware children. We are in a state of heightened awareness and sensitivity. But what are we doing? This is an essential question. People watching the movement sometimes say 'What *are* you doing?', not knowing what to make of it. The difficulties in labelling this movement can arise because spectators do not see in our movements a vocabulary like those of martial arts or formal dance. They just see ordinary, daily life movements.

With Amerta Movement we are in a physical, somatic discipline involving daily life movements and attitudes. Amerta practice also involves personal development, identity, hidden resources and potential, expression of self, creativity and art, including performance art and new ritual art, based on bodily movement. Finally, this movement includes ethics – just as Javanese classical dance used to include ethics and philosophical ideas – and ideas about serving human evolution*. In Amerta Movement, people are 'moving' and 'dancing' all aspects of life, narrating stories in an embodied form.

Likewise, since the turn of the 21st century, people in the West from many professions and disciplines have started to work with somatic movement, with the body from a sense of the physicality of the body, i.e. from 'body-nature' in Amerta Movement terms.

For Prapto, what was essential in Amerta Movement was not only the being, being-ness and expressive movement art, but also qualities like clarity, empathy, compassion, ethics, a spiritual approach to life, a holistic and an ecological approach, an attitude of living life with awareness and sensitivity from one moment to the next. Amerta Movement is about living life as a happening and a ritual at the same time expressed via somatic movement. Prapto was concerned with enlivening.

Amerta Movement, a practice- and art-based research, an artistic research

Any lessons that we learn about ourselves and about life while practising Amerta Movement come about through the movement practice itself. We explore ourselves and our environments, as well as responding physically to life and exploring movement as a vocabulary to form a language. As we have seen, we explore how to compose spontaneously while moving and are open to spontaneous crystallisations during a movement session – a kind of 'instant performance'. We also explore the movement process as an act of liberation. We do so by not identifying with our movements, as in purification meditation, where one lets go of inner stirrings and outer impressions, without identifying with what passes through one's body and mind.

We also study how to make the transition from movement as process to movement as art and as performance: we study how to create the performance on the building blocks of the creative process, while still improvising. In short, we learn through practice.

The method behind these activities, as we saw in Chapter 2, is called artistic research and follows the traditional Javanese idea of 'learning by doing'. Our explorations of how to create performance art and how to live life in an Amerta Movement perspective are carried out through free improvised movement and actions in the present moment and are only discussed afterwards.

Talking of the method behind Amerta Movement, Prapto said he had used an exploratory approach. He developed Amerta Movement by using his whole self, body, mind, spirit and personality as a starting point and as an instrument for movement, for studying development and growth, or for the 'blossoming of human life', as he put it. He has trained his senses by asking,

> *How should I do? How can I touch? How should I touch? How can I feel and how should I feel, see?*

Prapto studied what it means to crawl by crawling, to walk by walking, etc. So we may describe Amerta Movement in terms of method as a practice- and art-based research, an artistic research.

Four visual impressions

I formed the impressions below while watching practice in the main pendopo during a 'Basic' course. Students were working with tasks given them by Prapto. These seemed to provide a structure and theme to their movement, which formed bodily stories. The tasks concerned their relationship to space, to proportions, to individual rhythm within the group and to being focused in oneself and letting go. In between these stories, there was plenty of movement that had no clear meaning for me. Other spectators might have seen other stories. I have given each 'story' a title.

1. 'Territory' ~ relationship to space

The whole group is moving in the main pendopo. Prapto is observing from outside. The task is to practise one's relationship to space through the movement. A woman detaches herself from the group and develops a dynamic movement pattern, making spectacular circles between the pendopo's four central pillars. She takes this centre space for herself like a queen so that it is difficult for others to come into it. All the others remain at the edge of the pendopo, while moving. After a while, the woman seems to get tired and brings her movement to an end by lying down in the centre of the pendopo, in the manner of a sleeping beauty. Only then do the others start to approach her, drawing closer and closer except for one woman who only walks into the centre of the space and starts to move alone, after 'sleeping beauty' has left it, helped by the rest of the group.

My impression is one of a story told through movement about two rivals fighting over territory.

2. 'Sculptures in movement' ~ relationship to proportions

After the above 'scene', there is a change in atmosphere. By this time, members of the group have become more used to one another. My impression arising out of the group's movement is a story I call 'Sculptures in movement'. I connect my association with sculpture, i.e. with a fullness in the practitioners' moving bodies, an awareness of all sides of the body, to the task given to them by Prapto. Students appear visibly conscious of trying to allow their body to fill out its proportions in the space without bumping into each other. They seem to be aware of the presence of the others. They appear to be listening to their inner body sense, the kinaesthetic sense, as well as using their eyesight, and they manage to express the input received on that basis in their physical movement.

3. 'Clockwork' ~ relationship to rhythm

The task given by Prapto is training in one's relationship to individual rhythm within the group. My experience is that the students are moving in harmony, possibly a little too much for students studying how to 'stand on their own legs'. Their individual movements might be compared to cogs of different sizes in one large clockwork mechanism. Sometimes they are sucked into the group energy. This is a common challenge in a 'Basic' course. Later, when I took it up with Prapto, he agreed. He added that to his surprise, unlike during the 1980s, Westerners on his courses in the 1990s seemed very dependent on the rest of the group when moving and less individually based in their movement. As Prapto put it: "they are all in the same pot now".

4. 'Meditation in the stream of life' ~ letting go

Gradually a shift occurs in the students' way of moving in the space. In the next session, their task is training in being 'focused in oneself and letting go', i.e. being inside oneself with awareness and letting go of sensations, feelings and thoughts arising, instead of reacting to them. We might say that being focused in oneself means inhabiting the body (mind and feelings) in a state of heightened awareness. Letting go means that the practitioner lets go of the sensations, emotions, feelings and thoughts of which they are being aware. That way their whole body and self is in focus not just one part. Thus, two women, have arrived in a sitting position on the floor. Their eyes are closed as when one turns the attention inside in meditation. Gradually some movers join them, while others continue to move freely in the space. So my impression is one of 'meditation in the stream of life'.

The garden surrounding the main pendopo stimulates students' movement and makes them attentive. It also affects spectators with its varied beauty and its aliveness. There is no wind at all. Butterflies, yellow, white and brown, the colour of Central Javanese *batik*, cross the space. The atmosphere and the tropical heat contribute to the quality of the movement.

Experiencing stories of one kind or another while watching people moving in Amerta Movement is not uncommon. Whatever the spectator experiences, one cannot help but recognise that 'something is happening' to the students moving together. It is evident that choices are being made by the individuals moving, and that they are sometimes being 'pulled' or 'caught' by the group atmosphere, so that these choices can be made both consciously or subconsciously. Prapto used to suggest, for example, that placement in the space during practice might be revealing of one's [ambition for] position in life. If I place myself in the centre of the space, Prapto 'read' it as an indication of my determination to be the centre of attention. Similarly, if I immediately rush to the top of a temple where we have gone to practise, he would see me as someone who wants to go to the top of society or life without looking elsewhere. It was not meant in a sense of moral judgement but rather as an indication of someone's pattern of behaviour. Focus in 'Basic' is on being conscious of one's inner intentions, as well as of the environment.

In conclusion, we may say that instead of following a predetermined form or choreography, students compose spontaneously while moving. Nevertheless, there is a framework within which they perform and compose their improvised movement, albeit an open and flexible one. This framework is the student's own body, its structure and functions, as well as the attitude with which students practise and the degree of their aliveness in the present moment. Part of this framework is also constituted by the pendopo space itself. Added to this, the task given to students by Prapto for each session provides a structure and a theme for their free, improvised and non-stylised movement expressions.

Chapter 6

Vocabulary 1: The Hill and Sukuh

Introduction

The Vocabulary, Nature and Life course, hereafter referred to as 'Vocabulary', formed the second of three *Pribadi Art* courses. Students were taken on a learning journey through the Javanese landscape, through its nature, culture, life and history. The course programme is as follows (again I will often write in the present tense for immediacy):

Vocabulary, Nature and Life. Offered for the people who has [have] already work[ed] with me or one of the teachers [sc. dialoguers] (min. 80 hours). Reading the Borobudur Temple, [S]pace on the [H]ill at Wonogiri, Time at Sukuh Temple, [E]xpression in the changing of nature at Parangtritis Beach, Crystallisation in communication with the society on the stage. Rahayu … [4]

Students start this cultural journey through studying *space* at Prapto's private property, called the Hill, in the Wonogiri Mountains east of the Lemah Putih School. From there they go on to the temple Candi Sukuh on Mount Lawu, to study *time*. From there this cultural journey takes them to Candi Borobudur to study *reading*, and finally to Parangtritis Beach to study *expression*. After this, students return to the Lemah Putih School for their crystallisations.

The cultural sites where students practise during 'Vocabulary' are described in detail in this chapter and Chapter 7. The full title of the course, 'Vocabulary, Nature and Life', suggests the three main subjects to be studied.

The course's aim is to create a movement vocabulary among other things by going to cultural sites in natural environments and being exposed to Javanese history and style of life at these places, and to move there based on one's organic being, on one's natural self in the present moment, in a state of a heightened awareness and sensitivity.

---

[4] This is the course description for the 1995–1996 'Vocabulary, Nature and Life' course. It is a direct quote using terms and spellings from the programme's text. *Rahayu* means peace in Javanese and is often said at the beginning and end of a meeting such as at a communal meal or meditation session within the mystical movements of Central Java.

Purification

For Prapto, in order for us to create a vocabulary, based on our life and nature in the present moment, purification of self is needed. This is to ensure the students' movement originates from what Prapto calls their 'genuine being' or 'true self'. According to Prapto, the human body at the outset of movement practice is normally dominated by desire, so our 'readings', our perceptions of ourselves and the environment, are unclear. That is why it is essential, as part of the process of physical practice, that my body (body-mind-spirit) be purified, turning it into a clear mirror to reflect my physical and mental condition. This is achieved through awareness and sensitivity. Prapto compared this to the Javanese tradition of undertaking spiritual retreats to study nature and the natural elements as well as to honour the temples and the historical sites of their heritage. The Javanese make pilgrimages to these places, meditating there and performing ascetic exercises (*laku*). Many do so in order to become a better human being. They do so by purifying themselves of personal desires, of prejudiced attitudes to life and of that which they have accumulated but do not need any more. So a mother or father will commonly undertake meditation with fasting in natural environments in order to become a better parent. The king and the shaman will do the same in order to be a successful king or a better shaman and healer and the student will do so in order to get better grades. But there are no ascetic exercises in Amerta Movement, only a relaxed, but engaged and aware attitude to the body, to self and to life. In Amerta Movement, *Pribadi Art* is not a therapy, but a contemporary art of life, an ongoing practice for human development through enhanced awareness and sensibility. The Vocabulary course, according to Prapto, was designed so that 'one can see the individual student's development generally in relation to nature's life, society, religiosity or the sacred'.

Because Amerta practice is carried out with heightened awareness, it makes me aware of inner impulses, sensations, desires and shortcomings as well as inner resources and positive potential. These traits are no longer camouflaged by my will or habits but crystallised from my body into movement as my 'reading' and practice proceed. In this way, I can purify myself of what I want to release and of that which is not necessary or not part of my genuine being and try to develop – yes, embody – my inner resources and positive potential.

Aim of moving at cultural sites

The aim of studying 'nature and life' at the sites and of practising movement there is to develop a bodily movement vocabulary specific to me and to each site, and to widen my outlook on life, my receptiveness and acceptance.

The movement vocabulary through which I express myself is made up of bodily postures, gaits, arm, hand and finger gestures – i.e. movement 'words'. These words arise out of the practice, as seen above, and in their form, atmosphere and contents as well as in the way they 'make sense' they are characteristic of me (person-specific) and of the site (site-specific).

According to Prapto, a movement vocabulary is formed by repeated practice under all sorts of conditions and in all kinds of places. All the new input that we meet at the different sites helps to expand our outlook on the world, our frame of reference and our physical movement vocabulary, just as it contributes to our personal development.

So we can say that the idea of taking us to different sites is to make us experience new dimensions of life, widen our outlook on life and create a person-specific physical movement vocabulary which is also site-specific.

'Basic' compared to 'Vocabulary'

'Vocabulary' is also about becoming aware that our movement communicates something when seen from the outside, although it might not make clear sense to the spectator. This is because the language through which students express themselves, although based on daily life movements, is a personal one, specific to each student. There is no recognisable common movement vocabulary in Amerta Movement as seen in other movement and dance styles.

A practitioner who had studied with Prapto for a year compared the 'Basic' and 'Vocabulary' courses as follows:

> *[In 'Basic'] you learn to read the energy inside and outside.*
> *That means that you learn to feel it and sense it. You know you*
> *are expressing something or saying something with the*
> *movement, but you do not really know what you say.*
>
> *But in the next course, the Vocabulary course, you can better*
> *play with the energy and find a vocabulary and a language.*
> *You more clearly know that you are saying something through*
> *your movement and that it is a language.*
>
> *If you ask Prapto he explains it on a deeper level. But what Prapto*
> *does with his movement one has to feel by one's own body.* [5]

---

[5] A European Amerta Movement practitioner and Messenger Art dialoguer/teacher in his mid-twenties with a background in *Butoh* and in political science studies.

So 'Vocabulary' students work to become aware of their movements not only from inside, but also as seen from outside as an expression of self in relation to the site, i.e. as a vocabulary. They start to practise how to build a personal vocabulary, or how to expand the vocabulary they have already created. As Prapto said, a movement vocabulary is developed via the practice itself through the different body postures, expressions and attitudes I choose while moving. In this way, references are created in my body and used by me to create a person-specific movement vocabulary.

> *It is not only about your being, your attitude but also about your many kinds of approaches* [bodily positions and activities] *in moving. When you are walking or crawling or sitting and lying down with variations or relaxing, stretching or communicating, this is giving reference for your body, so that later it becomes a vocabulary.*

> *When I practise from the element in the sense of gravity, in the sense of material I do from the sense of my being* [of my self] *and then my being becomes so that my being has a sense of meaning: 'Oh ya, I have meaning for myself!' And also I'm touching of your* [my co-practitioners'] *meaning, and then after that I start growing of my being as a language, but starting from me not from you.*

It is worth mentioning that, especially after the turn of the century, Prapto thought it essential for 'Basic' students to start paying attention to communication, without waiting till the Vocabulary course, as was usual during the early period covered in this book.

No predetermined form

Why is it necessary to study how to make a vocabulary, we might ask? And why is it necessary to be conscious, to be aware and alert all the time during practice? The answer is that Amerta Movement is a free, non-stylised form of movement. It is free in the same sense that the movement of an ordinary person in daily life who decides to go for a walk, is free as to *how* to walk, slowly or fast for example, and free as to *where* they go, at least more or less so. Of course, as we walk around in our daily life, we must adjust to other people in the streets just as we must adjust to the traffic around us when driving. So, when I move around in society in my daily life, whether walking on foot, bicycling or driving a car, I need to be alert all the time and make decisions as to where to walk, in order not to run into other people, be hurt by the traffic or the conditions of the terrain and so on. Likewise, when I practise free Amerta Movement this demands the same kind of alertness. I must pay attention to the surroundings, constantly making decisions as to where to go, how to go there, and which positions to take in the practice space. There is *a priori* no fixed goal, no fixed way of getting about in the space or, for that matter, of getting about in life. Thus in the practice, as in my life, I have to navigate myself but, as Prapto said, while I do so, I can express myself on the way and have a good time. However, I really need to be awake, alert and aware as to what is possible, aware of what is happening inside me and out there in the world. Returning to the practice of free Amerta Movement, the question is: What can I do? What do I do? An answer is that I compose in a spontaneous manner my positions, gait, gestures and so on, while moving. Doing so is what Prapto described as: "choosing composition in living measurement". I use my own living body as an instrument for the shaping of positions and for the understanding and the measurement of proportions in the space. So I may measure the floor by walking through the space, counting the steps or using an arm's length for measurement.

In 'Vocabulary', our skill is not just to act out our impulses. Within the moment of improvisation, this skill consists of shaping impulses in a manner that Prapto called to 'make costume'*. In the 'Basic' course, movement comes directly from the body, so I have no 'distance' from what I am doing, i.e. there is no awareness of what the movements might mean or express in terms of vocabulary. When I have learnt to find greater awareness in the moment of improvisation, then movement based on that awareness is slightly delayed thereby giving me some 'distance' from it. This delay probably does not mean a time delay but refers to my state of heightened awareness and sensitivity. But the 'Vocabulary' student is more aware than the 'Basic' student and can encompass more of reality, i.e. more information and input or more of the present moment within their conscious mind. This larger capacity is experienced in terms of a time interval, i.e. as a delay between the impulses arising in me and the body's expression or translation of those impulses into an embodied expression, an embodied movement vocabulary in the outside world.

In other words, in 'Vocabulary', I am more 'outside' myself in terms of awareness than in 'Basic' and thus able, not only to be inside myself with the awareness, but also able simultaneously to 'look' at myself and at the movements I am forming. The distance experienced between impulse and expression means I have the time to give form to or actively influence the form of my movements. I have time to 'construct the body' actively, in Prapto's terms. Alternative movements are possible, because this distance allows me in some ways to decide through my conscious mind how to express or shape movements based on material from internal experiences. It allows me, in Prapto's terms, to 'make costume'. We can compare 'making costume' in movement to situations in everyday life where people choose which clothes to wear according to their mood or according to an image they want to convey, as well as suit the situation (work, partying and so on). Or we could say that to 'make costume', i.e. actively contributing to the shaping of the improvised movements, can be compared to using masks and textiles, or even to using a *mudra*, i.e. a stylised hand- and finger position, as we do when we move at Borobudur Temple – for embodying a 'story' in Messenger Art courses, see p.175.

Aims of the 'Vocabulary' workshop

Prapto tells students that it is possible to create a language by starting from our genuine being and from what he calls our 'element' or 'material'. By this he means movement based on my specific characteristics as a whole person, as an organism living within life's material and immaterial dimensions, i.e. within the Reality World (another term for *Pribadi Art*) and the Dream World (another term for Messenger Art). A physical movement vocabulary based on my genuine being will crystallise from the process of the practice itself, according to Prapto. This statement formulates an essential and characteristic feature of what is meant by movement in Amerta Movement:

> *Movement is not only a language for communication but also*
> *an expression of being, (an expression of self).*

This crystallisation, based on my being or self or my element seen as 'material', or energy, occurs as an organic process of transformation. This approach from the material world refers to the 'Reality World' or *Pribadi Art* World. A student grows and blossoms through the process of practising movement. One day this language 'speaks'. My expression of being, (of self), comes about in a dialogue with nature's being, i.e. it comes about while I simultaneously pay attention to, am sensitive to, nature outside me (the natural environment) and to nature inside me, receiving input and impulses from both.

It is important that we understand that nature, the organic world, and objects in the outside world are living 'materials' that transform and crystallise. They change just as people change. Nature has 'its own being'. It can 'speak' and 'communicate', according to Prapto. The bamboo tree, for example, like the pillars of the pendopo, does not just exist in relation to me, but has its own being, its own self and its own 'language'.

An approach for developing vocabulary

At the different sites where students practise, a framework is created through exercises in body-consciousness, attitude-consciousness and space-consciousness, and through physical and spiritual contact with these places. 'Attitude-consciousness' refers to my ability to consciously perceive and contain my attitude or approach to life, i.e. my thoughts, feelings, emotions, likes, dislikes, will, bias and judgement while practising, not only in relation to myself but also to my environment whereby I achieve 'space-consciousness', an awake knowledge of the space surrounding me in terms of form, material and atmosphere. Exercises in attitude-consciousness and space-consciousness help us, moreover, develop a vocabulary especially related to these sites as well as serving as tools to expand our sensitivity. This framework, consisting of body-awareness, attitude-awareness and space-awareness exercises, trains us to perceive clearly our approach to our inner and outer world. The sites presuppose our ability to grow in these forms of consciousness. By an acceptance or recognition of the state of affairs in relation to these three areas, I consciously expand my sensitivity and can thus receive more reality into my conscious mind.

Exercises in the skills – acceptance and the three forms of consciousness, so as to grow as a human being, and in the composing of a vocabulary – consist of the usual sequences of 'walking, crawling, running and so on', as well as of free movement in and across the floor and training of the senses. Students also study how to separate reception of an impulse from acting on it. The aim here is to avoid reacting automatically to impulses, i.e. 'not to go in karmic' as Prapto called it, i.e. to react in an automatic, non-conscious manner, but to respond consciously, based on a conscious choice. It is like the approach we use when studying 'catching' and 'being caught' (see Chapter 4).

We try to be aware of what is going on and from there we either actively agree to the ensuing action, actively allowing it, or we frankly disagree with it. We train in consciousness of attitude by training in receiving, in being open and sensitive. As part of our movement, we read ourselves and our environment. While doing so, we practise receiving and accepting rather than rejecting impulses and sensations from inside as well as impressions from outside. This means that we recognise the existence of the phenomena we receive, whether we like or dislike them. And we are aware of our inner attitude while doing so: 'Can I accept or do I reject?' 'Can I respond to the material received by making a free choice with my conscious mind?' 'Or do I react automatically in a knee-jerk way, controlled by my passions, desires or subconscious ('going in karmic')?'

So we practise receiving impulses and impressions from outside in a relaxed and attentive way, recognising what is happening without judging or analysing. We try to feel impulses from inside and outside in our body as well as our genuine response to them, before acting. In the same way, we also practise sharpening our senses, i.e. we train in how to use our sight, hearing, touch, smell and taste. In this way, we start learning to separate the reception of an impulse from action based on that impulse. We learn to respond in a conscious way.

Prapto would lead an exercise based on hearing as follows:

When you hear something, just hear it, that's receiving.

Receiving sounds and impulses from a relaxed position, calmly allowing them a space, containing them, does not prevent us from being alert. We remain, like a cat, simultaneously relaxed and alert.

Exercising receiving and accepting

Students practise receiving, first alone, then in pairs. When alone I work with myself as an object, walking, crawling and so on, receiving what comes up in the process and what happens in the space. When in pairs, the task is to try to listen to and be faithful to my own self or being in my manner of moving and to make my own decisions while still accepting my partner and giving them space. This exercise can be carried out close-up with physical contact, or with little or no physical contact. At the same time as listening to myself, I have to accept my partner and go along with their impulse in movement, at least to begin with. To accept my partner in this context means receiving their impulses and movements constructively, integrating them into my own flow of movements.

Preparing for the cultural sites of the Hill and Candi Sukuh

Now we will follow 'Vocabulary' students at the Hill in the Wonogiri Mountains and at the temple of Candi Sukuh. The different sites visited during 'Vocabulary' are tools to enable students to develop a movement vocabulary. The movement vocabulary that we build, as we have seen, is based on 'nature and life' at the site in dialogue with our own 'nature and life'. 'In dialogue with' means that, just as I am perceiving my own inner condition and reactions to the present moment, I am also receiving 'nature and life' from outside, i.e. impressions, impulses, input and responses from the natural conditions of the practice site and of the environment including the vegetation, animal life and people there. Dialogue means that I draw input from both inside and outside simultaneously for my movement expression and for building a 'vocabulary by movement', and that sometimes I compare my inner input or responses from moving, with the responses from outside. I conduct a dialogue between these elements.

'Vocabulary 1995-1996'

I will use the 'Vocabulary 1995-1996' group and course as a case study. The group consisted of 18 Western students, fourteen women, four men and a five-year-old child. There was also one Javanese participant. A few Javanese guests joined the practice for three or four days off and on. Professional backgrounds were mainly movement pedagogy, health and (performance) art. The course ran for some eight weeks with one or two sessions a day taught by Prapto five days a week, constituting a total of 180 hours. It started and ended at the Lemah Putih School with three days at the beginning and three and a half weeks at the end. During the intervening period, teaching took place at the Hill, at Candi Sukuh, at Borobudur Temple and at Parangtritis Beach, with stays of four to five days at each site. There, practitioners worked on a theme specific to each site. A crystallisation-performance of the whole process, one for each group, was scheduled to take place at the end of the course.

On the first day, Prapto focuses on the course's aim of developing a vocabulary of movement. It is possible to create a language by starting from my being or, in Prapto's terms, my 'element' [material]. A physical vocabulary or a 'language' through movement based on my being will crystallise from the process of the practice itself, according to Prapto.

This crystallisation, based on my physical body, being or material, occurs as an organic process of transformation: just like a plant grows and blossoms, the practitioner via the process of practising movement 'grows' and 'blossoms' to create a 'language' through movement. One day this language 'speaks', i.e. conveys a message or an expression which can be understood by someone from outside, a witness or a spectator, something, which, for example, can be seen in the 'Communication' course. My expression of being comes about in a dialogue, i.e. in an exchange with nature's being: in Amerta Movement it is not only humans who have an inner being, self or essence. Trees, flowers, birds and animals are animated by an inner being, self or essence. Hence, when I move in natural environments expressing myself, I also pay attention to the site, to trees, flowers, birds and animals there. I am also influenced by them in my movements, receiving input/impulses from them. I might be inspired by their qualities of stillness or movement or I might register how my presence and movement influence my surroundings. This is an example of what is meant in Amerta Movement by carrying out a 'dialogue with nature's being'. Nature can 'speak' and 'communicate'. An example of the latter is when commonly some people know right away by looking at a tree or a flower whether it needs water. Also the pillars of the main pendopo at the school, according to Prapto, have their own being and language, even if they have already been worked on and styled (organised one may say) by humans.

The Hill

The Hill is situated on a limestone plateau of the Kidul Mountains with panoramic views. The landscape is wild, barren and majestic and the theme connected to the Hill is space: space outside and inner space. When viewing the vast panorama from the property's *stupa*, placed as it seems between heaven and earth, it is clear why the Javanese think humans are not the centre of the universe, but only part of it. Recognising this invites us to humility, contemplation and prayer.

The Hill consisted of one or two hectares of land surrounded by trees. In the middle stood a simple pendopo with a large, flat, rectangular open area in front of it. The inner space of the pendopo was quite dark. It had bamboo walls, a concrete floor and, at the back, an altar with a Buddha placed on a small dais. At the front a small *stupa*, surrounded by *bodhi** trees above the lake, stood in memory of Prapto's wife. Students who stayed with the family at the bottom of the Hill started the day by climbing up to this area: an interesting exercise in warming up once the rainy season starts and the soil is slippery. Students did not normally meet any other inhabitants – they were alone with themselves and nature's elements, though the presence of a local population is obvious from the sound of dogs barking somewhere nearby.

Practice

The group worked in two sessions, one in the morning and one in the afternoon, both taught by Prapto, with time for individual practice. Usually everyone stayed together the whole day at the Hill's pendopo or on the land outside, even for meals. When working, a favourite place was the *stupa* overlooking the lake below. Its smooth surface was like a mirror. Practice started with full group sessions followed by explorations on our own and in smaller groups. The first step was to work with adapting ourselves to the new site, exploring space inside-outside. We read our inner sensations, feelings and thoughts as they arose in a dialogue, an exchange, with the outside world's conditions of soil, wind, sun, rain, sounds, smells, co-practitioners and vast space. We responded to these phenomena by receiving them, letting them transform themselves in the body and be expressed in physical movement. Prapto recommended that we find our own way to place ourselves physically in nature, as a pillar so to speak, a being between earth and sky, and to have an open attitude, i.e. an attitude of welcoming or acceptance. Thus when practising movement in a dialogue with the vast space of the Hill, we would receive wisdom. This wisdom could take the form of an insight from beyond the conscious mind. Receiving such insights entailed responsibility. This consisted of trying to follow and to implant that wisdom in one's life.

Exploring space in four steps

We explore 'space' at the Hill in four different ways.[6]

1. Finding one's own space in relation to the changing construction of the body while moving. By construction, Prapto means the changing form, expression or *'gestalt'* of the body from moment to moment during practice.

2. Entering into a dialogue with co-practitioners and their space. The others then become like a mirror of oneself.

3. Finding together the same view of the space. This is achieved through moving together within the same practice space.

4. Looking at space not only from one centre, i.e. from the perspective of one's own position. It is important also to look at space from other perspectives, for example from above, from the trees, or from the perspective of the birds. Prapto says:

    Think about the falcon looking for chicken steak.

Sound: 'Singing and Praying'

Students also responded to life, inside and outside, in terms of sound and vibration. This meant that my body, inner organs and being, as well as outer objects as trees and nature, were perceived in terms of sound and vibration as in rhythm and movement. We also explored sound as religious singing and spiritual/sacred expression while moving. In Amerta Movement, this is called 'singing and praying'. This is an open 'forum-space' where anyone can explore and express their sense of the sacred through movement and sound. The spontaneous sound and singing is seen as an alternative to the conventional way of channelling or translating through one's whole body feelings of the sacred into sound and movement in the outside world.

Prapto was singing and moving, using Buddhist *mantras* and songs from the Javanese shadow puppet plays. His movements centred on circling around his own axis in a slow, intense way with a sense of prayer and sacred dance rather than free movement. Was this part of Prapto's instructions via physical

---

[6] Space is used in two ways: First, it refers to a physical location and its form, material quality and atmosphere. Second, it refers to the specific attitude or approach to oneself, to the practice and to the environment, i.e. to the site and co-practitioners, with which students practise movement and which results in a specific atmosphere or 'space'.

demonstration? Was the spiritual energy involved in his movements a deliberate choice in keeping with the energy of the site? Or was it simply his personal response to the site's atmosphere of contemplation? The latter is most likely. The source of Prapto's movements, when he moved at the Hill, was less in the instructor and more in Prapto the monk. He would sometimes describe himself as not only a father, a lover, and head of a family, but also a monk, a person with the spiritual needs of a monk. Anyone practising movement with Prapto soon discovered how the sacred part of existence is as important to him as his breathing in and out. Sometimes this aspect of life was so vital to him that he thought of becoming a monk. So, while moving, Prapto stayed mainly with religious and spiritual/sacred expressions. Sometimes he practised for himself making specific movement patterns and expressions, which looked very much like praying through movement: one day he was standing under the enormous vaulted open sky stretching both arms vertically upwards. His hands were in the praying (*sembah*) position, i.e. with the palms of the hands together pointing upwards. Slowly he opened his hands by letting the fingers part from each other without letting go of the hands' contact at the wrists. It looked like a lotus flower opening. He then started to turn both open hands, still touching at the wrists, in opposite directions, and made a new movement pattern. It was not a demonstration. It was Prapto praying to life in the open space of the mountains.

During the first sessions, students seemed much influenced by Prapto's movement patterns, sound and spiritual energy. This was especially true for the movement pattern of circling around one's own axis, the vertical axis of life in Java connecting 'Mother-Earth' and 'Father-Sky', as the Javanese say. When they explored sound and singing, as well as their sense of the sacred in connection with the Hill, several used the circling movement as an expression of the sacred. This pattern might also have arisen in response to the Hill's position half way between earth and sky, as it seemed. Some may have chosen it because they had not yet found their own way of expressing the sacred dimension in their movement, or simply because circling is an archetypal movement.[7] Circling around one's own axis, in Amerta Movement, may also be seen as a physical manifestation of the practitioner's individuality as in the term *pribadi*, on one's own, or standing on one's own two feet. Students would include their personal inner being/inner self, as a creature between earth and sky, by circling around the vertical axis.

---

[7] Circling is often used in sacred dance. It seems to provide a kind of framework, almost like a choreography, facilitating the exploration of sound and singing at the same time as moving physically.

In one session, students were exploring sound and rhythm collectively. One of the men accompanied the group's movement by beating two bamboo sticks together. After a while, a common beat arose in the group's movements. Soon the whole group was starting to make rhythmic movements as with one body and uttering sounds of 'ha ha ha'. There were also sessions where one of the students accompanied the rest of the group with a flute or saxophone.

Movement and music

When accompanying someone's movement the musician has to follow the practitioner's movement, respecting its rhythm, speed and style, supporting it, never directing it. In this way, the practitioner remains free to improvise. It is a delicate balance between the mover and the musician. For this collaboration to work well it often demands that musicians be familiar with Amerta Movement from having practised it themselves. This explains why music accompanying a practitioner needs to be live. Music was not part of Amerta's original concept in the 1980s, at least not during ordinary practice.

When there were silences, the sound of the wind, birds and sometimes a dog barking could be heard. This was also a kind of 'musical accompaniment' influencing movement. When the wind became strong, this was a sure sign of the oncoming tropical rains. They soon made everyone seek shelter inside the pendopo, where they carried on with their practice.

The brief stay at the Hill gave students a sense of spiritual retreat and prepared them for a new beginning in life, one more in tune with their 'genuine being' than before. It prepared them for the temple of Candi Sukuh.

Candi Sukuh

Candi Sukuh was built in the early 15th century at the end of the Hindu-Javanese [Hindu-Buddhist] period (called the Classical period of Java). The temple is 910m above sea level on the western slope of Mt. Lawu, Central Java's mightiest volcano. Preserved as part of Indonesia's national heritage, Candi Sukuh is closely linked to Java's history, mystical practices and shadow puppet theatre. The temple contains references to a major part of Javanese mythology. [8] Locally it is of great importance in a cultural and a religious sense, not least for modern spiritual artists who, like Prapto, look to it for inspiration and knowledge.

---

[8] My description is mainly based on Prapto's presentation. I am not trying to give a full description of the temple. See also Holt (1967) and Pemberton (1994), whose view of Sukuh has been challenged by Jo-Anne Sbeghen (2004). Here, I keep to the ideas about Sukuh that Prapto offered his students.

Candi Sukuh seems to be built in an almost primitive style. It contains a number of reliefs, pylons, obelisks and statues, all executed in a simple, almost awkward, but forceful style with sculptures roughly hewn. Because of this, Candi Sukuh is commonly said to stand apart from Central Java's more famous temples of the Hindu-Buddhist period, Candi Prambanan and Candi Borobudur. The latter are more elaborate and elegant. People commonly compare Candi Sukuh's architecture and style to the Maya temples of the Aztecs, while others see it as modelled on a prehistoric megalithic style.

Candi Sukuh is built on four levels of three terraces. The main temple building is situated on the third terrace as a compact, step-formed pyramid of large boulders. Like huge Lego bricks, these are piled on top of one another without mortar. The pyramid seems cut off near the top, giving it a flat roof. Three huge stone turtles, symbols of life on earth, 'guard' the entrance to the temple. A flight of stairs leads the visitor from an opening at ground level through the temple top onto the roof. One can thus get up onto the temple's roof, but not into its inner chamber.[9] As Prapto said:

> *I like very much the idea passing the pyramid. You go in and then you going up. The pyramid gives you sense of liberation, come back to nature again.*

From the temple's roof, there is a panoramic view down to the fertile Solo plain bordered by a line of volcanos on the horizon. On the mountainside in the midst of luxuriously green vegetation, here and there roofs of the characteristic Javanese shape come into sight. Looking up you see Mt. Lawu's peak. Most often shrouded in steamy mists, it emerges as glimpses of a wall of grey granite.

The three wide terraces forming the temple yard on three different levels are connected by gates and stone staircases. These form a straight line from bottom to top. Visitors in earlier times had to ascend to the main temple by walking up the many flights of stairs from the temple's ground level. Thus, they approached the main temple following the way indicated by the temple's architecture.

First, they passed an entrance tower 'guarded' by the mythical eagle Garuda and the monster Kala, the god of time. In the entrance tower the visitor steps across a relief placed horizontally on the ground.[10] It shows a realistic portrayal of a *lingga-yoni,* a large phallus (*lingga*) pointing towards a large vulva (*yoni*).

---

[9] According to Prapto, the inner part of the temple was probably a burial place. Maybe it contains the remains of the temple's constructor, a Majapahit queen.

[10] Today we cannot enter the entrance tower but look at the *lingga-yoni* from outside.

The *lingga-yoni* placed here indicates that life starts with the meeting of male and female. It then unfolds in time as represented by Kala, under the auspices of Garuda.

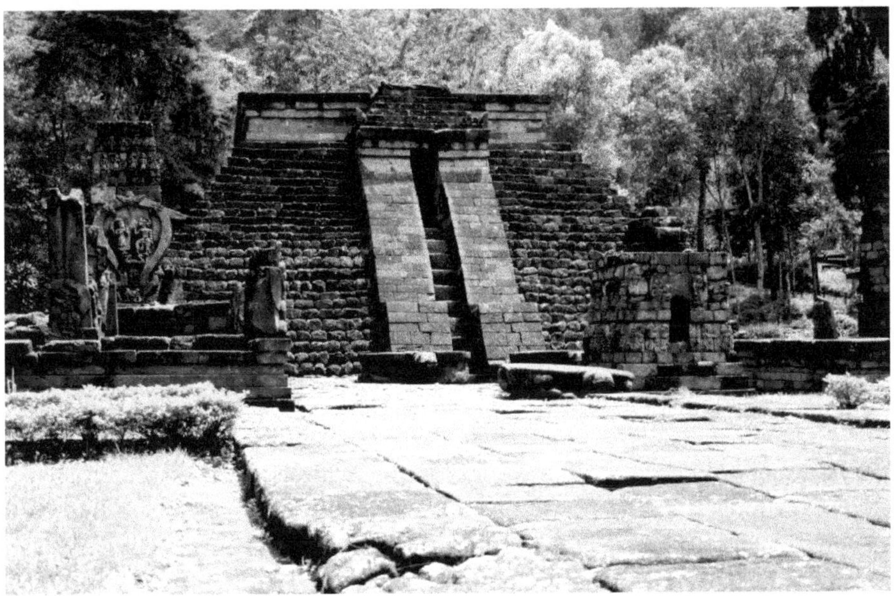
Candi Sukuh

Religion and mysticism in Candi Sukuh

The two royal dynasties of Solo still carry out traditional mystic practices on Mount Lawu. The younger family has its own temple for meditation on Mt. Lawu and even now in modern times, when Candi Sukuh has the status of a museum, one can still see offerings of flowers and incense on the *lingga-yoni* or in front of the monument containing the temple's spirit [*kyai*]. This occurs especially in connection with Javanese New Year [*Sura*]. Mostly they are placed there by local villagers, but sometimes also by practitioners from one of Java's many mystic groups. It was still a tradition among Javanese mystics in the late 1990s to go up Mt. Lawu to carry out exercises of asceticism and meditation leading to higher spiritual insight and transformation and for receiving blessings (*pangestu*). The aim was for both spiritual and material advancement.

Candi Sukuh is also a tourist destination. Many young Indonesians disavow the traditional mystical practices of their parents and find them old fashioned and incompatible with modern times and modern Islam. They come to Candi Sukuh as tourists, having fun looking at the fertility symbols. Usually they are very proud of the temple as part of their cultural heritage. Most tourists, including those from abroad, go straight for the *lingga-yoni* symbols and then onto the temple's roof for the panoramic view of the mountain and its valley. After that, they disappear almost as fast as they appeared.

The 'Vocabulary' course at Candi Sukuh

After about half an hour's car-ride in the heat of the day across the Solo plain, the two cars transporting students reached the road climbing Mt. Lawu. Here the air became cooler, the vegetation changed as rice gave way to vegetables and flowers, which cannot grow on the plain. The road passed fresh mountain streams, a sure sign of the rainy season. It wound up the mountain through coffee, tea and rubber plantations.

For the last kilometre of steep ascent to the temple, pine trees lined the road on the valley side, making the atmosphere seem Alpine. People walked along the road carrying on their backs large baskets full of merchandise, collected wood or fodder for their animals. These mountain people appeared very shy compared to the people of Solo. The road ends on a small plateau containing the local hamlet, a public square and a pendopo overlooking the Solo plain.

Sukuh temple itself is situated next to the village square on the mountain slope. We lodged in the house of the temple's custodian opposite the main temple. The nights were very cold compared to Solo, as was the clear water in the bathing quarters coming straight down from the mountain. The toilet holes were heart-shaped and cut from solid rock. There was an atmosphere of mountain village life with chickens running between banana-palms, children playing and the villagers working on their houses and land.

Four days were spent at Candi Sukuh. Our day started at dawn in order to be ready for practice which, as at the Hill, was divided into two sessions, one in the morning and one in the afternoon. If the rains came, as they did for a few hours about every second or third day, the sessions would take place in the village pendopo. They consisted of students' individual exploration of the temple and its grounds via their movement practice and of Prapto's instructions to the whole group as well as to students individually. Whole group and individual sessions guided by Prapto most often took place on the stone-paved upper terrace, which led to the temple's entrance.

Prapto's introduction to the practice

On the first day, Prapto introduces Sukuh temple and the theme of time. He says that Sukuh was built by a ruling queen from the Majapahit. He incorporates in his teaching what he calls bowing, i.e. showing homage to the temple and to life. According to Prapto, 'the right timing' and genuineness depends on three things: consciousness in the present, purification and spiritual quest. These themes were all illustrated by stories Prapto tells, giving students an open framework for their movement practice. Students are free to do what they like with these stories but are asked to practise bodily movement responding physically to the temple in a conscious way. Through the stories, Prapto illustrates themes we are going to work with at Sukuh in order to create our vocabulary through movement.

Time has an inner and an outer aspect. In its inner aspect it is interpreted as genuineness in one's inner attitudes, i.e. in one's approach to one's thoughts, feelings and emotions. In its outer aspect, it relates to appropriateness, i.e. to being in concord, or not, with an outside situation.

The *wayang kulit* stories. Time as genuineness, rebirth/new beginning

Time is studied by practising movement in dialogue with or in an exchange with, the temple's architecture, inspired by stories from the shadow puppet theatre, relating to Candi Sukuh and portrayed on its reliefs. In particular, on the upper third terrace there are reliefs portraying scenes relating to the themes of purification and liberation and to rituals of exorcism. The way the reliefs are carved reminds me of puppets on a screen. For the 'Vocabulary' course Prapto concentrates on the story of Bathara Guru (Shiva), Uma and Kala from the Murwakala, a ritual of exorcism. He narrates three episodes representing the 'wrong time': Honeymoon, Curse and the Indonesian term *Sperma*. He then briefly and without interpretation refers to the *Sudamala* after which he finishes by narrating the *Dewaruci* story.

Interpreting some of the themes of these stories, Prapto suggests how these themes might apply to the practice. He tells the old stories in his own style, using contemporary references and a lot of humour but still in a respectful way, bringing the stories alive. His aim is to inspire students, to introduce them to Candi Sukuh, to Javanese myths and to traditional Javanese mystical practices, according to which one has to be aware of one's desires (*nafsu-nafsu*) through meditating, for example. The desires are represented by the colours yellow, red, black and white, and traditionally regarded as dangerous for the meditator/the mystic. If one seeks spiritual liberation one must step back from desires. But in more modern techniques of meditation and spiritual liberation, for example Sumarah, the desires are seen also in a positive sense of energy which can be transformed positively, helping in one's process of liberation.

Murwakala: Honeymoon, Curse and *Sperma*

> ***Honeymoon.*** *On a beautiful day, the patriarch and god Bathara Guru took his wife, the goddess Uma on a honeymoon-trip on his flying bull Andini possibly going to Palm Beach in Florida.*

The scenery was beautiful, Uma was beautiful and Bathara Guru wanted to make love with her. But she refused. The time and place were not appropriate for her as a spouse and a mother. Moreover, she was not at all thinking about sex. She was absorbed by the beauty of the scenery they were flying across. However, Bathara Guru could not control his sexual appetite. After insisting several times and being refused by her several times, he forced himself upon her. She pushed him away at the moment he reached orgasm. The result was that his sperm fell into the Indian Ocean fertilising it. From this erroneous sperm (kama salah), the giant Kala was born.

__Curse__. Bathara Guru, the god and patriarch cursed his wife Uma for her disobedience. She was transformed into a giantess, Durga, and relegated to live on earth.

__Sperma__. Bathara Guru's sperm fell into the ocean and gave birth to Kala. Thus Kala, who was a giant full of supernatural power (sakti), was the result of Batara Guru's erroneous sperm and his lack of control of his sexual desire. Kala devoured everything in the ocean including atomic garbage left by the French. The goddess of the ocean was alarmed by this. She asked him to find his parents so that they could feed him. Kala set out searching for his father. First, he looked for him on earth, but in vain. Then he looked for him in the heavens. Here he found his father on the Mahameru Mountain. At first Bathara Guru did not want to acknowledge Kala, even though he saw that Kala was his son. They fought but were reconciled again. Then Bathara Guru told Kala to go back down to earth to find his mother: "Son, go to your mother. What is in your heart is your mother, but on the outside, she is your wife." Kala obeyed his father. He descended to earth and married Durga. She was, as Bathara Guru had said, actually his mother Uma who had been cursed to go down on earth and live as the giantess, Durga.

Prapto's interpretations. Bathara Guru, Uma and Kala

The stories of Bathara Guru, Uma/Durga and Kala represent the 'wrong time' and are specifically connected to Candi Sukuh. Prapto compares them with the Oedipus myth. Prapto sees Bathara Guru as representing the way of the archetypal patriarch and Uma as representing the way of the archetypal matriarch. Kala, the god of time, the monster eating everything, is a result of the patriarch's will being imposed by force. It is not appropriate (*cocok*) to time and place, something which is very important in Java. Kala is 'out of time' in Prapto's terms. That is why he has become a monster. Candi Sukuh is the temple of Kala and the 'wrong time'/ wrong timing.

Prapto also talks about Uma's feelings. She refuses Bathara Guru because she is absorbed in the scenery. In contrast, Bathara Guru is absorbed by his animal sexual instinct. The story illustrates the 'wrong time' in that Bathara Guru's question and Uma's answer 'do not fit one another', as Prapto terms it. The story also raises the question of drives like sex and hunger. Is sex to be motivated by evolution and the animal instinct to procreate, thereby following nature's instincts? Or is it to be approached in a human sense, based on choice?

As to Kala searching for his father in the heavens and his mother on earth, on a universal level, this relates to patriarchal or matriarchal societies. At the individual level, it relates to identity. I find my identity through the personal father and mother. Prapto interprets the Oedipal aspect of the story as follows: when a man does not have good *karma* with his sperm (as with Bathara Guru) he will get a son or a wife who is not really adult. The karmic result of Bathara Guru's erroneous sperm was the marriage between son and mother as in the Oedipus myth. Prapto adds humorously that the Javanese man likes his wife to be like his mother, taking care of him. On the outside, however, the wife must of course look like a wife; inside a mother. According to Prapto, this situation will continue until the wife, Durga, is fed up with being a giantess. Through a purification process, she is transformed into a human again. Prapto says, "I am as the son of the Durga!" and that, according to legend, Durga built her palace 20 km from his Lemah Putih School. He concludes by saying that the *wayang* stories he had narrated were meant as inspiration only.

> *I think you are not Durga and Kala, but it's good to understand it. The main [thing is] that we would like to become ourselves whatever, as a child, a lover, a husband, a wife, a friend, a god or goddess.*

Sudamala

> *This is the story about the Pandawa hero Sadewa liberating the giantess Durga from the curse placed upon her by Bathara Guru. Hereby she turns into the beautiful goddess Uma again. At the same time as liberating Uma, Sadewa liberates his own mother from slavery.*

Dewaruci

*The wayang story Dewaruci is about the warrior Bima, second
of the Pandawa brothers. He has borrowed his identity from the
Indian epic Mahabharata, but is a local hero in the Dewaruci,
which is a Javanese story. Bima has to find the 'secret of life' in
order for the Pandawas to win the war. The story runs on two
levels, an outer and an inner one. On one hand, it proceeds as an
action story relating the warrior's journey through the Javanese
landscape. On the other, it proceeds as a meditation relating the
mystic's inner journey through his feelings, emotions, sensations,
fears, desires and temptations in order to unite with his eternal
essence, also termed 'the water of (eternal) life' (tirta amerta).
This is impersonated by the miniature-god, Dewaruci, also
referred to as the 'true teacher' (guru sejati). The Dewaruci story
indicates that the human being is not only material, but comes
from a spiritual source as well.*

Prapto selects parts of the *Dewaruci* story for special emphasis. He does not
hide the fact that his narration and interpretation is coloured by his Javanese
meditation teacher, Sudarno Ong, whose relaxed attitude to spiritual liberation
he shares. There are no ascetic exercises within Amerta Movement. However,
the Amerta practitioner, like a person meditating while moving physically, also
enters into an inner spiritual process where they face an inner world of desires,
emotions, and thoughts, through an inner journey towards meeting their true
self. In this sense the *Dewaruci* story, in some ways, can be seen as an
illustration of the Amerta Movement practitioner's inner journey towards
spiritual liberation, while moving physically in Sukuh. According to Paul
Stange, as seen below, the *Dewaruci* story is a roadmap helping in how to
proceed on one's inner journey of liberation.

*Before setting out on his journey, Bima was first led astray by
listening to his teacher's advice. His teacher Durna, who is loyal
to the Kurawas, the enemy, advised him to look for the water of
life on top of the mountains, as for example on Mt. Lawu where
Sukuh is situated. But after having done so, Bima found that the
water of life was not there. He only found it at the bottom of the
ocean, as possibly near Parangtritis Beach. After having
conquered many dangers and overcome many temptations,
Bima met the miniature god Dewaruci, a replica of himself, at
the bottom of the ocean. After many long dialogues, he merged*

with Dewaruci by creeping into Dewaruci´s left ear. Bima did not think he would fit but Dewaruci assured him to that he would. "The whole cosmos is lying inside," he said. Having entered, Bima at first was disoriented so that he lost all sense of direction. The space seemed totally empty. However, gradually everything returned to view although in a somewhat different light. Bima then saw four colours, yellow, red, black and white.

These colours portray desires. Finally, Dewaruci himself appeared and launched into a long explanation of an esoteric doctrine about attitudes to desires. This included the revelation that the water of eternal life was everywhere suffusing all beings. After the instruction, Bima was reluctant to return to the world. He found the realm of teachings exceedingly satisfying. But Dewaruci reminded him that he still had many unfinished duties in the world. Bima agreed and re-emerged into the world, transformed.

Prapto's interpretation of Bima and Dewaruci

According to *kejawen*, life is a divine power consisting of an eternal essence, which is both inside and outside a human being. It is all-permeating, comprising the totality of life. The *Dewaruci* story illustrates this. Life as a divine power is related to in terms of 'eternal essence', the 'water of (eternal) life' and the 'true teacher'. Prapto translates this in different ways depending on the context, as we will see. He uses terms such as 'nectar of life',[11] 'inner soul', 'true self', 'true inner teacher', 'truth *guru*', 'first ancestor' or 'God' or *Tuhan* in Indonesian. These terms all relate to the belief that we are spiritual beings in the sense of coming from a non-material source to which we return again and, as such, we are part of life's eternal essence, part of the divine.

In his interpretation of the Dewaruci story, Prapto stresses that Bima's way to spiritual insight and liberation is through the body. He refers to the temple relief where Bima and Dewaruci are portrayed inside a womb according to Prapto. Bima has to re-enter the womb to become one with his 'inner soul' or 'true self'. This means being reborn into a pure state of open reception like that of a baby.[12] His process of liberation takes place within the physical body. It proceeds as a journey, both in the outside world and the inner one.

---

[11] Prapto also uses the term 'the nectar of life' about *amerta*.

[12] In Javanese mystical practices, this relief is also seen as portraying the mystical union between master and servant, high and low, the mystic and the Supreme Being (*manunggaling kawula-gusti* [Jav]).

I must be aware of the whole body and open to receiving impulses from inside and outside while practising. The feelings and passions, as they arise when I turn my attention to an inner world in order to merge with the true self, constitute material that is then transformed into physical movement. In this way it is opposed to out-of-body techniques where one leaves the body and travels in spirit only. I can be liberated in the sense of starting again and experiencing the world afresh. This technique entails growing anew in the physical body, forming new attitudes based on the 'true self' (*jati diri*) and thereby facilitating rebirth into wholeness. This also means

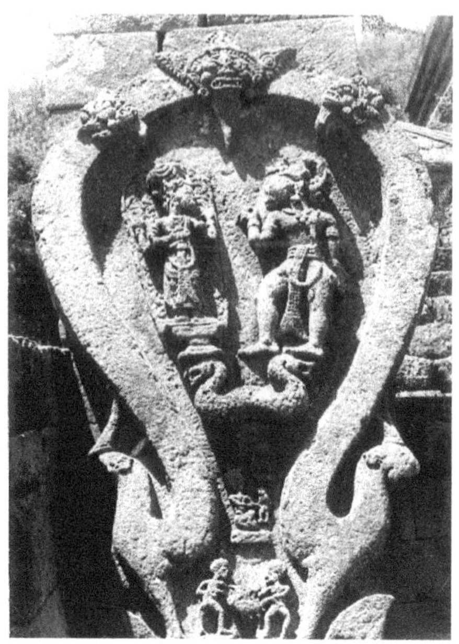

Bima and Dewaruci, Candi Sukuh.

development in a physical sense, just as children develop by growing physically. This liberation, by being contained within the physical body, as well as nourished by it, can be termed 'limited liberation'.

Patriarchal story

According to Prapto the story of Bima and Dewaruci is also a story about the authority of a patriarch/teacher.[13] The son follows the father and the student follows the teacher. He calls Bima's teacher, Durna, the 'false teacher' because Durna leads Bima astray. By sending Bima up the mountain, Durna cheats him. In contrast, Dewaruci is Bima's 'true teacher', 'truth guru', in Prapto's terms. He helps him find the 'nectar of life'. Bima obeys both of them in the sense that he listens to them and does as he is advised. In relation to Bima and Dewaruci, this is expressed symbolically when Bima, who is very large, has to enter into the miniature god Dewaruci's ear. Bima has to make himself small or humble. His ego has to be reduced so he can fit into Dewaruci's ear, the small entrance to cosmos where, through inner transformation, Bima reaches liberation.

---

[13] According to Prapto, the *Dewaruci* story deals with how Bima tries to find the right vibration with the right frequency. If he can do this, he can then reach out into the cosmos, i.e. reach 'God' and the whole world including life's origin. Prapto compares it with going to church. In Java at one time, there was the concept that it was unnecessary to have temples. The human being was a temple.

Bima asks Dewaruci the truth guru for the nectar of life [water of life]. Dewaruci speaks to him and gives him teaching telling Bima where is the nectar of life. He tells Bima that his teacher Durna who's sent him is not right and not good.

The idea of Bima's meeting with Dewaruci is that when he meets with his truth guru or his true inner self, then he's in the cosmos, then he can see many colours, like black, white, red, and so on: he can see the desires.

What Prapto relates to here is the Javanese attitude to human desires. Red, associated with fire, relates to anger; black, associated with earth, relates to food; yellow, associated with water, relates to sex; and white, associated with air, relates to purity, (Stange, 1977: 111). Each desire has two sides, negative and positive – they are not only dangerous but also like a blessing. Bima, to find what he really needs, first has to understand his true self, i.e. to meet himself. By listening to Dewaruci (the 'truth guru') Bima is led to spiritual insight, which transforms him. It makes him into a whole human being so that he is no longer split in two.

Lessons from Bima's story

According to Prapto, one can only assimilate teaching from others after one has met one's own self, i.e. after one knows one's own character and has achieved body-consciousness and attitude-consciousness. If not, the teacher risks leading one astray as Durna did Bima. This is also true with regard to the practice.

If I can feel oneness with myself when I hear something, with [the person] who teaches me, then I feel I can move with myself. I can move with my self who teaches me.

For Prapto, the story is also about following or not following a *guru*. Sometimes it is necessary to follow first in order to know whether it is the right way or not. This is as Prapto says to Bima in the story.

'OK Bima I Prapto follow you', and after that I can say, 'I need not follow you', but I can say 'I love you' (big laughter).

Prapto says the lesson of Bima and Dewaruci is important because it relates how Bima, a person on a mystical quest, meets his 'true self' or his 'truth guru'. Bima found a mirror in which he could mirror his 'little I'.

Sukuh is very important, the teaching there, because Bima is meeting his truth guru [who is identical with him] same with him. This is mirroring. It is his big I and little I.

Practice and time

Time for Prapto means different things, the most important being 'farmer's time' and 'city-time', 'own time', 'in time' and 'on time'.

Farmer's time and city-time

Prapto sees the farmer's sense of time as connected to nature, to the sun, the moon and rain in relation to planting and harvesting. If I watch the processes of nature, for instance a tree growing, I can see this in terms of time: let's say that I have planted a little tree outside my house, and then I have to go away for a year. When I come back, the little tree has grown and its growth can be measured in terms of time, i.e. one may measure the time that has passed in relation to how much the tree has grown. Growth in nature has its own sense of timing in harmony with the universe and wholeness. When one lives in a city, one experiences time differently. It is something artificial, regulated by (industrial) production rather than by nature. In cities, natural vegetation is often lacking, so one cannot measure time from year to year like the farmer.

Own time

'Own time' is related to personal identity, to becoming oneself or to finding 'your own inner yourself', in Prapto's terms. Finding 'your own inner yourself' or your 'genuine being', is connected to my attitude to myself and to the world. It is connected to purification because, by reading myself in an honest, neutral way, with regard to my attitude to myself and to the world, I become purified of distorted or biased approaches. In this way I can meet myself in the sense of meeting my 'genuine being'. Hence, 'own time' indicates my genuineness.

In time and on time

'On time' means making an appointment with another person at, say, 4 o'clock and coming at 4 o'clock sharp. 'In time' means showing up comfortably in the flow of things, i.e. not at 4 o'clock sharp, and finding that works out well. (And when one has really found one's 'own time' that would then lead rather to 'in time' than 'on time'.)

Own time and Sukuh

Practising at Sukuh was also about becoming oneself in relation to time. As we have seen, Prapto calls this 'own time' or finding 'your own inner yourself'. For this Prapto normally refers to Bima's spiritual quest to unite with his 'inner essence'. But Prapto also related to the myth in a new way. To follow Bima in order to find one's 'inner essence' now seemed old-fashioned to him. It was just another way of following tradition blindly, he said, and might become an excuse for doing nothing in the sense of development in one's life.

> *What for finding your own inner teacher? Maybe this is good*
> *for finding your own hammock.*[14]

> *I think that more and more it is not about finding the inner*
> *teacher, this is the projection of the old understanding.*

Rather it is a question of finding authority in oneself. This means that the practitioner is going to be their own authority in life. We need to become ourselves. We need to become absolute authorities for ourselves.

It was evident that Prapto here in the mid-1990s wanted to bring his teaching of Amerta Movement up to date for his Western students. These students often liked to see themselves as being in absolute control of their lives. But Prapto continued to use the Dewaruci story and other stories related to Sukuh. For finding 'own time' in Sukuh, Prapto often advised students to do so through breathing, relating this to Bima.

> *In Sukuh much speaking about the wind we call bayu. Bayu*
> *means the god of the wind. Bima is the son of the god of the wind.*

> *Find your own time in the practice in Sukuh through breathing.*

> *Finding your own breathing, own-time, life, space, finding your*
> *own understanding.*

Awareness of breathing while practising movement means a condition of heightened consciousness and sensitivity. One's own breathing is part of one's 'own time'. It facilitates a rebirth in the sense that it helps me be in tune with my inner life force in the sense of expression, genuine rhythm and speed. Moreover, in order to understand Sukuh, the starting position in the practice has to be based on one's 'own time', i.e. based on one's true self or genuine being. The focus on breathing does not, however, indicate use of specific breathing techniques. It refers to breathing in terms of a natural life impulse or energy, 'breath of life', through the whole body.[15]

---

[14] The term 'hammock' here may indicate taking the easy way out by relying on tradition, instead of personally finding one's own way and identity in life.

[15] According to Prapto, the focus on breathing for heightened consciousness and sensitivity might be compared to the Theravada Buddhist meditation where one concentrates on breathing to enter the state of meditation. For Theravada Buddhist meditation practice, *Vipassana,* in modern times, see Jane Hamilton-Merritt (1976).

Exploring and practising 'in time'

Students sometimes had difficulty in relating to this ancient temple. Finding the right balance between oneself and the temple had to do with time, according to Prapto. Thus, 'on time' had to do with how to make one's own time/timing in movement and expression fit with the time outside, i.e. the time of Candi Sukuh, which, due to its ancient style is described as being 'in time' and very different from modern styles of temple. Because of this Sukuh could be difficult to understand for someone in the present day. The first step for someone moving at Candi Sukuh was to try to adapt one's 'own time' to that of the ancient temple. This might of course result in a unity whereby the student managed to move/chose to move in tune with the outside, i.e. with Sukuh, its terraces and ancient atmosphere. Conversely, it might not be possible for a student to be (completely) in tune with Sukuh. In that case, the student would practise by engaging in a dialogue with the temple. This dialogue could take the form of a 'bargaining', an inner discussion in Prapto's terms, between one's genuinely felt manner of moving and the temple.

Students started to work with 'in time' and 'on time' by exploring whether their own physical timing, rhythm, speed and manner of moving as modern human beings (on time) fitted with the ancient temple (in time). For the individual practitioner, physically this meant weighing up how much activity and how much passivity felt right. Attitude-wise it included probing oneself for how much openness and receiving and how much closedness felt right.) 'In time', apart from practising at the temple, for the individual practitioner could also be to practise with a co-practitioner who moved with a different timing, speed or rhythm from their own.

To find their 'own time' in relation to the time of Candi Sukuh, students were asked to go to the bottom and the top of the temple while practising Amerta movement. Going downwards in the temple to its *lingga-yoni* meant going downwards in the body physically to its primal instincts. It also symbolised the earth and the mother, the female. Moreover, it indicated a new beginning for the individual practitioner in the sense of inspiring them to integrate, in a new way, female and male, within themselves: going to the top of the temple, on a symbolic level, represented going to the head, the sky, the father, the male, or the top of society. Alternatively, it could be to gain a new 'top' in oneself by achieving a new skill. In short, students practised moving in between earth and sky, mother and father, matriarch and patriarch, body and mind. This exercise helped them to explore their identity individually within the themes of female-male and earth-heaven.

One student was assigned the task of doing nothing but practise free movement between the temple's bottom and top. This involved moving constantly on a line formed by the pathway linking the temple's three terraces. This can be seen as a journey from the beginning of life to its end or simply as a journey from body to spirit. Others might see this exercise as a movement meditation starting from the root *chakra* to the crown *chakra* and back again in a circular movement. In terms of movement, this exercise provided a clear outer form to the free Amerta movement. In that respect, it was akin to practising with a kind of choreography and scenography.

Passive-active 'dependent' and 'not dependent'

Students, working in pairs, practised passive-active in order 'not to be dependent' on each other. During this session at Sukuh, students were taught first to practise 'passive-active, as two separated phenomena' ('not dependent'). The second approach, the complementary manner, ('dependent'), was illustrated by the meeting between male and female in the *lingga-yoni* at the temple's entrance-gate. In order to become whole, independent beings, we must first integrate the male and female aspects of our personalities. During practice with another practitioner, passive-active 'not dependent' entails a female-male relationship where each person stands independently of the other. The aim was to train in making one's own decisions.

Students were shaped and processed, so to speak, by Sukuh's physical form and atmosphere and they developed their physical vocabulary and their being on that basis. As practice proceeded, consciousness and sensitivity were heightened and students began to wake up to life in the present. They would avoid reacting in an automatic way and avoid being caught in a karmic pattern, like Bathara Guru in the story above. However, if we were caught in karmic patterns or became dependent on each other, this was all right, although it had consequences. When it happened within the practice, we had to recognise it and make a clear choice as to whether we were to be dependent or not.

Each other useful but not depending [dependent] on each other!

Stop! Find your position who is active, passive, not dependent, not holding. You are not to depend your life, your space, your time, your most important your breathing… [on someone else]!

Stop! Understand if you are dependent already or not! Go on!

Stop! Understand if you are dependent on the time, space, the body, the energy!

Stop! I see the active is greedy for the time. Don't give your time to the other!

See what you do to the other! You still can recognise your own space and time being not dependent, but still can receive what the others do.

You can practise in your country all of your life.

Circling: Fertility and bowing

The temple provoked awe and an almost monastic austerity, which the circling movement seemed to satisfy. At the beginning, students often went into the circling movements learned at the Hill. This was partly due to Prapto who continued his circling pattern.

Full group sessions often had an almost shamanic sense. This was partly due to the drumming, which almost constantly accompanied the movement. There was also an artistic element in the movement brought about by Javanese guest artists taking part. When watching them it was evident that they knew Candi Sukuh well. It was interesting to see the respect and, as it seemed, the natural religious feeling, even awe, the temple called forth from several of them. But their free movement seemed much less free than that of the Westerners. Rather they practised a kind of improvisation based on Javanese classical dance positions and patterns.

Prapto, dressed in black with a small white, triangular scarf covering his hair, looked like a local holy man or a Javanese shaman and his way of moving hands and fingers was not unlike that of the Javanese dancers. In contrast, his circling around his own vertical axis was not. Circling is not a characteristic pattern of Javanese classical dance in the strictest sense. It is maybe rather a manner of bodily movement belonging to the Javanese shaman or to Prapto's own individual expression.

At Candi Sukuh, Prapto spoke about bowing in the sense of praying and honouring ancestors, both as bearers of family culture and the origins of one's life. He openly showed his respect for Candi Sukuh, for the ancestors and the fertility connected to the temple as manifested by its *lingga-yoni* and other fertility symbols. He saw the first ancestor as an equivalent of god or Tuhan (in Indonesian), in animism. In traditional Java, it is part of every individual's duty in life (dharma) to pass on life by begetting children. Fertility in itself is holy as is the mating of husband and wife. Hence, fertility has to be revered and dealt with in the proper way.

The male-female union on the level of mystical practices in the spiritual sense represents rebirth through mystical reunion of the male and female aspects of the individual person. As I understand it, Prapto primarily related fertility at Candi Sukuh to personal development and creativity or blossoming in the sense of the movement practice.

Students were visibly influenced by the temple's sacred atmosphere. This showed in their individual ways of expressing their feelings of the sacred through physical movement. They also made small altars of green fern leaves and mountain pebbles interspersed with small red and white flowers oriented along the eight directions of the compass forming a kind of mandala pattern. Sometimes they burned incense and rang Buddhist style bells. This was not so much because they were Buddhists, although some of them were, but because they found the sound suited the atmosphere. In the afternoons when the rains came, students had to practise in the village pendopo. Then they also worked on how to generate sound within their movement. They did so by responding via sound to their own inside stirrings and to input or impulses from the outside world. They also accompanied each other with spontaneous sounds. Some made sounds while watching the others. Hence, sitting on the edge of the pendopo floor, they were tuning in to the movement of their co-practitioners in the space, responding to it through sounds and by making overtones*. Bringing sound into the practice was a feature of the 1990s.

Chapter 7

Vocabulary 2: Borobudur, Parangtritis and Crystallisation

I. Candi Borobudur ~ Reading

This chapter covers the second part of the 'Vocabulary, Nature and Life' course. After their stay at the Hill to study space and at Candi Sukuh to study time, students were taken to Candi Borobudur to study reading and afterwards to Parangtritis Beach to study expression, before they returned to the Lemah Putih School for the crystallisation that ended the course.

Before introducing Candi Borobudur, which is a Buddhist temple and which has inspired Prapto in developing his movement technique, 'reading', let us first look at Prapto's relationship to Buddhism.

Prapto and Buddhism

In the 'Vocabulary' programme, Prapto presents himself as a Theravada Buddhist, but the course is addressed to everyone regardless of religious adherence. In his role of instructor and spiritual artist taking students to Borobudur, Prapto naturally related to the whole Buddhist spectrum. This includes Mahayana, Vajrayana, and Theravada Buddhism. All of these have influenced Java. Modern Theravada Buddhism, (re)introduced in modern times in Indonesia, is represented by the Buddhist *vihara* at Candi Mendut near Borobudur. Prapto's Buddhism as applied to his teaching of Amerta Movement was probably also inspired by his Sumarah meditation teacher Sudarno Ong, who was a Theravada Buddhist. Sudarno Ong's terminology, according to Stange (1980), can be linked to the continuity of awareness exercised in Vipassana.

Candi Borobudur

This description of Candi Borobudur is meant only to present it as a practice site for Amerta Movement. The temple is part of Indonesia's national heritage and a UNESCO World Heritage Site. It is a tourist destination, visited daily by hundreds of people from all over the world and is among the most popular tourist destinations for Indonesians themselves. Only once a year at the *Waisak* festival, commemorating the Buddha's birth, enlightenment and passing, is the temple officially used for religious purposes.

Seen from a distance, Candi Borobudur looks like a huge lotus flower. It is, in fact, a huge stupa with many small stupas clustered around the main one.[16] Each stupa reaches for the sky in the same way as the jagged mountaintops of the surrounding volcanos, which might have inspired the construction.

The temple was constructed about 800 CE around a natural hilltop and forms an artificial mountain. Its base is in the form of a square and its top is circular. By combining the form of the square and the circle, the temple makes a mandala. Its quadratic base symbolises the earth and the circular top the heavens. Prapto called the temple a 'mandala chakra in nature'. The temple measures 123m x 123m in its ground plan and is 34.5m tall. It is crowned by the 7m tall main stupa shaped like a large bell.

Around the main stupa on the three descending circular terraces forming the temple's upper structure are 72 small stupas. These are perforated with latticed openings permitting one to see that a Buddha sits inside each one. They are probably a representation of the historic Buddha, Sakyamuni. The main stupa might have contained an incomplete Buddha-statue. One cannot look into it from outside. The tripartite circles, the three descending circular terraces forming the temple's upper structure, rest on the quadratic base. This in turn is composed of six increasingly larger quadratic terraces. The lowest forms a paved way for religious processions around the temple. One part of this procession-way constitutes the corner-platform where Amerta practice starts in the morning. Four of the six terraces are walled in by balustrades to form passages or galleries all the way around the temple. These are connected by staircases going from the foot to the top of the temple, one on each of the four sides, so that no staircase forms the main entrance. The temple's ground level is covered by a wall probably to consolidate the construction. The reliefs there cannot be viewed today except for a few in the southeast corner where part of the wall has been removed exposing reliefs from the *Karmawibangga,* an ancient Tibetan text that discusses good and bad deeds and their consequences.

So Candi Borobudur is composed of ten levels symbolising the ten levels of the way of the future Buddhas, the Boddhisattvas. These levels are divided into

---

[16] A *stupa,* a reliquary, is also called a *dagaba.* The word is a combination of the Sanskrit *dhatu* (relic) and *garba,* (womb, chamber, receptable). The implication is that the relics, planted in the womb of the structure like a quickening seed, exert an animating influence on this seemingly dead mass of masonry, generating and perpetuating for all time and for all men the spiritual power of the Buddha. (Hoadley, 1998).

three spheres representing the three cosmic worlds: *kamadhatu*, *rupadhatu* and *arupadhatu*. The first is the world of desire at the ground level (*kamadhatu*). The covered reliefs relate to the story of Buddha's life and deal with karma – how good deeds are rewarded and bad ones punished and how this mechanism binds the human being to endless cycles of birth and rebirth.

The second level (*rupadhatu*) is today the lowest level to which the visitor has access. It represents the world of form. Here human beings in their purified bodies are engaged in meditation and preparation for Buddha-hood under the guidance of the Buddhas whose statues are built into the temple's niches. At this level the Buddhist pilgrim has let go of desire (*karma*) but not yet of form (*rupa)*. It is the level of the Bodhisattvas (the future *Buddhas*), their way in Buddhism and their message. The reliefs on the walls of these galleries illustrate the *Jataka* pre-Buddha stories. Thus, when pilgrims walked through these galleries studying the reliefs, they were gradually brought to higher levels of Buddhism on their way towards enlightenment. The temple functioned as a textbook in the Buddhist doctrine for aspiring monks and religious pilgrims. It was a *yantra* or an object of meditation. The temple's third level, the circular top level with all the stupas, is the world of non-form (*arupadhatu*). Here the walls are unornamented. One guesses at the presence of the almost invisible Buddhas behind the small stupas' wall openings. Once at the level of the main stupa, one is under an open sky with an unhindered view of the landscape. Most spectacular among the surrounding mountains is Mt. Merapi, an active volcano located here in one of the world's most densely populated areas. It is also one of the most fertile ones because of the volcanic ash. The landscape's palm groves and rice paddies attest to this.

On each of the temple's four sides, the many Buddhas sit in niches.[17] They belong to the Dhyani group, the so-called meditation Buddhas and represent the four most important moments in the life of Buddha. This is indicated by their different hand and finger gestures or mudras. The four different Dhyani-Buddhas sit in meditation in the *padma asana* bodily position i.e. in the lotus or the cross-legged position.

> *The symbolic structure of the monument is as follows: The whole building represents a Buddhist transition from the lowest manifestations of reality at the base, up through a series of 'regions' or psychological states, towards the ultimate condition*

---

[17] For the names of the Buddhas and the mudras and other information here, as far as possible, I have followed the terms and spellings used by the Indonesian Tourist Board in the *Borobudur Archaeological Park Indonesia*, 1991, pamphlet.

*of spiritual enlightenment and release from corruption and
error at the summit. At the same time, since the monument is a
unity, it effectively proclaims the doctrine of the unity of the
Cosmos in the light of Truth, and does not – as other religions
may – banish 'the world, the flesh and the devil' to an eternally
'different', negative region. In this Buddhist doctrine, not only
is the entire creation redemptible it has never been anything
but redeemed, and the ordinary state of existence is, if only we
have the eyes to see it, no different from the state of enlightened
bliss. The difference between enlightenment and ordinary
corrupt life is not a difference in the world, but in the eye and
mind of each beholder. Someone who has reached the top of
Borobudur should be different from the one who started up.*

(Rawson, 1995: 228-230)

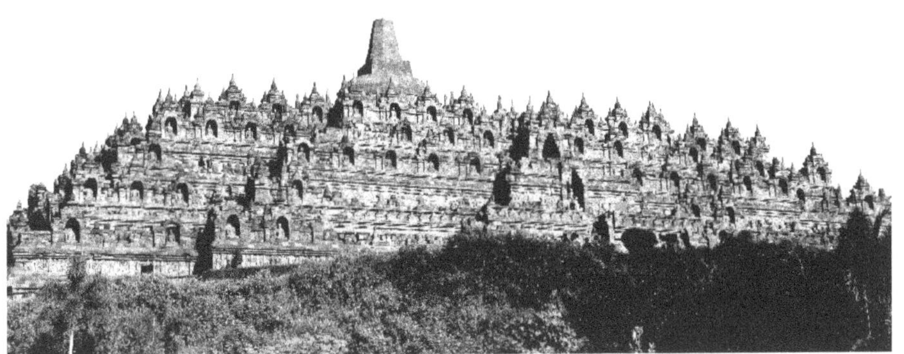

Candi Borobudur

'Vocabulary' course background at Borobudur

Vocabulary students arrived at Borobudur on an evening at the beginning of
December in a fierce but refreshing downpour of tropical rain. We were going
to stay there for four days. During the last part of the journey to Borobudur, we
passed through a landscape of rice paddies and small hamlets surrounded by
high volcanos. We lodged in a hotel, in a cluster of homes very close to the
temple. The inhabitants are proud to live on the doorstep of the temple
complex and call themselves the Borobudur-people (*orang Borobudur*).
Although they are Muslims, they feel connected to Borobudur in the same way
that they feel connected to their ancestors.

The temple lies in a large well-trimmed park with a few coconut palms and
small flowering bushes. We could enter the park directly via a back entrance

close to the hotel and only had to walk about 500m to reach the temple's procession-way via a wide flight of staircases at the end of the park's main avenue. As it was the rainy season, the view of the surrounding volcanos was clearest in the early morning. On some days, however, clouds lay like a girdle of ultra-light white gauze across the mountains and under their peaks. The heat came very fast as did light drizzles. These were not unpleasant but sometimes as early as 8am a mist descended.

Early in the mornings the whole group would practise outdoors on the corner-platform next to the temple's procession-way in its southeast corner. From about 10am until 1pm students practised in the temple's museum and/or outside it in a coconut palm grove. In the late afternoon we practised in the hotel pendopo. Individual practice would generally be very early, before group practice with Prapto, and again afterwards, at one of the temple's four sides, studying our chosen *mudra* for up to an hour.

Practice sites and practices

At the meeting-place where Prapto talks, everyone sits on the ground amidst a stream of visitors. Several large Bodhi trees growing on the grass slope below offer some shade. From here we can see a whole side of the temple from bottom to top: this includes its beginning at the procession-way to galleries, Buddha-niches, the upper terraces' small stupas and the main stupa.

The corner-platform is an enclosure with a stone floor. It is next to a small staircase from where guided tours normally start, because it is here that part of the wall has been removed, allowing one to see some of the otherwise hidden reliefs of the *kamadhatu* level belonging to the world of desire.

The museum is close to the temple. There are two pendopos, which can be used for practice. They have marble floors and a set of *gamelan* (Indonesian percussion) instruments, which students can use if they like. In front of one of the pendopos is a mandala, a compact circular stone floor made of rocks with a large Buddha statue in its centre (the Buddha-mandala). This Buddha, according to Prapto, is the most important one in Borobudur. Officials and their guests are always brought into the museum to see it. Practice in the museum usually takes place on the marble floor of one of the two pendopos, protected by the roof from tropical sun and rain. Practice also takes place outside on the Buddha-mandala.

Students normally practice until lunchtime in the museum or at the coconut grove in the park. The coconut grove is a grassy area with a few slender coconut palms which provide a structure for practice. Tourists usually do not come close but one day an elephant walked past carrying a tourist. The grass in the grove is soft and pleasant to move on, opening new possibilities for movements. This is especially welcome after moving on the stone of the corner-platform, the rocks of the Buddha-mandala and the marble floor of the museum pendopo*s*.

At Candi Borobudur, students have ample opportunity to work on two important Amerta Movement qualities: patience and acceptance. All day long, a continuous stream of visitors arrives on the procession-way, accompanied by a loudspeaker and explanations in different languages. The loudspeaker at the nearby mosque also calls the faithful to prayer. One might say the course takes place in the middle of the stream of life at Candi Borobudur.

'Reading' and 'writing' at Borobudur Temple

Reading

The 'Vocabulary' course at Candi Borobudur deals mainly with the theme of 'reading Borobudur Temple'. As with the entire course, the aim is to build a vocabulary through movement. Students do so by reading Borobudur's form, proportions, material, texture, atmosphere and story. They learn to become aware of their attitude or approach to themselves and to life, based on four mudras, one for each of the temple's four sides. They start their movement practice from their own being, their own self, from earth or, in Prapto's terms, from the *Pribadi Art* or the 'Reality World approach'. From that basis, they form their opinion or ideas, the 'sky', in Prapto's terms.

According to Prapto, as we read the temple we are also being read ourselves i.e. we are being processed and influenced by the temple's form, atmosphere and story in our movement's form and in our attitude while passing through the aisles of Borobudur or at other places in the temple grounds.

To complete the course, it was essential that students had begun to develop a heightened consciousness and sensitivity as to their identity in terms of their concepts and their felt bodily sense. This meant that they tried to register consciously how they met with the spiritual or sacred concepts of the temple. How far could they follow them? Furthermore, as seen above, the temple, by its physical layout, imposed a form on their free movement. When they walked in the narrow galleries, for example, they were almost pushed forward in the ascending spiral. As Prapto said, the temple could absorb each of us so that we did not clearly have our own space. By this, he meant that we might lose our sense of identity and become part of Borobudur. However, this mechanism maybe played a lesser role in the course practice, or at least a somewhat different one, from what might be expected. The general practice sessions taught by Prapto did not take place within the ascending spiral of the temple. They were taught in places that are open or half-open spaces of different form from that of the spiral, such as the corner-platform (square form), the coconut grove (linear form), and the square pendopo*s* at the museum and hotel. So they contrasted with the prevailing ascending spiral. Only on the last day did Prapto instruct students to practise in the ascending spiral form.

The course's practice technique allows us each to read the temple as we wish. This is unlike the Buddhist pilgrims who circumambulate the sanctuary in a clockwise direction studying Buddhism and reading the reliefs. While Amerta practitioners might do so on their own, this is not an explicit part of the programme taught by Prapto. So we were less influenced by the ascending spiral form and the Buddhist doctrine at Borobudur than might be expected.

Writing

In 'Vocabulary 1995-1996', Prapto introduced the term 'writing', indicating expression by movement as a result of responding to Borobudur via reading. It also includes responding to inner impulses and sensations. We might see 'writing', as presented by Prapto on this course, as a kind of calligraphy performed by the whole body. This calligraphy is seen as specific to the individual practitioner and to the site they are responding to. Prapto asked us to be clear in ourselves about our intention when 'reading' Borobudur. Did we really want to read Borobudur and 'write' i.e. to express our readings transformed into bodily movement? Or were we only going to 'scribble' a little down in our subconscious?

> *… or if you are just as scribbling in your inconscient mind [subconscious] from this all programme or you let go that you have a plan studying together, reading together the spiritual concept and working in the park.*

In general, however, Prapto lets students themselves take the initiative at Borobudur. This corresponds to the method for seeking and obtaining (esoteric) knowledge, which the temple itself illustrates by its construction, i.e. by being constructed as a textbook in the Buddhist doctrine.

'Landscape' and 'skyscape', body and mind, people and king

We were encouraged to find our own understanding of Borobudur on the basis of our own nature. As Prapto said, practitioners were foreigners to Java, to its landscape, nature, sounds, smells, climate, culture, architecture and art. Since Prapto is Javanese, students might be tempted to 'hook' his mind. Instead, students should develop their own relationship to Java and to Borobudur.

*As Westerners in Java, you start from this landscape in order
to finding your own skyscape. The cosmos potential is in
starting from the landscape.*

*You would see me as a landscape here, and then you would use
me to find your landscape here. By me, using me as your hook,
you can find your landscape here.*

*I have stay here. Maybe you can feel my home sense, me as a friend,
a lover, a husband, stimulator, source of all Eastern people.*

Here Prapto uses the expressions 'landscape' and 'skyscape' as metaphors for the practitioner's body and mind.

Prapto warns students against over-identification with him as a Javanese and also with Javanese nature and culture because these are very different from their own nature and culture.[18] However, he adds that if students are ready to be 'caught' by Java or Borobudur, this is OK.

Mudras and attitudes. Instruction for practice

The four different *Buddhas* seen at Candi Borobudur are associated with four different mudras and with four attitudes in Amerta Movement.

Temple side	Dhyani Buddha	Mudra	Attitude
East	Buddha Akcobya	Bhumisparca mudra	Witness
South	Buddha Ratnasambhawa	Wara mudra	Offering
West	Buddha Amithaba	Dhyani mudra	Channelling
North	Buddha Amoghasidha	Abhawa/Abhaya mudra	Less fear

Mudras and attitude in Amerta Movement

The *Buddha Akcobya* in the east calls the earth to witness his enlightenment and the beginning of the new teaching. His right hand rests on his right leg, palm downwards. The left hand rests in his lap, palm upwards. As Prapto said, the *Buddha Akcobya*, when calling the earth to witness his enlightenment, touches his body as a symbol of the earth. Prapto saw the *Buddha Akcobya's* gesture in terms of movement and not as a fixed bodily position. The witness can see and then can make statements like: 'oh yes it's happening like that' or 'this is new' or 'this is green' and 'that is white-green' and so on.

---

[18] Carl Gustav Jung warned Westerners travelling and studying for long periods in African and Asian cultures very different from their own, against a similar mechanism. He used the term 'to go black under the skin', see Jung (1993: 273).

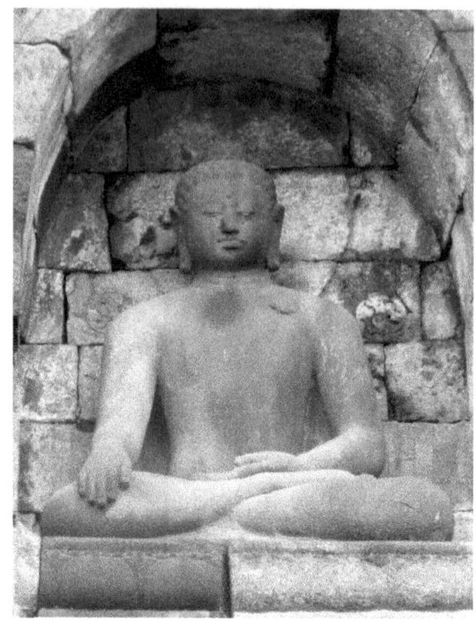

Bhumisparca Mudra:
Wikimedia Commons. Photo: Anandajoti

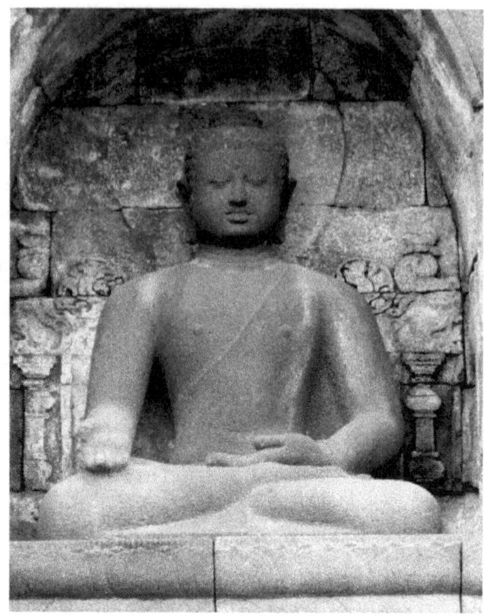

Wara Mudra:
Wikimedia Commons. Photo: Anandajoti

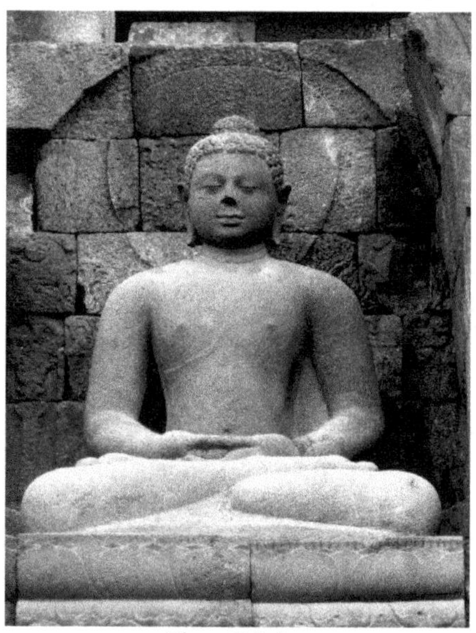

Dhyani Mudra:
Wikimedia Commons. Photo: Anandajoti

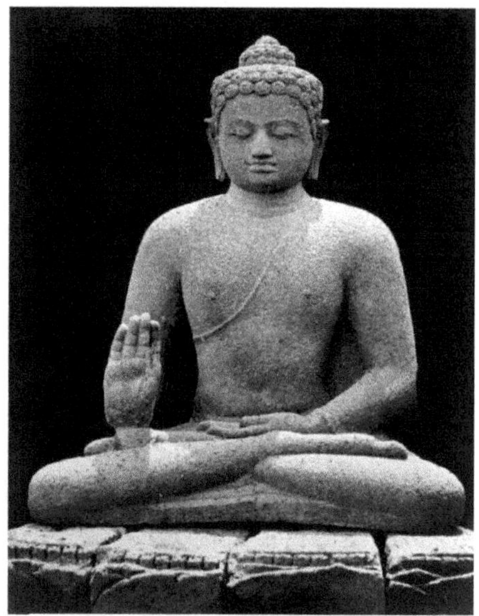

Abhawa Mudra:
Wikimedia Commons. Photo: Anon

The attitude of offering is represented by the *Buddha Ratnasambhawa* with the *wara mudra* giving blessing or showing the way to salvation. The *Buddha Ratnasambhawa's* right hand rests on his right leg, palm turned up; the left hand, also with the palm turned up, rests in his lap.

The channelling attitude is represented by the *Buddha Amitabha*. He sits in the well-known position of meditation: hands in his lap, palms turned up, right hand placed on top of the left. The two thumbs are touching at the tip. He directs his attention inward to meditation. This is connected to meditation in the sense of receiving. Traditionally in Java, the person receiving is like a pillar, a living link between heaven and earth, acting as a channel for the message from the sky without questioning the message but passing it on to the meditation community.[19] But the channelling attitude in Amerta Movement involves responsibility. This means I am fully aware and in my body while channelling, responsible for what I channel with my bodily movement. This is the opposite of a traditional medium or traditional Javanese trance dancer, for example. The difference is that the Amerta practitioner's ego is awake and active while, at the same time, they are in a condition of heightened consciousness and sensitivity.

The less fear attitude is represented by the *Buddha Amoghasidha* in the north with the *Abhawa mudra*. He sits with his right palm raised. The left arm is resting in his lap with the palm turned upwards.

In order to choose a mudra for practice, Prapto asks students to explore Borobudur on their own, going around the procession-way in free movement, sometimes referred to as 'walking walking'. In this way, we can see the four different Buddhas with their mudras. We make our choice by exploring them all in our physical practice. Prapto asks us not to copy the Buddhas and their mudras. Instead, we should use them as a basis for our movement, including in our reading the attitude of our chosen mudra. Then, when we go 'walking, crawling, sitting and so on' with our chosen mudra, we will experience what the mudra meant. Prapto takes the example of the mudra representing 'to witness'. Students who choose this simply include the attitude of witnessing in their movement and in their different body postures. When they crawl, walk, sit and so on, they do so in order to witness. In this way, they bring to life their inner witness and are animated in the form of a witness.

> *To put the idea of witness in your crawling, crawling for*
> *witness, lying, sitting in your witness, walking in your witness,*
> *stretching in your witness, give life in your witness.*

The same applies to practising with the other mudras. The offering attitude might be translated as having an attitude of bowing to life and of giving in a

---

[19] Channelling is the common attitude to receiving practised in Javanese mystical movements, according to Prapto. He gave Sumarah as an example, where one starts practice from an attitude of receiving from the sky. This implies that the guide is channelling energy from the Almighty to his followers during a meditation meeting.

spirit of compassion without taking back. For the channelling attitude, we are recommended to receive material from the sky or from outside ourselves via our whole body. It is important to let it pass through our body before it is transformed in the body and communicated via movement. For the *Abhawa mudra* of less fear, Prapto recommends that we practise with it not by forcing ourselves to get courage but rather trying to go forward with less fear.

> *Do not just push yourself for making courage, but you can go forward with less fear and give form to your courage in Borobudur. Who has fear is not only you. Before someone like the Bodhisattva, all have fear. I also have a lot of fear, but the fear can transform. The fear can help me to wake up my awareness of how I can make less the fear itself.*

Students can also choose to be personally creative in the sense of finding a new mudra for themselves if they prefer to do so. For those who are not ready to work with the mudras in their movement, Prapto recommends that they go 'walking walking' in Borobudur in a manner of free movement and in an atmosphere of development and creativity. Not forcing an exercise on a student is characteristic of Prapto's way of teaching, and of the Central Javanese in general.

Through their choice of mudra, students receive a theme and a form, even though they are free to explore and apply these. The aim of choosing a mudra and one of the temple's sides for individual practice is to help students create their own vocabulary at the temple, providing them with a tool for developing their own form and expression. Using the mudras in this way also serves as a model for helping students develop their own ways of applying their movement experience from Java after their return home, where they might replace the theme and form provided by the mudras with a similar tool appropriate to their own culture. Thus, connecting the practice in Borobudur with the Buddhas and mudras may be seen as introducing an element into Amerta Movement practice that is close to choreography, although mainly meant for inspiration. (Starting in this way from a point outside oneself and one's private autobiography in movement practice is a Messenger Art technique. So, in the midst of this *Pribadi Art* Vocabulary Course at Borobudur in the mid-1990s, Prapto introduced a Messenger Art technique. See Chapter 9.)

Practice on the corner-platform

It is eight o'clock in the morning. A group practice session is under way. These sessions often have a strong spiritual energy. Students have already placed small flower-offerings and incense on the temple walls. They respond to the temple and its atmosphere through their movement and with prayers and singing. This feels natural at Candi Borobudur both for the students, who are open to their surroundings and for the Buddhist Prapto, who is in his element. As the floor is made of hard stone, it invites practitioners to move in the standing, walking and sitting positions, rather than running or crawling. At first, the session is full of solemnity, but gradually it grows lighter and full of joy. Students practise alone on the platform, i.e. not as a group but individually. Prapto in high spirits sits on the temple's balustrade above the corner-platform, making sounds and singing. It seems to be an expression of his own personal response to students' practice and to Candi Borobudur: sitting in the lotus position, dressed in black like a traditional Javanese mystic, his right foot beating the rhythm against his left lower leg. Little by little we join Prapto's singing. First, quietly humming his tune then gradually singing a song with words, and then Buddhist mantra-singing, following Prapto, who seems ecstatic. His voice continues going up and up until it ends with trills in the treble. His joy catches the students so that their movements became more lively and expressive. It spurs them into expressing more freely their bodily-based spirituality in the middle of the chaotic swarming crowd at Borobudur.

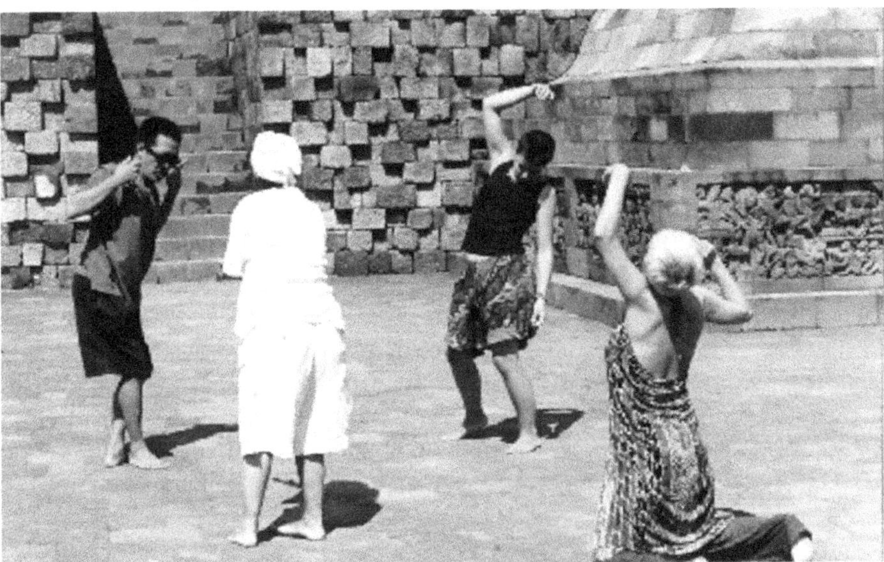

Practice on the corner-platform

After this full group session on the corner-platform, we spread out throughout the temple in order to practise individually with our chosen mudra at one of the four sides. Alternatively, we set out to go walking-walking, wandering in the temple exploring its galleries, reliefs and terraces before group practice resumes at the museum.

Practice in the museum. 'I and You' and 'I and Buddha'

Students start their practice in the museum on the Buddha-mandala. First, they practise movement in three dimensions with the Buddha statue, in their own individual ways through free movement. Then they start working on exercises which Prapto terms 'I and You' and 'I and Buddha'. They practise these exercises in the same way as they had trained with the pillars in the 'pillar-in-situation' exercise on the 'Basic' course, i.e. based on identification or dialogue. (see Chapter 5, p. 78). In other words, they practise the 'I and You' and 'I and Buddha' exercise in two ways: first in a manner of identifying oneself (seeking unity with the other person: You/Buddha), then in a manner of dialogue and exchange with the other person (You/Buddha) as an independent being.

Students first practise the 'I and You' exercise in pairs, reading each other from an attitude of unity, of identifying with the other practitioner, and then proceed to practise from an attitude of dialogue, of exchange, in the sense of being 'not dependent' on the other. This exercise prepares students for practising with the Buddha in the 'I and Buddha' exercise, which they also practise based on the two attitudes. When practising from the sense of unity, Prapto says their attitude will be: 'I am Me' and 'I am Buddha'. In this way, the Buddha is seen as part of the practitioner. For the dialogue approach, students enter the practice with the attitude that the Buddha and the students are two different beings and, moreover, not on the same level. Having finished these exercises students also read the temple from unity and from dialogue in order to understand and get to know about it, to relate to it, based on their own being and on their bodily movement in the temple.

These two approaches – The Unity Approach and the Dialogue Approach – are also respectively referred to as the 'Fertility-Approach' and the 'Hero-Approach'. When carrying out the exercise with the Buddha on the mandala, Prapto adds that personally he would never "put himself as Buddha", meaning that he would not practise with the Buddha from an approach of unity, i.e. of identifying himself with the Buddha "for we are not one, we are two". Prapto would rather practise from an attitude of dialogue, of exchange, with Buddha. Students, however, are free to practise how they like.

Prapto guiding in the coconut grove

Prapto continues to be in a process of development himself as Amerta Movement develops. Students may find his way of guiding strange, because he sometimes embodies different human characters or archetypes, which are not immediately understandable. According to Prapto, the characters he embodies may be an as yet unseen part of a student's personality. This way of guiding or even teaching is not uncommon in Java within ancient mystical practices, and even in modern mystical practices like Sumarah. Furthermore, bodily communication is important in Java, not least due to the multi-ethnic character of society, the different dialects and different educational levels.

This is an account of Prapto guiding in the coconut grove:

A woman, a movement-teacher in her late thirties, begins an individual session on the grass. Prapto is standing calmly outside the area used for movement practice in the coconut grove. He watches the woman moving, guiding her. At the same time, Prapto explains to the rest of the group some guiding points. The woman's movement is light and flowing, like a fish in water. It is unusual to move with such ease and speed in the intense and humid heat under the open sky. These factors normally encourage slowness, but the woman turns and twists going down to the ground and coming up again, spinning on her own axis, all in an incessant flow. Her bodily lightness is impressive and only a few times does it go off the edge and make her begin to 'fly', as Prapto calls it. To fly means that the practitioner loses her grounding in the physical body, so that her mind takes over, forcing too much speed on her. Otherwise, the lightness of her movements is physically initiated. For this to be possible the woman, in her movements, has to focus her attention inside her body in a physical way, rather than being in her mind. At this point, Prapto starts guiding her by shouting: "Good, yes, good, go on!" Simultaneously, he talks to us all and says that in this way, by supporting the woman with his 'good', 'yes', instructions, he is stimulating her to find for herself her own physical limit. He points out when her movement is initiated from the physicality of her body and when instead, it is her mind which takes over and makes her 'fly'. 'Flying' indicates a way of moving that takes her 'out of her physical body' and into the mind, so that she might misjudge her physical capacity and hurt herself physically. By making these comments, Prapto lets us follow his guiding while the movement takes place. He adds with humour that his guiding sometimes creates problems and sometimes helps. He says the quality of the movement initiated by the woman is from 'body-nature' or from 'body-body', i.e. from the physicality of the body, in contrast to movement initiated from the mind, which Prapto calls movement from 'body-mind'.

> *By this, I give stimulation. Sometimes I help sometimes I give problems. I remind [her to] find the physical, finding inside of physical, finding, feeling in the sense from the physical. By this, I can stimulate and help her so that she can realise where her boundary is.*

Prapto wants to help her to become more body-conscious while practising by experiencing through her own body in movement whether her movements are initiated from her mind (body-mind) or from physicality (body-nature).

> *By mind or by physical in working with her movement she can realise her boundary.*

Movement initiated from energy as *chi*

Two women enter the movement space for the next session. They set out very slowly. Prapto points out to the group while guiding the two women, how their movement is based on energy as in *tai chi*, rather than on the muscles working, as in the woman's movement from body-nature of the previous session. He tries to show us that movement can derive from different sources. It may be initiated from physicality, primarily related to muscles working in contracting and relaxing, or from energy, i.e. from the flow of energy through the whole body as in the latter example and finally, it might be mentally initiated, i.e. from the mind. None of these sources is seen as superior to another. Rather it is a question of being aware of one's own source, when moving. [20]

Practice at the students' hotel

The students are all staying in a small hotel just outside the temple, where they are away from the noise and the curiosity of the local people. All the rooms are set around the hotel's pendopo where students practise in the afternoons. Here the group is more of a unit than when practising on the public or semi-public sites on the temple grounds. They are also freer to express themselves. This means that not only do they explore new physical vocabularies and expressive skills but sound and music are also included differently in their movement as they do not have to pay attention to curious onlookers.

Sound: first session

The whole group is moving on the floor of the pendopo. Prapto is instructing sequences 'lying, crawling, side-wards, forwards, backwards, up and down'. Then he asks us to make sounds to accompany our movements. After a while, one of us makes a sound, responding to the situation as a child or an animal might. It is not ordinary singing. This sound is followed by others from other students. They turn into a cacophony, more like sounds of the jungle than adult humans. The students seem to enjoy this very much, becoming more expressive

---

[20] See Gunna Brieghel-Müller (1979) pp. 94, 95, 69.

in their movements and more and more rhythmic. Some start running, jumping and singing while clapping their hands, bubbling with joy. The energy level gives the feeling of a 'language of liberation', according to Prapto.

Sound: human-made, nature-made

During a pause between sessions, a student asks Prapto:

> *What about things like rhythm, melody and sound like 'da da da'?*

Prapto asks him to distinguish between human-made sounds and nature-sound. Human sounds and rhythms can be found in composed melodies. Prapto demonstrates, starting with a harmonic Western style melody with 'da-da-da-da da da'. This is already a human-made melody Prapto says. He starts again singing a long melody going harmoniously up and down in pitch and finishes with a 'hym hym ha' on a low pitch as songs often do. Organic sounds are different, Prapto says to the student. They involve us using the whole body as an instrument for making sound, not just the lungs as a resonance-chamber.

> *You have to be clear with your question first. Is it human*
> *rhythm, human praise, human melody you mean, or sound in*
> *the sense of organism of nature, of your body-nature?*

Prapto suggests that students try to explore sound not only as human sound but also nature-made (or organically-made) sound. They can start by singing human sounds and, by listening to them, they can then explore their personal sound and rhythm of life, their own nature-rhythm. However, they can also start right away from nature-sound or rhythm i.e. from their own nature's sound and rhythm. So they can more easily find their own natural rhythm.

> *But, can also be it is like this first: I try to find my own rhythm,*
> *nature rhythm or life as I can feel it to be in there.*

By working with sound in that way in my movement practice, my movement becomes integrated with my sound. It takes some time to explore, but during that time a merging of movement and sound will start to take place. This will continue until finally a kind of alphabet, language or melody arises.

> *So when I have sense so, how in my movement I can be in one*
> *with my sound, and then as the sound comes back again to me,*
> *this gives me a sense of form, sense of alphabet, sense of work...*
> *and then I have melody, I have language.*

Prapto then takes the five-year-old the daughter of one of the students as an example. The little girl often follows the students as they practise moving in

Borobudur. According to him, the little girl naturally makes sounds without really knowing what she is 'saying':

> Her 'bab bab, bab bab' means she is also reading, but she cannot yet do in expression. She's reading unconsciously. She knows what happens and makes description. Sometimes it's so pure like children are in the kindergarten age, so joyful, so without any interpretation. She has no sense of army strategy and no sense to make plans.

Nature-sound, where we use the whole body as an instrument, does not mean sound expressing raw emotions. It is sound transformed via the physical body.

Ecstatic sound

In the next sessions, Prapto supports students' movement with his kind of nature-sound. Its quality resembles that of shaman-sounds with its 'heya hey haw!' sounds. These become wilder and wilder and have a neighing quality, ending in orgasm-like sounds. At a certain point, Prapto stops and looks at the students with an eloquent gesture: "This is new strata!" Does he mean the high level of energy or the sounds? Probably both. At the end, Prapto picks up a drum and starts drumming. The session ends on a trance-like, ecstatic level, though students are still in a state of full awareness.

More sessions

The composition of the group on the floor changes constantly. Some stop moving and go to sit at the edge of the pendopo, resting, watching or accompanying the others by clapping their hands or singing. Others continue moving on the floor. At one point, a woman and two men are moving. One of the men in his mid-twenties has put himself as a counter-balance to the wildness, manifested in the movement it seems, by placing himself outside the pendopo in the yard. There he sits in the squatting position, both hands on the ground as a kind of lightning conductor, his face turned calmly towards the people moving in the pendopo.

In another session, a group forms spontaneously. It consists of five women and a man. The women crawl into the centre of the pendopo and move on the floor keeping full bodily contact, their movement resembling that of reptiles. The man enters and walks around inside the space, ending by circling nearer and nearer to the women as if around a prey. Then Prapto, who has been sitting silently outside, enters while making deep sounds. All of a sudden, he changes these and his sounds become dynamic and rhythmic, again suggesting shamanic songs: "hee hee ha ha heya ha, waw awh awh, awhr". Some time later, the atmosphere changes to one of serenity. Now the sounds start to have the quality of a mantra or prayer. The session ends in meditation. And at the very end, everyone is standing in the pendopo and it seems as if the group has made a journey from the deep level of reptiles to that of humans and, moreover, that the journey has taken place spontaneously without anything being spoken or planned. Such developments, happening spontaneously in the group, going from an unknown chaos to series of movement expressions providing a story and a meaning, are characteristic of Amerta Movement practice.

The art of Prapto

Then follows a movement session where one person moves alone, guided by Prapto. At first, Prapto who is sitting outside, instructs movement sequences with "stop, go on, stop!" and so on. Later, having entered the space again, he sits on the floor still guiding the student with shouts like "*ya*, right, good, - 'no'!" He has his back to the student. Nevertheless, his instructions seem accurate. This ability of Prapto's precisely to attune to his surroundings reflecting the inner condition of a student or reflecting in his movements the atmosphere of the site as well as expressing this in front of his students, seems mystical to the Westerner experiencing it for the first time. But many people say his way of guiding is uncannily accurate in seeing their problems within a situation. They also say that he is normally capable of helping them with whatever they need or at least pointing them towards positive solutions.

What kind of pedagogy is this? It is not that of an ordinary movement teacher nor even that of a charismatic course instructor. It is rather akin to the approach of a Javanese shaman (*dukun*). Or is it simply a special talent of Prapto's? According to Prapto himself, it is normal. He spends much time and energy telling his students that he is not a healer, nor is he a paranormal, and he does not want to have anything to do with the traditional Javanese way of channelling energy, which according to him, very often is done without any kind of responsibility for what is being channelled. In spite of this, he appears to be not quite free of his heritage in this respect. He is certainly no ordinary movement teacher and it is not easy for others to pinpoint his teaching or guiding methods, which are largely based on his personality and his experience gathered over many years of physical, emotional and spiritual training and through many crystallisations. They are also based on his ability to be awake to the present moment/to seize the moment and to act accordingly.

The last day's practice at the temple: recognition

On the last day at Borobudur, students are asked to walk from the temple's base up through all the galleries and terraces using Amerta Movement techniques. Before starting, Prapto reminds us that we are not tourists. We are to 'process Borobudur and be processed by Borobudur'. However, he says, at the end of our stay at Borobudur, it will be a different and much deeper experience for us. Under these circumstances, to undertake walking up and around the temple's spiral will have an impact, possibly causing a change in us and in our lives. Our experience of reading Borobudur will however, create 'a world of difference' for us, because it has given us an expanded consciousness, a greater sensitivity, and a new perspective on life. Prapto's last instruction is to be aware of any changes in attitude, movement and sensitivity. He adds that his minimal requirement of us is that we pay attention to any changes in ourselves in these areas: "After five weeks of work on the Vocabulary course, the main [is] that you can recognise."

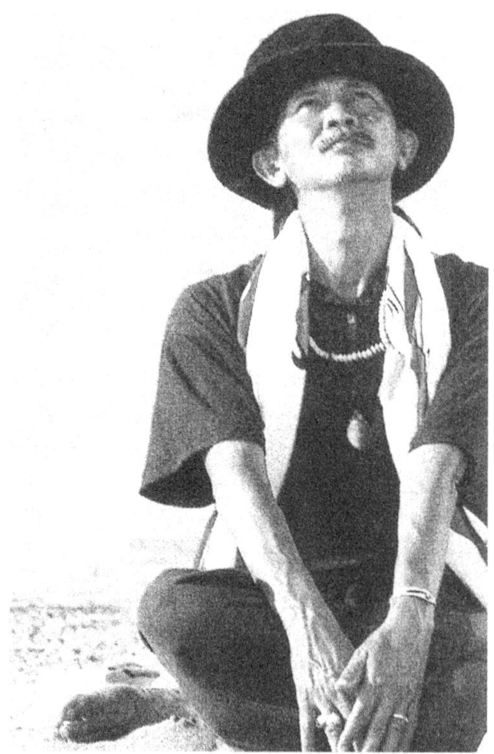

Suprapto Suryodarmo. (Originally published in *Jakarta-Jakarta*, 27 April-3 May,

II. Parangtritis Beach. The Ocean, the dunes and the wind. Expression

The theme at Parangtritis Beach is

> *'expression in the changing of nature at Parangtritis Beach'. Crystallisation in communication with the society on the stage. Rahayu …*

At the ocean

Leaving Borobudur Temple, students arrive at the Indian Ocean. Driving across an open plain with slender coconut palms, the freshness of the sea is distinctly smelled. Prapto characterises Parangtritis Beach as,

> *… the most complete of places that has water, shadow, sunshining, stars, land, hills.*

Parangtritis, with its cliffs, caves, sacred springs, hills and sand dunes, is not an ordinary fishing town or resort, although it has at least one international hotel. The ocean can be violent with strong undercurrents. No wonder that no boats are anchored at the beach or even sailing nearby. Only now and then can large tankers be seen far out to sea. The violence of the ocean is attributed by locals to supernatural powers and to the fact that there is no land between this coast and the South Pole. According to Javanese belief, the ocean's violent breakers symbolise emotions that Javanese warriors or mystics must conquer on their journey to reunite with their own essence, as the warrior Bima in the Dewaruci story studied at Candi Sukuh. However, the ocean can also be so calm it looks like a mirror. Sometimes at dawn, villagers walk along the beach digging in the sand looking for mussels and other fruits of the sea.

Because it is full of healing springs and grottos, Parangtritis is considered to be a holy and magical power-site (*kramat*), where spirits are consulted.[21] Its many caves are believed to house spirits. Instead of attracting ordinary tourists, the caves draw people interested in mysticism and meditation or who are seeking advice from the spirits. Even modern politicians come to ask the spirits for advice. Traditionally, Parangtritis is a place for meditation and for spiritual retreats, involving purification exercises with some form of fasting and abstinence (*tapa*). People following Java's traditional mystical practices often meditate at Parangtritis, and, among other things, ask advice from the Goddess of the Ocean. Mystics sit on the beach meditating all night. To a lesser degree, artists and *pencak silat* practitioners of Javanese martial arts also choose to visit.

---

[21] For Parangtritis as a traditional site for magical and spiritual power, see Pemberton (1994: 270-279).

Ratu Kidul, Goddess of the Ocean

Intimately connected to Parangtritis is Ratu Kidul, the Goddess of the Ocean and the story or myth about her: According to legend,

> *Ratu Kidul, Queen of the Ocean, is the spiritual wife of the kings of Java, of the Mataram dynasty as well as their protector. This means that land and sea are united, as are the Queen of the Ocean and the King of the Land. Indonesians when talking about their homeland call it 'our land and waters'. Moreover, there are close connections between the goddess, royal power and both sexuality and mysticism. Ratu Kidul is very beautiful and has to be treated with great respect – like the ancient Greek sirens – and all Javanese respect her and are afraid of her. Anyone going to the south coast is warned not to wear green, which is her favourite colour. If you do, she might pull you to the bottom of the ocean. The fact that Ratu Kidul is the spiritual wife of Java's kings is not merely a belief or a symbolic story, but a living reality to traditional Javanese.*

> *Every 35 days, the tradition goes, she emerges from her palace at the bottom of the ocean to personally help at the royal palace with training for the sacred ritual dance symbolising her union with the kings of Java. This dance is performed in modern Java at the king's palace on the day of the king's ascension to the throne, marking the anniversary of Ratu Kidul's wedding with the king. Hence, at the beach, every 35 days, Ratu Kidul is offered flowers and incense by mystics who sit near the ocean, meditating while they await her coming just before dawn.*

The Ratu Kidul story is one of many stories from Javanese tradition used by Prapto, who often relied on narrating a myth connected to a practice site both for entertainment and as a pedagogical strategy. It is a form of teaching that allows students to take or leave what they chose without 'losing face' – they are not being confronted individually as when they are told directly what to do or not to do. This indirect approach is typically Javanese.

Prapto described himself as a modern mystic. Thus he did not follow traditional mystical practices every 35 days in relation to Ratu Kidul. He saw the story as a metaphor for the meditation process. It is an expression of what happens when one is meditating and something rises, like the goddess coming to the surface at dawn. It is like an insight from the subconscious emerging into consciousness. Prapto saw the relationship between the goddess and the kings of Java as an expression of fertility. His attitude to the story was, however, ambivalent. He did not really see Ratu Kidul as only a symbol. In some ways, she was as real to him as she is for many other Javanese.

> *At Javanese New Year (Sura), traditionally the most important day in the Javanese calendar, there is a special ceremony on the beach initiated by the Solo royal palace, Hadiningrat. It continues with a purification ritual in the form of a shadow puppet performance. The King attends, accompanied by specially invited guests from among Central Java's nobility and Indonesia's higher governmental officials.*

Prapto was asked if he was not worried about taking his students to sites reputed to be full of magic and spirits and if he was he not afraid that he or his students might be possessed by evil spirits. He answered that evil spirits can enter people anywhere. It does not especially have to be at Parangtritis.[22] Moreover, the students' ignorance of all the magic and spirits connected with Parangtritis protects them. For comparison, Prapto pointed to children saying that evil spirits cannot possibly harm them.

> *And when people [as the students] are not so aware of the spirits, usually these have nothing to do, can do nothing, because their way of doing is by contacting the awareness. It's like children, no one can harm the children in spiritual. They [the children] have not so much thinking about that.*

Practice theme: expression

Prapto's theme at the ocean is 'expression in the changing of nature at the beach of Parangtritis'. The movement vocabulary that students are creating here is not only based on experiences with nature at the beach itself, but also draws on the other sites visited earlier in the course, where they have studied 'space', 'time' and 'reading'. After their stay at the ocean they are going to finish the course with a public crystallisation back at the Lemah Putih School.

---

[22] Prapto said that for hundreds of years Parangtritis had been seen by the Javanese as a power-site, a place of spirits and used as such. Prapto personally respects Parangtritis' life, its nature and spirits. If the spirits had rejected him, he would never have forced his presence on them. Prapto did not reject the question as to the existence of spirits as being irrelevant. He felt, however, that believing in and bowing to a god-concept, affords him protection.

Practising movement at the beach is very popular with most students because it offers a refreshing change from inland Java. They are met by roaring seas, wide horizons, panoramic sunrises and sunsets, kilometres of beach, sand, dunes, cliffs, and a hospitable local population. Also, there is an atmosphere of life and not just in the sense of freshness from the ocean with its fish and bird life. Students live in little bamboo huts on the beach. Behind is a small enclosure with primitive washing and toilet facilities, as well as a simple shed with domestic animals. There always seem to be new creatures arriving at the same time as a new group of students. This contributes to the atmosphere of birth and new beginning, of new forms and expressions and fits well with the students' process in creating a vocabulary as a new physical form and expression in movement.

Prapto's introduction and instructions

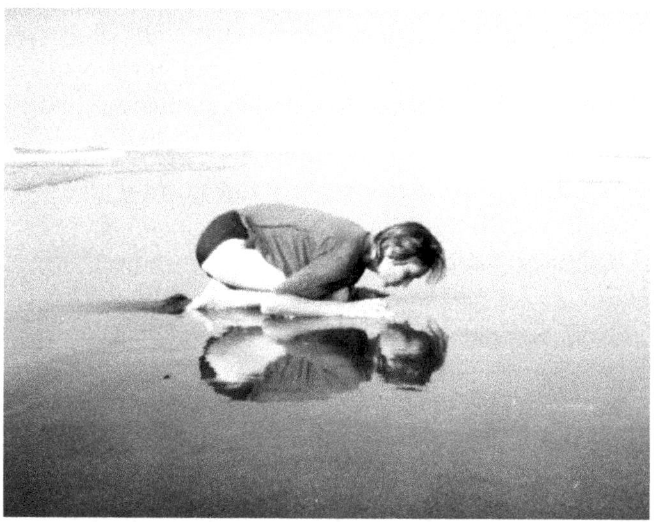

A practitioner, Parangtritis Beach

As students practise on the beach, Prapto starts by warning them about the dangers of the ocean, personified by *Ratu Kidul*. The waves and currents are so powerful that one must not for a second lose awareness. He also points out the pulling force of the wind and of the whole of nature here. He tells students not to identify themselves with the ocean: I am one entity, the ocean is something else. It is always important to distinguish between myself and the ocean so as not to be pulled by its strong forces. We should move in a way that is grounded physically in the body and on the sand. At the same time, we should recognise nature's pulling elements, as well as the many different pulling forces within our own nature.

> *Do not try to be the sea, the wind and so on, but try to*
> *recognise these elements in you, the elements of the water, the*
> *wind and so on.*

Prapto recommends that students practise from the dialogue model with the ocean (see the exercise 'pillar-in-situation' in Chapter 5). I observe the ocean and enter into a dialogue with it trying to recognise in a concrete way the physical power of this ocean but also trying to recognise how I contain within myself, in my own nature, elements similar to those of the ocean. Prapto continues:

> *Try to find your position and try to find how to move in this*
> *nature where everything is already moving, the wind, the*
> *water, the sand and the light.*

Students are to express, in time and space, movement experiences from all the other practice sites on the beach with its changing weather conditions. They are to do so by constructing their own personal movement, in a manner specific to each one of them. This can be done if they let themselves be moved not only in the sense of bodily position but also in the sense of allowing changes to occur within themselves.

> *And then by the changing of the nature we try to construct our*
> *movement and be constructed by movement, by changing.*

Students can 'cook up' something. Moreover, they will 'be cooked' themselves by the elements and the whole environment. They will be in process themselves, as they had been at Candi Borobudur. By 'being cooked' Prapto means that they will be formed by life at the ocean as they have been formed and influenced by the other sites. They will also meet reactions to their movement from their environment. But what is essential in the midst of all those influences is to distil or extract something from the process, something usable for their crystallisation and for their life in general.

In this way, students will hopefully create their own motor abilities, their own body dynamic expressions as an embryo for creating a movement vocabulary and finding their own crystallisation. Some students are helped in this process by writing a diary or making video recordings or paintings. The process is seen as a seed, whereby students can grow in terms of creating their own bodily language.

> *And then the second thing by understanding all your*
> *experience, you are remembering in your writing, in video, in*
> *image. Maybe you take materials as points for orientation, for*
> *recording and then you can 'cook' in the life and be 'cooked' by*
> *the life. Of course, your life is in it and then on your journey in*

space and time you can find a crystal, a diamond. And then
you can use it for you in your life, and for the life of the others.

Prapto expects students to have, by the end of the course, an awareness of what it means to have a vocabulary. By that he means a bodily language based on 'nature and on life in nature', i.e. one based on the natural environment at the beach, on the plain and in the mountains and based on their own inner nature, i.e. on their quality as organisms of nature.

Practising near the ocean

Students do not seem to be afraid of the ocean. Neither do they go in very deep. The hot wind, the sharpness of light and the softness of the sand make it difficult to move dynamically. These factors often make students choose a slower mode of movement. Besides, there is no drumming, as there sometimes was when outdoors during this course. (However, musical accompaniment was not a standard part of Amerta improvisation at this early period.)

The students' movement expressions vary, comprising movement, sound, and play. Students build sandcastles and mandala-drawings and small altars in the sand. They are exposed to a movement dialogue, an exchange, between themselves and the elements, wind, light, moving sands, as well as the ocean's roaring and sounds from the local community. One of the young men, like a warrior mystic or a boy at play, is building a sandcastle. He moves with his sandcastle while he is constructing it. A girl from the local village approaches. She talks to the young man and after a while naturally enters into his activities of building and moving. The same happens a little later with some local children. They are also curious. This is what Prapto terms a scene of 'society in the middle of everyday life', a mixture of play and seriousness.

Themes for discourse

As a result of their practice and the natural elements, students become intensely aware of feelings and emotions. While my emotions and feelings, as well as the stories connected to them, are not important in themselves in Amerta Movement practice, their substance or energy is essential for transformation into movement expressions and thereby also for the practitioner's liberation. When moving with feelings and emotions, it is important that we do not express them directly in our movement nor make stories of them; we should simply accept them or allow them to be, with a clear mind, leaving an analysis of them for later, outside the practice. It is our attitude to our feelings and emotions that matters, more than the feelings and emotions themselves. Feelings and emotions are recognised as common human challenges. If we are overwhelmed by them, we may be advised to spend time outside the practice facing them, meditating on them maybe, since there is much valuable energy in emotions, and not try to repress them or be ashamed (or proud) of them.

Prapto gives feedback on our movements in the form of generalised stories. In these, we are portrayed as characters or heroes of a given gender, cultural background, nationality and so on. So students are referred to by Prapto as in a play, which makes a lot of fun. At the same time, these stories provide a useful tool for conveying feedback in a manner the individual student can accept.

After practising on the beach in the mornings, students move in the sand dunes behind the beach in the afternoons.

In the dunes

Prapto, with his long black hair, is dancing and moving in the dunes. The sun has almost set and the sky is turning golden red. The continuous sound of a drum, a Javanese *gendang,* can be heard as well as that of a saxophone played by an American jazz musician. Prapto is dancing and moving in an endless pattern; sometimes jumping, sometimes lying down, then squatting or stumbling and wobbling through the sands. He is humming a Javanese melody.

When asked by a journalist present what the American saxophonist, taking the course, gets out of the movement practice apart from accompanying Prapto, the latter answers,

> *This saxophone musician studies how he can tune himself like*
> *an instrument, how for instance, as now in the dunes, he is 'in*
> *tune', he can enter into the atmosphere with his condition in*
> *an active and passive way, with the sea, the sand, the wind, the*
> *water, the heat, himself and his friends [co-practitioners].*[23]

The element of wind inside and outside the practitioner

In the dunes, in the afternoons, students practise movement in relation to the wind. One of the male students has arrived early for the afternoon session to fly a kite. The wind is very strong and while he tries to get his kite off the ground, one of the women has already begun to move on her own.

Prapto starts his teaching by turning slowly around on his own axis to demonstrate what he means by practising with the element of wind. The wind

---

[23] For using oneself as an instrument of expression, see Jodjana Raden Ayou (1981: 22), which states that the Javanese hold that the body is an instrument which receives information about itself and about the world. It is a very complex and subtle receptor.

in this context can perhaps be compared to the Chinese notion of *chi.* Prapto talks about the warrior Bima, the son of the god of wind. He reminds students that the wind also has to do with the mystic's inner quest for wholeness. This is because of its relation to breathing as in the expression 'the breath of life', and because of breathing being part of meditation techniques. The element of wind is also inside each of us, according to Prapto.

Prapto introduces the wind as a technique to apply during practice at the dunes. He says the wind has a house, which he calls the 'hole of the wind'. One can compare the 'hole of the wind' with what Prapto calls the 'hole of the night', which is the gap between sleep and being awake. Prapto relates the 'hole of the night' to the transition or meeting point between me as both a passive and an active person, which is symbolised respectively by the night's non-activity and the day's activity. In terms of movement, the 'hole of the night' and the 'hole of the wind' relate to the transition between movement initiated from the autonomic nervous system not under the control of the conscious mind and movement from the willed nervous system, which *is* under the control of my conscious mind. The technique that Prapto introduces is based on relating to the wind in terms of its non-activity (instead of its activity, as one might expect). In some martial arts, for example *tai chi,* this consists of evading the opponent, i.e. of a non-confrontation: by a turn of the body one steps aside. In this way, the aggressor is pulled off balance by his own aggression. In the same way Prapto indicates a way of using the wind based on our non-confronting action vis-à-vis the wind. Symbolically this is what he means with his expression, 'un-gravity', something very different from flying normally.

Prapto has constructed the word 'un-gravity' as an illustration of his point of view. When asked if 'un-gravity' means the force of lightness, Prapto replies that it is alright to say lightness, but what he means with 'un-gravity' is that it is not the same as flying. He also uses terms like 'find your own desert' in movement and 'hit the hole of the wind' in the practice.

Prapto demonstrates the 'hole of the wind'. He shows it as a 'stop' in his movement's flow, calling it 'tek!' Students can try to 'fly' normally – think of the kite mentioned above – but the most important thing is:

> *It's good if you can find the 'tek' of the wind.*

The students spread out, working for the most part individually. Some start to practise grounding as far as this is possible in the sand. From there they go on to move more freely or rather they try to move more in accordance with their individual way of adapting to the sand dunes. They then proceed to explore un-gravity or 'the hole of the wind'.

Practising 'un-gravity' can be illustrated by my standing upright, properly aligned in a vertical axis. Then standing in the balance point between gravity and lightness, between earth and sky, so that the body's weight is properly placed in relation to these two in a vertical line, i.e. my feet on the ground supporting my balance and lightness. Now I am using only a minimum of muscular energy to keep an upright position with my muscles mainly working in a static way to stabilise my bones and joints in this position. In contrast, when I swing my body forward, I project my centre of gravity forward. To keep balance in that position without being pulled to the ground by gravity, my muscles, the so-called anti-gravity muscles, are forced to work much harder to keep me in this position, against gravity. Hence, un-gravity may be found in the balance point between gravity and lightness, rather like the space between night and day, and between the inhaling and exhaling.

Students practise the 'hole of the wind' exercise in three ways:

1. Some find a place where they can stand still while exploring the 'hole of the wind'. They try, for example, to position their body on the sand so that they can move with a minimum of effort without being pulled to the ground or without losing their balance in the moving sands.

2. Others do the same exercise, but they do so while moving.

3. Yet others start the exercise, as a child would, by first feeling the wind in the normal sense, feeling how it almost makes them fly. They let themselves experience the wind as a force pulling them here and there, like the ocean currents. From there they can detect more clearly the wind's non-activity and recognise when they meet the wind's 'holes', i.e. how they can keep balance without moving very much.

Creating a vocabulary

The barrenness of the dunes makes it a special challenge to create a vocabulary through movement. Prapto compares the dunes to a desert. The technique for coping in deserts, and hence in the dunes, is to accept their nature and to use a minimum of energy, Prapto says:

> *The dunes are the sons or daughters of the desert. Please receive the dunes and the dunes will receive you.*

When trying to adapt to the conditions of the dunes, students also have to open up to a new dimension in consciousness. Prapto asks,

> *What will happen if I welcome the dunes without being welcomed by the dunes?*

What will happen, if the dunes welcome you and you cannot receive the dunes? That is the question.

To inspire us, Prapto asks us to imagine that we are alone in the desert and want to make a plant grow: we have to find water. In the same way, when trying to develop a vocabulary, we have to find ways of responding, through physical movement, to the barren landscape. Prapto compares the barrenness of the dunes with students who are all head and cannot get into their body. To create life in the desert, making a plant grow, is like finding ways to create a movement vocabulary. If I am only doing so mentally, my bodily landscape will be like a desert – barren. This might also be true for feelings. If I feel as if I am 'walking in the desert', I need to draw from the well of my inner self, inner being, to create a vocabulary. This is like watering a plant in the desert. I must open my heart, my inner feeling, my compassion and let the unknown resources in my inner self trickle out:

You can do from the well in your heart here in the dunes.

So, when we start creating a vocabulary in the dunes, we start by working on how to accept the dunes while moving there. The idea is not to fight, but to collaborate with the conditions. This is a typically Javanese way of coping. But it makes it difficult to do anything in terms of movement. The sands make active movements exhausting. Also, it is hard to keep our balance and not fall over, roll down or sink in. Sand blows into our eyes. We have to practise using a minimum of force in order to keep our balance. As Prapto says, while we are struggling to do so, we might discover that we are moved by forces other than muscle power. We are also moved by energy.

The beach, a stage for cultural expression

Our expressions on the beach, however modest, constitute a personal manifestation of our inner journey through movement, and through the Javanese landscape, through its culture and nature. As such, these expressions are valuable, forming part of the learning process.

The journey has taken students across Central Java and culminated at the Indian Ocean before returning to the school for their public presentation, their crystallisation and to finish the whole course.

For a few days, this beach changes into a stage for 'cultural expression in nature' as Prapto calls it. Students' experiences from practising movement at all the sites where they have moved, are 'written' on their bodies, inscribed in their bodies, in the sense that they have been internalised. Subsequently, through an ongoing process of movement, these experiences are transmitted via the students' bodies and expressed in bodily movement here at the beach where students practise in its atmosphere of spirituality and nature.

III. Back at the school for crystallisation

By the end of their stay on the beach, students have finished the main part of 'Vocabulary'. Prapto expects students to have achieved an awareness of how their improvised expressions are influenced by the different sites where they have practised. The crystallisation that will end the course will be based on their understanding of 'human, nature and life' while they have been practising movement in the different sites. This understanding will be manifest in an embodied physical expression.

Students now return to the Lemah Putih School which, with three and a half weeks of the 8-week course left, gives us time to prepare and carry out our crystallisations and re-adapt to the land and the mode of practising there. An important part of our daily practice, on our return, is digesting our experiences from the sites and assimilating them into our bodily expressions.

On the first day Prapto asks us to 'construct' ourselves in the space and to 'construct the space'. This does not mean choreography or for us to think about what movements will be appropriate for the crystallisation. Instead, we have to decide what materials to include in our crystallisation, for example textiles, rocks, flowers, sticks, music and so on. We also have to consider how to do our crystallisation: in our own small group, with another group, alone, or if we want to form a group with a Javanese artist or spiritual person. We must also choose the site: one of the pendopos or a 'nature-stage'? Usually such choices are made by students trying things out physically or moving with them, letting the decision take its form through practice and experience. This way of making a choice can be compared to how one can solve a problem by 'sleeping on it'.

Practice for vocabulary

Group sessions take place mainly in one of the pendopos but also in the open practice sites in the school's grounds and which are also used as 'nature-stages'. The usual practice sessions are soon supplemented by sessions where, guided by Prapto's instructions, we focus on 'constructing' ourselves in the space and 'constructing the space'. His instructions are aimed at bringing our attention to construction in an organic sense while we are moving. Prapto points out how our physical positions make up the movement's flow. When he shouts 'stop', we freeze and our physical positions become structures, constructions in the space or 'organic compositions', as Prapto calls it, rather than process. These positions become a kind of a vocabulary of gestures specific to each of us.

> *Stop, understand the surrounding of you. By that you can
> understand what is organism composition [organic
> composition], what is going on, what is processing on.*
>
> *Go on!*

From our position, we continue our movement.

> *Stop!*

We freeze again.

> *By that you understand in your process what is composition
> this land [how this land has been composed]. Go on!*

Changes

There has been a remarkable change in the quality of our movements since our return to the school. They are less closed and 'speak' more, communicate better. They are more precise than at the start of the course, with pauses in the flow of movement when necessary. We allow the impulse of the movement to finish naturally. Like ocean waves, we let the movement follow its own natural timing instead of trying to control it. So our movement tends to form whole 'phrases' and seems more like a kind of language. It is also clearer because we avoid a lot of empty movement. We have sharpened our bodily suppleness and sensitivity and are more in touch with ourselves, so we can encompass more awareness in the moment of improvisation. There are longer periods without music. Only the sounds of the village and the students' feet on the ground are heard. The drumming which has supported our movement off and on is now supplemented by other simpler rhythms – like rocks or sticks being knocked together.

Group rhythm and tempo

The whole group is on the floor of the main pendopo. After a while the students' rhythm becomes faster and they end by moving at a terrific speed. They rush in and out, through the pillars and all over the space like swallows. Prapto immediately enters the students' energy level in his guidance.

> *Good. You can see this is the field of mind. Good, ya, ya.
> Connect with the form. The form and the speed.*
>
> *Right good. And at the same time, also go down, go up, crawling.*

By form Prapto means bodily position. It is alright to initiate the movement from mental energy but this must be grounded in the body or it will make us 'fly' and lose our felt contact with the body while speeding along. We will be out of our bodies, as mentioned before. Laughter follows as we adjust our speed to what suits our own bodies and in relation to the group's speed. Slowly we come down from the whirling speed, attuning ourselves better to our own body's needs in the situation. We continue to move fast but our movements take on a more expressive quality and are more like a vocabulary. This way of moving allows individual differences of expression and a more genuine interaction between students. This manifests itself in the form of a 'story' told through movement when seen from outside. In spite of the high speed, one young man manages to create his own space by going into a much slower mode. By the end of the session he is stretched out, quite still. He forms a counterpoint to the other students, who form a group, which looks like a flock of birds around him.

Crystallisations

Preparation

The main pendopo as well as the 'nature-stages', (square, circle or oval), are especially important for presenting crystallisations. The *mandala*, an octagonal platform in red cement under some large trees, is a popular choice for many. It is especially dedicated to crystallisations with the theme of purification and to shamanic expressions, i.e. expressions based on the natural, the organic world, or based on the student's inner nature in a dialogue or an exchange with the natural world around. But some students prefer to practise on the grass itself.

An important part of preparing for crystallisations are the full group sessions that take place in the main pendopo under Prapto's supervision. The group explores how to 'construct a performance space' through their positions, by placing different materials in the space while moving. There is an atmosphere of theatre and ritual celebration with music coming from the students themselves or from celebrations going on in the village.

As the day for the crystallisation draws closer, local artists come to observe the practice. Sometimes they join in for a day or longer. One day a Javanese puppeteer accompanies the group's movement by responding to it with songs from the *wayang kulit*. His friend, a classical actor-dancer, joins in by playing on a bamboo flute. Both have practised Amerta Movement with Prapto and, while accompanying the students, the two musicians tune in to the movement, attentive to its rhythm and pattern. They follow and support it, rather than directing or controlling it.

Performance

The aim of making a crystallisation is not to make a theatre performance but to extract the essence of the course's movement process and express it in free, non-stylised movement in improvisation. It builds on the entire experience of the course and is typically based on the theme of one of the practice sites on the land – each of these sites being linked to one of the three themes of: 1. Physical/Bodily expression, 2. Prayer and 3. Purification. What matters is my relationship to my own nature, to the site of my performance and to the spiritual dimension. Before relating to any spectators, I will first relate to the vertical axis of life, that is to my human nature, to the spiritual dimension of life/the source of life, or god, and, to the physical conditions of the performance site.

Since the 1980s, crystallisations have come to involve more special preparations. Some 'Vocabulary' students make flyers inviting friends and local residents, others have new outfits made or buy flowers to make an altar or a place of prayer; others again involve the spectators on a voluntary basis or collaborate with a local artist or spiritual person as described above. Some students, however, do nothing special but just 'practise' as usual for the crystallisation. That way their crystallisations become part of the whole process, just another link in the chain of the practice. Many times over the years, the day of the crystallisations ended with a kind of celebration or jam session usually taking place after dark in the tropical night lit by torchlight and the glow of fireflies. Spectators as well as students would move at such events, sometimes singing and praying as well.

Chapter 8. Communication

Introduction. Course background and programme

The last *Pribadi Art* course is called 'Movement in Communication, Dialogue' (hereafter referred to as 'Communication'). It is the third and final *Pribadi Art* course. This chapter takes as its point of departure the 'Communication' course in 1996, which had the following programme description:

> *Offered for the people who have [ever] studied with me in Vocabulary seminar. To read for understanding the being of Borobudur Temple, Nature and Human. For sharing of understanding in human life. Movement is not only a language for communication but also an expression of being. The practice would start with distinguishing between road-society and home-society and should lead to a dialogue [crystallisation -performance] in society at the village, market or also at the theatre, the art centre, and so on.*

Students create new ways of communicating and dialoguing with their surroundings by 'crawling from their cocoon' as Prapto termed it, and by 'making a new step in life', for example by making a crystallisation of their process in society. For this to happen the realisation of an inner potential in the individual practitioner is needed.

This chapter also draws on Prapto's early communication courses in Java of the 1980s and 1990s also entitled 'Movement in Communication, Dialogue'. The course's full title indicates its aim: to create changes in current ways of communicating and in conducting a dialogue. In this context, 'dialogue' means a crystallisation where students communicate their process to society.

The 1996 'Communication' course took place over seven weeks at the Lemah Putih School, with one session of three hours a day, five days a week, 120 hours in all. In the third week, students visited the cultural sites for practice, two and a half days in all at the Hill, Candi Sukuh and Parangtritis, and five days at Borobudur. The sixth week was reserved for the crystallisation.

This chapter will focus on communication – the cultural sites of Candi Borobudur, Candi Sukuh and Parangtritis Beach will not be dealt with here as they were covered in the last two chapters.

Crystallisations most often took place at the Art Centre, the *Taman Budaya Surakarta* (TBS), and/or at 'nature stages' at the Lemah Putih School. Among these, as seen above, we especially focus on the 'square', 'circle' and 'oval' practice sites, both physical spaces on the land and a kind of 'nature-stage'.

The course was offered to people who had already done a 'Vocabulary' course, so some of the students came from a newly finished 'Vocabulary' course, while others came to Java directly from their home countries, having done 'Vocabulary' earlier. There were ten participants aged 25-49, seven of whom were women and nine of whom were Westerners. Various visitors, mostly from Java, joined the course for a few days. The students' professional backgrounds were in dance, theatre and office-work and there was one academic. Among the artists, five were also teaching dance, movement and physical theatre and three were also working as therapists.

Aim of the course

The aim of the 'Communication' course is, as we have seen, to create changes or new steps in our way of communicating and of conducting a dialogue. A key component is that students communicate their process by presenting a crystallisation. In this they must demonstrate a change in their ways of communicating through movement, by managing, for the first time, maybe, to embody inner potentials in the outside, physical world, thereby daring to leave their 'cocoon', in Prapto's terms, i.e. their shelter.

In contrast to 'Vocabulary', the crystallisation is not only to be a public display of students' process, but also aimed at showing students' individual ability to 'take a new step' in relation to their private and professional lives.

So it was important to bring themselves to the stage of an embodied, personal 'blossoming' or unfolding, in the art of communicating. New ways of relating to others were also essential. There was no doubt that 'Communication' places greater demands on students than 'Vocabulary'. In relation to the movement practice in 'Communication', students carry out their own movement-exploration every day. Prapto leaves time for this by teaching only one session a day instead of the usual two. Students are also expected to travel to one of the cultural sites to practise, either alone or with their chosen group. This was all in order to prepare for their crystallisation, their new step and personal blossoming.

Difference between 'Communication' and 'Vocabulary'

In 'Vocabulary', students had created a personal movement vocabulary, a 'person-specific' one, but they had not learned how to communicate it. Now, in 'Communication', students are not only expected to express their being or self in movement through a personal, person-specific, somatic vocabulary or somatic 'language', they are also expected to communicate this language to a public. We may illustrate the difference between the two courses by thinking of a child learning to ride a bicycle. At first, the child has to give all her attention to riding the bicycle. This is like the 'Vocabulary' student who first must get to know her instrument, i.e. her body as a tool for expression in order to create a bodily vocabulary. With training, the child can relax while riding the bicycle, which now allows her to carry on a conversation at the same time as she is cycling. In terms of the movement practice, this is like the student who has completed the 'Vocabulary' course and started on 'Communication': this student has learnt to be aware of her bodily language and what it means. In 'Communication' she moves with ease based on her personal bodily language, i.e. she composes her expressions and movements while moving with a certain ease from one moment to the next, but crucially she must now also start to communicate with other practitioners in the space at the same time, like the child carrying on a discussion whilst riding the bicycle.

Creating the framework for practice

Prapto introduces the course by telling students that at the Lemah Putih School they are mostly going to work with process. They are going to create, as they would do in a workshop. Only later, they will have to communicate their creative process to the world through their improvised crystallisation:

> *Here [at the Lemah Putih] we more create and then put out*
> *there in society sense.*

Forming groups

The course's daily programme is similar to other Amerta Movement courses: students each choose a group at the start. We do so by choosing a practice area on the school's land. By choosing one of these areas, we also choose our group members and a theme with which to work, because each practice area is connected to a specific theme. As soon as we have done so, Prapto asks us to discuss our process and to continue to do so throughout the course. What is important is that the members of each group help one another to develop a new attitude, as a new step 'for presence and future', as Prapto says. This may also be seen in terms of the individual practitioner developing the courage to take a new action in her life and to move into new territory, into new circumstances and challenges making a new step, as seen above. Or in Prapto's terms by moving outside 'home', i.e. outside one's familiar territory.

On a personal, developmental level, the aim of taking a new step, i.e. leaving 'home', is achieved by developing a new attitude to life in relation to one of the chosen themes of the course. Prapto calls embodying this new attitude, 'going out to the road', in contrast to not changing one's current ways of moving and being (called 'staying at home in the house' in our familiar surroundings and with our familiar ways of coping and relating). 'Going out to the road' means opening all my senses, being curious and following what happens, daring to take this new step in whatever new direction is revealed in my process.

In this way, we proceed to a new behaviour, a new attitude to life, bowing to life, and a new way of moving, enhancing our sense of presence, bowing and growing, as well as that of healing, i.e. of becoming whole human beings interconnected with life's being and with society. This is where Prapto says,

> *Movement is not only a language for communication but also an expression of being.*

> *We try to crawl from our cocoon from before and then to go out to the road and the society. …We also will work with new attitude, new behaviour for our being now and for our future in sense of presence; bowing and growing; and healing.*

The personal themes that students work with relate to the Amerta Movement themes of 'Physical/Bodily Expression', 'Prayer/The Sacred' and 'Purification', but in 'Communication' these themes are called: 'Presence', 'Bowing and Growing' and 'Healing'. Students choose one theme by choosing one of the three practice areas of Square, Circle or Oval.

Theme	Presence	Bowing & Growing	Healing
Overall theme	Physical/Bodily Expression	Prayer/The Sacred	Purification
Practice site	Square	Circle	Oval
Student's attitude based on	Human Culture	Respect, Praying/Sacred, Spirituality, Homage, Thankfulness	Nature and animal/organic life. Nature inside/outside
Field of life	Society. Culture. Human/secular art. Campaigns	The Sacred, Spirituality	Purification
Application	'Creation in reflection', Art/Performance Art, Cultural Events.	'Bowing in Praying' New rituals	'Purification in circulation', Health, Healing, Therapy

Communication framework elements

Students of 'Communication' who choose *Presence* are interested in growing by expanding their orientation to life in relation to society and culture. *Bowing* indicates a spiritual attitude to life where one grows as a human being through the act of bowing to life. It includes expressing spirituality/the sacred in a physical way, through gesture and movement – a sacred language for communication, like the one used when praying or participating in rituals. Finally, those who choose *Healing* want to expand their orientation to life by purifying their inner and outer nature. The purification takes place through a process of heightened awareness and sensitivity in order to become whole beings, interconnected to the surroundings.

Prapto says that in the 'Communication' courses he allows himself to rely on the students. By this he means that he starts a course, taking his point of departure from students' process with no specific aim, allowing the aim and the method of the course to emerge by itself: material made up of all the students' experiences during the course will form a 'common view' or a 'common basis' not only for the movement practice, but also for the crystallisation. So his method here, seen in Western terms, is process-oriented and exploratory. It is clearly one of practice-based/art-based knowledge also termed 'artistic research' (see also pp. 28, 39 and 87). His methodology is seen as deriving from *kejawen,* according to which one only learns by input and experience [*pengalaman*], felt by one's own body. [See also Chapter 3.]

Light and shadow

High up on the school's land, Prapto introduces a new, large practice area called the 'shadow-place'. This embodies 'time before', according to Prapto. 'Time before', among other things, refers to the individual student's hidden potential – i.e. the material or inner energy which is in the 'shadow' or between shadow and light, between being invisible and visible, or between the unconscious and the conscious of the individual practitioner. In other words: awareness of this material or energy is on the verge of entering the student's consciousness. Once it has, it can take form in the outside world, by becoming embodied as, for example, a new skill or insight. So, in the 'shadow-place', students practise with the past and/or the personal unconscious in terms of potential abilities or skills, which, though still dormant, are ready to become active.

Another important feature of the course is the concept of light or 'body-light'. Here, the body is seen in terms of clarity, thought, creativity, vision and aura. Eyesight is important in 'body-light', as are subtler forms of seeing: Prapto talks about insight, even 'enlightenment', and of 'our being as light'. This 'enlightenment' in relation to 'body-light' is not enlightenment in the traditional Buddhist sense. Prapto compares the process of going from darkness to light to that of going from unconscious to conscious and to becoming aware in the sense of achieving a heightened consciousness/sensitivity and of working towards obtaining 'enlightenment'. His sense of light includes the physical (e.g. daylight) and the metaphorical (e.g. insight and self-knowledge).

Seeing based on 'body-light' is primarily achieved by 'seeing' through the mind and differs from insights achieved primarily through 'feeling'. Mind means not only the intellect but also higher consciousness and it is always seen as an integrated part of our whole being.

Shadow and light, female and male, passive and active mode

Within the practice, Prapto views shadow and light also in terms of female and male, passive and active. He uses 'female' and 'male' to refer to a passive and an active value respectively and not to gender in the sense of women and men. For him, 'female' refers to a neutral passive value and 'male' refers to a neutral active value. As we shall see below, this system of female and male, passive and active ways of moving can be used by all practitioners irrespective of gender and may be seen as two different, neutral modes of moving.

In Amerta movement, students' attitudes to mind and body can be based on passivity, receptiveness and softness, or on the active, energetic and sturdy. We can compare this passive-active dynamic to playing the piano, where the minor keys may be seen as the passive mode and the major keys as the active mode. The 'female' approach to movement and to the attitude of body and mind when moving in Amerta Movement is sometimes characterised by qualities like closeness and empathy, while the 'male' approach is sometimes characterised as one of expressivity, sturdiness, roughness and distance.[24]

Space: passive and active

Human functions are both passive and active, 'passive-active' in Prapto's terms, and female and male, 'female-male'. In Amerta movement, the female and male dualities are also called 'spaces'. Female 'space' contrasts with male 'space'. The female space has a male aspect and the male space a female one. Moreover, on

---

[24] This distinction is characteristic of traditional and classical Javanese dance which has female and male dance-styles, the former having a more passive, soft and refined energy (*halus*) and the latter having an active, robust and sturdy energy (*gaga*). Both are neutral energies, modes or modalities and dancers of either sex can dance in either style. See Brakel-Papenhuyzen (1995) and Koentjaraningrat (1980: 300-303), who calls these dances *alusan* [refined] and *gagahan* [robust] in Indonesian,

Communication courses, Prapto worked with what he terms 'passive-active space' interchangeably with 'female-male space'. According to Prapto:

> *Passive space is also active and active space is also passive in the practice. In the same manner, female space is also active and male space is also passive.*

In movement practice, students nearly always start from a 'passive space', from an attitude of receiving not only with their conscious mind or ego, but also with their whole body. However, if they like, they can also start from an active space, from a space of actively producing movement, by actively shaping movement expressions based on their ego or conscious self. Students train in passive and active in relation to each other and to the natural elements, like the wind.

When practising in passive with the wind or with other students, for example, practitioners let themselves be moved by the wind or by their partner or the group. While this is happening, they try to be attentive to whether they are completely passive or to some extent active. They also try to be aware of how they react to the pull of the ocean, the wind or other people. They are attentive to whether they can ignore their own urge to act regardless of the partner, the group or the 'melody' of nature's elements, as Prapto called it. They also try to detect whether they can be spontaneous in their expressions, always with awareness of how being passive or active feels in the body.

Groups and sites are also characterised as 'female' or 'male'. Parangtritis beach with its ever-changing elements of nature and no architecture is a 'female' space. Borobudur Temple with its stone structure is a 'male' space. In relation to people, 'female' space is seen as more passive and 'male' space is more active. A group of mostly women naturally forms a 'female' space, and attitudes to life and to movement in such a group will be 'female' and vice versa for a group of men. To take another example, our muscles, when they help us to carry out some action, move while collaborating in an active-passive rhythm.

Taking a first step, an example

As we have already seen in 'Communication', before moving onto the practice floor, the student has to 'take a first step'. This means making a decision about going forward in my life and forming a clear intention as to direction and end goal. If I reach a 'crossroads' and need to change my destination, this trains me in decision-making. That way I can grow. The idea is that the ability to make a choice is crucial for development.

People often get many chances in their lives. However, as Prapto says, if they do not have a clear understanding of where they want to go, i.e. if they are not able to form a clear intention as to their direction and destination, a new step in life might take ten years to complete. That is why students on 'Communication' need to practise how to have a clear position in the space, so as to form an intention as to their direction and end goal not only in the practice space they are working in, but also in their lives.

Clear position and a 'window' for looking out

Students practise 'clear position' and how to make a 'window' for looking out in the space and beyond. They do so by placing themselves at different spots in relation to the pillars in the pendopo, using these as a frame or a 'window' for looking out.

In this way, students, while moving and using the whole body, are creating their personal outlook or 'window' on the outside world, while at the same time being aware that they are being looked at by others from outside. As Prapto points out, the 'window' thus created is a living organism in three dimensions. It is not the same as an ordinary window, which is just a square frame in two dimensions. My outlook in the practice is three-dimensional, alive and in flux.

> *In the pendopo between each pillar, it's like a window. You have a frame. You have frame in seeing.*

Practising 'clear position' and at the same time practising intention of direction in the space helps us to make choices. A clear choice also helps us to face the issue of communication, because a clear choice as to positioning ourselves between the pillars helps us to move in space in a way that can be seen from the outside, if we so wish. Do I want to be seen or not? Do I want to dialogue, to make exchanges, to speak, with the outside world? Do I want to take it into my movements or not? At least we should try to be aware of an outside world while making our choices of position in the space. This fits with the course's aim, which is communication and dialogue or exchange between oneself and the environment, from a 'clear position'. It is like an attitude in the space of 'YES, I have made this choice', radiating through my whole body and a 'YES, I've seen you' message to the spectators: 'I'm paying attention to you', and 'I want to be seen!'

Training in a moving balance

Students also start training in a 'moving balance'. This is based on the concept of 'moving for moving' rather than on 'moving and stopping to gain security', which students practised earlier on in 'Vocabulary' and 'Basic'. In practising 'moving for moving', Prapto tried to make students understand that life is always in flux and that working with balance through a 'stop-go on' training as students have done so far, is not really the best way to find balance in life. According to Prapto, we only find balance in the practice and in our lives by learning how to move and change with life's moves and changes: we have to be able to respond and not stagnate. We can only find genuine balance through movement. As preparation for learning how to have a 'moving balance', we first practise the usual sequences of 'walking, crawling, lying, sitting, running, stop-go on'. In that way, when stopping we have time to recognise our internal/external condition and find our balance if we have lost it.

Then we go on to practise the second approach – 'moving for moving' – without stopping. Here we learn to keep our balance inside/outside until our movements naturally bring us to a stop. We do so by working on reducing conscious control and allowing the body to express its own rhythm as a 'melody' between activity and passivity, impulse and settling down. Prapto sees this rhythm of passivity and activity in relation to the student's movement as a 'dualism within wholeness'. It is comparable to natural rhythms like night/day, low tide/high tide in the sense of forming a whole. Moreover, in Amerta movement practice, I need to be aware not only through an awakened mind, focused in the present, but also through a heightened sensitivity of my whole body in the present. I achieve this by relaxing my mind's control over the body, allowing impulses to emerge from the body itself, i.e. from my physicality, from my subconscious, from my 'body-nature'. This rhythm corresponds to dualities within the practice, like 'focus/relaxation', and may be called a 'binary rhythm' between activity and passivity. This dynamic is also important in the context of working with clear position, where I need actively to make the decision of being seen by spectators from outside and yet at the same time must be able to relax – an ability more related to passivity.

Case study: 'Moving balance' at the Indian Ocean

One of the female students on 'Communication' particularly wants to work on balance when the group goes to the beach. There, she says, all the elements – water, clouds, sand and wind – are moving, so that there is no sensation of anything being permanent. She is motivated by a sense of being stagnant in her life, as well as in her physical practice. She wants to "move on and to make a 'new step'". It is essential for her to find her balance. At the beach, she starts by moving with the ocean as a partner and keeping her balance. In doing so, she needs to find what she terms her 'focus', which she defines as follows:

*Focus for me in this connection is to be able to see the light on
the water, to feel how my body moves with that light. To me it is*

the awareness of, the attention to the temperature of the water, to how the water moves and whether the waves are coming in one line or they are coming from different lines; that is focus.

I tried to do it with a sense of focus, so that I didn't become giddy or sick to my stomach or you know 'flying' or out of a sense of balance, working with the water and myself. I did that in a couple of ways. First, I began by trying to find my back, because I'm working with a sense of stagnation and I worked to open my back to not be stagnated. If I'm stagnated in a place where the ocean is moving and the sky is moving, I'd get sick, I'd lose my sense of clarity. So opening my back, feeling my body, working with my body, is to arrive and to be grounded.

She applies an important Amerta practice technique: being aware of one's back. This allows the student to relax, to feel and to be aware of the whole body, i.e. to have an open attitude to the *whole* body. If the student's focus is on one part of the body only, she will not be able to anchor herself in her whole body from a felt sense. At the same time, she focuses her mind: she is both relaxed and focused simultaneously. One might compare this, as Prapto sometimes did, to a person threading a needle: their whole body is relaxing but at the same time focusing, i.e. concentrating on the hand holding the thread while bringing it to the eye of the needle held with the other hand.

Interconnectedness

Students in full group sessions practise keeping a 'moving balance' between the inner and the outer worlds, i.e. moving without stopping the natural flow. They do so without giving priority to either inside or outside, but keeping a balance between the two. According to the same female student: "Being too deeply inside myself is out of balance in the same way as reaching too far out into the world". During sessions of practising a 'moving balance' between the inner and outer worlds, we often experience a new feeling, one of being connected to our surroundings and being included in one large pulsating rhythm of life. It is interconnectedness with those around us and with the environment in a way that is often new to us. We might call it a way of communicating that 'just happens'. Students do not seem to actively do anything for it to happen, but some people say they feel supported in their process on the course by the Javanese rhythm of life.

The female student goes on to say that she does not believe in her own potential as it unfolds in the practice and that she cannot step out of her stagnation, as she calls it. But towards the end of the course she succeeds in doing so, according to her, via her own inner development, supported by the kind of interconnected consciousness that, she says, you meet in daily life among the Javanese. The new step she takes is related to the communication style of her crystallisation, as we will see below.

Discussions

In group discussions, communication comes up. Students have just come back from a full group session practising communication together. It has not been satisfactory. One reason is that they failed to read the situation in the group before throwing themselves into group communication, i.e. into their movement practice together. As a guideline, Prapto has put forward four rules for communicating during the practice:

1. Make your situation and your position clear
2. Distance
3. Read until it is enough
4. Communicate

Prapto compares communication to hunger: when people are hungry, they throw themselves into communication as into a 'hole' and, in the process, they lose awareness of the situation. They forget to be attentive in a calm, non-attached way to their own condition and to what is going on in the practice space, including to the situation of the others in the space. Communication has to be a conscious choice. In the practice, this means that students must read the situation in a calm, non-attached way and find their own physical position before entering into communication. Otherwise they jump into communication and 'fall' into the 'hole', losing their clarity.

Student: *The main thing in communication in the practice is to find your own position, otherwise you jump into communication?*

Prapto: *Yes. You jump into 'hole' communication.*

Student: *And then it's difficult to get out. And then you say, Prapto, that there is an impulse of thirst or hunger, or an impulse of communication, but it's not clear, what you want to eat or drink. That is the 'hole', isn't it?*

Prapto: *Ya, ya. The mechanism of communication is making you hungry in communication, thirsty in communication. Communication itself is like you have no friend, and then unconsciously, you'd like to find a friend. This is speaking in general. Because when you are conscious and reading to make communication, you are making your position clear first, so that you have a sense of distance. You are not mixing first with the person(s) you want to communicate with.*

Another student: *…there's a lot of mixing we're not conscious of.*

Prapto: *Exactly! Please read again and again and then, after you've finished, you can make communication. So that's my experience, OK.*

Crystallisation

Preparation

The crystallisations are going to take place at Lemah Putih. Prapto says there are several ways for students to prepare. One is by making independent visits to one of the cultural sites with their special group, or alone. Another is process – meaning that each group prepares their crystallisation via their daily, improvised practice and process at the school, based on a theme. In that case, individual students do not have to look so much at personal relations but can give priority to the themes instead. If I can collaborate with the others in the group for the crystallisation, that is fine, but it is not the first priority. In that way, students learn something about how to function with people different from themselves. As one student says:

> *In order to develop our theme, whether it be in 'Presence',*
> *'Bowing' or 'Healing', we work with people in the group or it*
> *could be that we choose another colleague whether we like the*
> *people or not, feel a connection to them or not.*

The crystallisation gives students an opportunity to present their personal process to the public and represents a new step in their lives. Some students may never have stepped forward before and presented or performed in a public space. The 'Communication' course is not exclusively addressed at performance artists, as it includes people from many different walks of life. But even for professional artists in the group, it is new to communicate through the Amerta Movement approach, different from most other performance techniques since it consists of improvised, non-stylised movement based on input and impulses from the student's body, mind and feelings, the student's personality, identity, attitude to self and to life in the present moment. And as we know, the crystallisation, being not only person-specific but also site-specific, is also founded on input from the site of performance, the whole environment, including co-practitioners and the audience. This openness to one's inside and outside simultaneously can make a performer vulnerable.

Prapto gives instructions to help students create their crystallisation: it can happen when students have an open attitude, i.e. one of dialogue, as Prapto calls it, or one of exchange and interconnectedness with the surroundings.

The crystallisation is in deep contrast to traditional dance performance in the West. It also contrasts with the usual practice in Java, during the 1980s and 1990s where performers and spectators are separated as by a 'glass wall', as Prapto termed it, with gestures and steps being fixed beforehand.

What follows is a case study from Java in 1996 of two women: 'A' who we have met above, relating her experience moving at the Indian Ocean and, 'B', one of her co-practitioners on 'Communication'. They have formed a group to prepare for a crystallisation. They are both Westerners, performers and teachers of modern, dance- and movement-based theatre. A is 49, with quite an intellectual approach to life; she is articulate and talks easily about things. B is 45, goes about things in a practical way and does not talk much. Both have worked with Prapto for several years. They are in the same group primarily because they have both chosen the theme of 'Presence', part of the overall Amerta Movement theme of Physical/Bodily Expression. Since there is little affinity between them, verbal communication or 'small-talk' is difficult. Hence, their relationship as a 'group' has developed only slowly.

However, Amerta Movement students learn to open the way for other forms of communication besides talking. Communication may take place tacitly, for example through movement with props, as when students prepare a framework for their practice in the space. For that, they bring props, like textiles, sticks and rocks to use as tools to 'construct the space', integrating these tools into their personal style of movement. Doing so normally involves some kind of communication through the way we handle the props and where and how we place them in the space and in relation to our co-practitioner(s). For example, when this kind of 'construction of space' happens in the pendopo at the Lemah Putih School, I might choose a specific place near certain pillars as my own 'territory'. By bringing the props and placing them in my personal territory, I am sending a signal saying: 'here is my home!' Others might from their own personal place or 'home', if they have created one, set out to move in and across the pendopo with or without tools, just as when we leave our home in daily life to go out and return later. In these circumstances, communication depends on improvisation, or rather, on what arises in the process from moment to moment in the space as well as on my attitude to it.

Let's follow the two women, seen through the eyes of A:

In the beginning I felt very uncomfortable with B, so we didn't
talk to each other. She'd clearly not come and practice with me.
I felt very isolated.

> *I felt a sort of a wall between us. At first we were alone in the*
> *space, then we were colleagues, not a group really, because only*
> *two of us, and I'd work in my own process, she'd work in her*
> *own process, but being aware, though, that by being in the*
> *same space, we worked at communication.*

Their difficulties, according to A, come from their being so different. Although they had both chosen the theme of Presence, they never talked about it. But a trip together to Parangtritis Beach, as part of their independent performance project – a task suggested by Prapto – brings them into closer contact and they begin to speak to each other and A becomes aware that B is very sensitive to things around her. So A begins to connect to B more on a feeling level, i.e. on a tacit level, than on a talking level.

Then one day, after their return to the school, they are practising in the main pendopo each with a cloth, sometimes using it as a kind of a dialogue-partner in their movement and relating to it through their senses, i.e. looking at it, smelling it, feeling its texture and so on. Otherwise they might also put their cloth down on the floor at a chosen place in order to indicate their private place/territory or 'home', in the space. They might also sit on their cloth and so on. A, besides her cloth, also has a bamboo stick and a thin bamboo mat, which she always carries with her:

> *I just put my cloth down, that's my 'home' [in the pendopo]. B*
> *had created this wonderful space, with this big wide cloth. I*
> *wanted to go moving. I took my mat and spread it out. Then*
> *something happened and it just happened, I wasn't thinking*
> *about it. My mat went from my 'home' to her 'home', and then*
> *I went in moving to find my stick.*

> *In that moment, she crossed over. I couldn't see whether she*
> *walked on my mat, but I imagine she didn't, and then she was*
> *moving in my space, in my 'home'. That made me feel, although*
> *it happened independently of me, that it was OK for me to work*
> *in her 'home'. I went and worked in her 'home'. What happened*
> *was that perhaps she saw me put out the mat which was really a*
> *coincidence and then she thought I made her an offer. This gave*
> *a bridge for her to come and move in my 'home'.*

Unintentionally, this experience helps the two women communicate. This shows how genuine communication is not planned by those involved, it just happens in Amerta Movement. For A, this is an illustration of 'Presence' or

'Physical/Bodily Expression'; i.e. the overall theme she has chosen for her practice and her personal development. It also illustrates to her what movement in communication is about: how, for example, a situation may emerge, becoming a catalyst for the communication process, as here. The two women had been unable to talk their way into this kind of communication, not because of hostility, but more because of feeling inadequate in the face of the task.

After relating the above experience of collaborating with a co-practitioner, A describes how she normally goes on stage when performing at home (in Australia or the USA, especially New York):

> *I'd often* [when performing in the West] *get an idea in my head -'oh! I think I'll put my cloth in the water and then wear my cloth' and so I'd enter the stage with an idea. Now, [after having studied Amerta Movement], what I try to do on stage, is having a moment, a time granted myself, feeling my body and being on the stage and letting my own inner perfect form [genuine condition] emerge. ...In the West, we come from function. There is usually a direct line, almost a set timing, it is not organic* [like in Amerta Movement], *it's more mind, in the West, in my understanding.*

Hence, according to A, the Western way of performing through movement in the 1990s did not leave much room for improvisation in dialogue with the surroundings, or for an exchange of impulses and input between the performer, the site, the audience and the atmosphere of the present moment. A's 'new step' as a performer (in relation to the course and the crystallisation), is that she now dares to perform in public, not only through improvisation around a theme, but by receiving her own condition first, i.e. feeling herself and her whole condition first on the stage, while performing, rather than just following a set idea, as she did before. The physical expression, whereby she now communicates with her audience, is spontaneous and improvised in the same way as when, for instance, one goes to the market.

Crystallisations at the theatre in Solo

Generally, students of 'Communication' perform, not only at the Lemah Putih School, but also at the city art centre (TBS), at its huge pendopo, or in its indoor black-box theatre. Below, for comparison with the 1996 crystallisation, are examples of crystallisations held at the end of the 1988 and 1989 Communication course in Java.

Crystallisations not only for entertainment

In 1988, I took part in a two-month 'Communication' course with Prapto in Java. The 10 students formed three groups each presenting a crystallisation based on a theme at the TBS pendopo. During the week before the crystallisations, we trained at TBS and explored theatrical props like body painting. Until then, tools and props had not played any role in the practice. Being at TBS, our training took on an atmosphere of classical Javanese arts: while we were practising free, non-stylised movement, Javanese classical dancers nearby, dressed in costume, practised the highly stylised, refined Javanese dance. Some danced with a bow and arrow, a sword or the characteristic dancing scarf. At the back, where the *gamelan* orchestra was situated, Javanese musicians, singers and puppeteers were at work. Traditional *gamelan* music and song filled the air. Sometimes children came to play or have a go on the *gamelan* instruments. They were not chased away by the grown-ups who seemed to think, 'Why not start to practise at an early age?'

What was important for our three groups was the intention to create new approaches to performance, including a daily life atmosphere and incorporating disciplines other than dance and movement, such as healing and social aspects of life. The groups had discussed this during the course, and their crystallisations were an embodiment of their discussions. They tried to create a holistic approach to theatre, where neither the performer's inner being and daily-life identity nor their physical surroundings are excluded from the performance. Our groups also tried to create a physical, improvised form of expression without a fixed or pre-planned structure or choreography and a performance in which the music follows the performer. We wanted to break away from the traditional model with performers, as it were, inside an aquarium with the spectators outside. Instead, through improvised free movement, we wanted to establish an open dialogue and communication with spectators and with the environment. By 'dialogue' we did not mean physical interaction between performers and spectators, but being open to receive influences and be inspired to create our performances in and by the present moment, in relation to the group of spectators present, and to the specific stage we were performing on, including its atmosphere. The performance, rather than being a spectacle in the ordinary sense, was seen by these 1988 groups to be a common sharing and ideally a kind of celebration.

The three crystallisations were as follows. The titles indicate the process leading up to them. They were accompanied by *gamelan* and flute music, but only at the performance itself. Music was not used in this way during the course.

1. This was a group of six people, (mostly from England). The crystallisation title was 'Hello Misterrr!' pronounced with the rolling Indonesian 'r', referring to some of the group's experience in Java of hearing the hearty greeting Indonesians, at the time, yelled after Westerners in Solo, irrespective of gender.

2. This group consisted of me and a German man. The title was 'Can I speak to you?' and was an attempt to form a meeting between two professions – healing/therapy and theatre/acting, based on improvised movement.

3. The third group consisted of a German couple. The title of their crystallisation was 'Hausgeister [Housespirits], A Couple on The Road'. It revolved around new roles for women and also for men.

Only some 30 spectators came, not many by Javanese standards. Afterwards there was a discussion with the audience. These were mainly artists, students and teachers from the performing arts' academy in Solo, from a nearby university and from the arts centre. The audience found the lack of story and of conventional gestures challenging but they seemed to respect the 'performances' as new expressions, although Javanese politeness might have kept critical voices at bay. Questions included, 'What is the story of these performances?' and 'Are you aware of your vocabulary through movement?' One of the people from the three groups answered saying: 'The story is what you saw'. The Indonesian who had put the question remained silent.

Similar questions were asked in connection with another crystallisation, at the end of a 'Communication' course in 1989. Again, the crystallisation took place at TBS and the group consisted of a Javanese man and two German women. The 'presentation by movement', as this crystallisation was called, was described as 'movement without scenario by three people expressing the three elements, earth, water, and fire'. The man embodied fire and the two women earth and water, respectively. Some 250 people came to watch, mostly local artists, students and teachers. After the performance, there was a 45-minute dialogue with the spectators. Most did not understand what the 'presentation by movement' was about. They asked what its aim and basic concept were. The performers answered by saying that the 'performance' was not only meant to be seen but also had to be felt. One had to have an attitude of contemplation. Another point raised in terms of criticism related to quality. The three performers' manner of expressing the natural elements had been insufficient. They were advised to train more. Some of the artists among the public, however, sympathised with the group's 'performance'. They found that the movement language could be used as a tool for creating new art.

After their crystallisation the three practitioners returned to the Lemah Putih School for practice in order to 'digest', i.e. to reflect on, analyse and discuss their own reaction to the performance. The Javanese man, who was both an academic and an artist, responded to the criticism as follows.

> *Until now, I have not found how to express my thoughts, my inner feeling and how to make a concrete form of my inner feeling in movement.*

In conclusion, we can see that it might present a challenge, at the time, successfully to use Amerta free movement from the *Pribadi Art* approach as a tool for professional performance art. It is not only a question of training in somatic movement or theatre skills. This is evident from the Javanese practitioner's reaction to the criticism. He judged that the problem lay in his lack of ability to express his thoughts and inner feelings adequately. When presenting the crystallisations, I have purposefully not said whether the 'performers' were trained artists or not as this is not an essential point within Amerta Movement, at least not at the time. The movement itself and the crystallisation have to be enlivening, with the performer being genuinely alive in their whole body and in a felt contact with the surroundings in the present moment. Crystallisations were not only for entertainment.

PART III: Messenger Art

Chapter 9. Messenger Art

On the road to a Professional Art Language

Introduction

Messenger Art was officially introduced in the Lemah Putih School's course programme in 1997, which marks the end of this book. However, Prapto, who for many years had been eager to develop Amerta Movement into a performance art, had already been teaching Messenger Art techniques unofficially, especially during the 1994-1997 period.

Prapto describes the Messenger Art programme as follows:

> *This is a three months program consisting of the 'Way of going
> to the Ocean', then 'Liberation of Sukuh Pyramid' and then
> 'Borobudur Circulation'. ... By the ocean, we purify ourselves
> in the sense of harvesting. ... In Sukuh, we study Candi Sukuh's
> importance in liberation. There we learn about Dewaruci, and
> about the architecture. As to 'Borobudur Circulation', we try to
> understand humanity and nature looked at from Borobudur.
> We study the mudras as interpreted via our own movement.
> We read the reliefs via our own movement.*[25]

Explaining his wish to start the practice from Messenger Art, Prapto said his aim was to develop Amerta movement as a tool for making professional performance art:

> *Already for long, long years, I struggle to bring up my sense of
> work in the sense of Messenger Art. In '82 when I worked in
> Germany and in Switzerland then the Amerta Movement work
> was growing more from the sense of individual growing
> [Pribadi Art]. There were then people from many different
> backgrounds, also many from an art background. At that time
> most of them practised from Pribadi Art, from their own
> individual source and being.*

---

[25] Interview with Prapto (Sartono, 1996).

Aim of Messenger Art

Prapto added that his goal in creating what can be described as an artist's training with Messenger Art, was "giving something to the society". The overall aim of Messenger Art is to let life be in tune with modern times without losing its roots.

For inspiration, Amerta Movement draws on the values of Javanese village culture rather than metropolitan values. The intention with Messenger Art, as seen above, is not just entertainment or aesthetics, but to have an impact on society, as well as on the evolution of the human being. It is not for personal but for collective development, whereby the positive potential of a society may take form and transcend the old one. It is about how society handles nature, the sacred, the planet and ecology, and about how our relations, attitudes to life, ethical values and behaviour, as well as cultural roots, are managed.

In Messenger Art, the practitioner starts with an attitude of respect for a higher dimension including ethical considerations in order to benefit humanity. Prapto does not point to a specific religion. But he clearly disavows a worldview in which human beings are at the centre and thereby placed above nature and the sacred. Amerta Movement is a holistic approach to life, 'whole and holy', and thereby also a holistic approach to art.[26]

Messenger Art: a language for professional art

The Messenger Art programme, aimed at professional artists and at creating a professional art language, is based on delivering a message and communicating a 'story' from the collective and cultural heritage through bodily movement. In this, Messenger Art contrasts with the *Pribadi Art* programme, which emphasises the individual practitioner and personal development.

At the outset, Messenger Art took place almost entirely at the 'retreat sites' of Parangtritis Beach, Candi Sukuh and Candi Borobudur. According to the school's programme at the time, the source of the Messenger Art courses is, 'retreat source based on a 'story' part of the collective culture, expressing its

---

[26] The practitioner's aim to become 'whole' like nature means trying to bridge the separation between body and mind or, at least, engaging in a dialogue between the two. We become 'holy' in the sense of being *reconnected* to nature inside and outside ourselves. (Compare this meaning of 'holy' to the etymology of the word 'religion' meaning to *reconnect*.) By extension it refers to being reconnected to divine power and to expressions of religious faith.

attitudes to life'. This means that the movement practice flows from a 'story' linked to the site where the practice takes place, and not, as in *Pribadi Art*, from the individual practitioner's body and being.

'Story' and Message

The Messenger Art practice is initiated from the 'story'. 'Story' in this context is a package of ingredients – the sum total of the cultural site where the practice takes place in its function as a retreat site, and is often termed 'retreat source'. The 'story' includes the site's form, material, atmosphere, energy, essence, myths, and, in the case of Candi Borobudur, mudras. The 'story' also comprises attitude, language, mind and ideas. An example of site-form as 'story' in relation to a cultural site is Borobudur's ascending spiral form; examples of site-myths as 'stories' are the myths of Dewaruci, Murwakala and Sudamala at Candi Sukuh (see p.110).

'Retreat source' tells us that the practice takes place at sites of retreat and, as such, is part of the 'story'. It also indicates the overall attitude through which the practitioner reads the site and communicates by channelling. This is not for personal development but for message giving. The 'practitioner-messenger' passes on a message through the body in an impersonal, non-attached way without expressing their own being as in *Pribadi Art*.

Messenger Art is communication through free, improvised Amerta movement, both on the vertical and the horizontal axis. In the vertical axis, the message is homage, reverence and thankfulness to life. On the horizontal axis, the message may be aimed at society, for example, at being a leader or a spiritual guide. As discussed earlier (p.38), even a message on the horizontal axis always goes via the vertical axis.

Crucial to Messenger Art is that the 'story' comes from outside, from the 'Dream World', in Prapto's terms, meaning the non-material world of the mind and the spirit. This contrasts with *Pribadi Art* where the material embodied comes from the 'Reality World', from the practitioner. The Messenger's message is non-verbal or mute, and although this message is not derived from my personal being, it is still transformed and expressed via my body into a bodily 'language' in the outside world. The message, in order to be fully communicated on the horizontal level in a performance or crystallisation, should be received by the spectator's whole body and being. In this way, the spectator in Messenger Art completes the act of communication of the message.

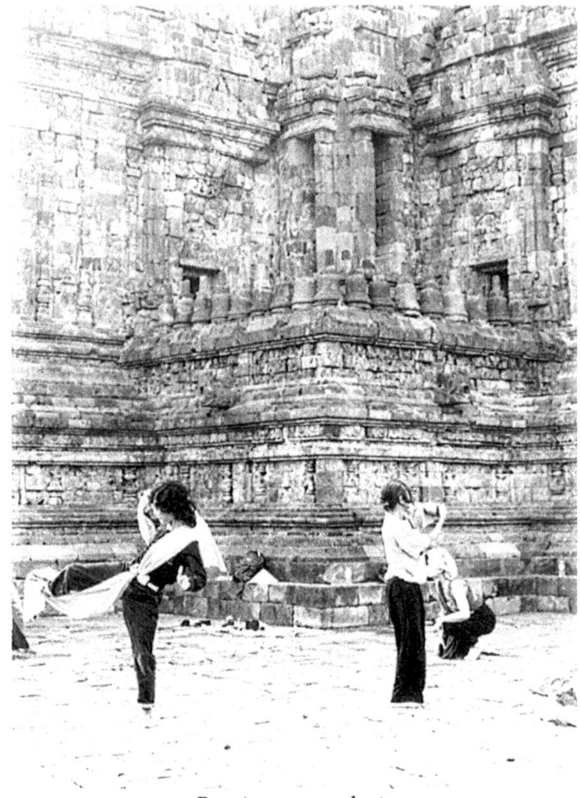

Practice at a temple site

Half-trance

The process from 'story' to message in the practice may be understood through the example of Candi Sukuh. As a Messenger student, I start the process in Sukuh from my ego – I rely on my conscious mind as is normal in daily activities. However, I am changed through interaction with the site. I become more aware and transform the 'story' to a message via movement. From the practitioner's point of view this process might be described as follows.

I start in Sukuh from ego; my ego identifies with Sukuh by tuning in. As the practice proceeds, I am changed; I am in a different state. Having transcended my ego I am aware with the whole body and hence relying on the whole body like a child or an animal. In that state I can communicate better. And that is what Messenger is about. I do not wipe the slate clean, i.e. suppress the ego. My ego is still there: in the phase of reception, when I read the 'story', it is passive – but when translating the 'story' into the message, i.e. when communicating, my ego is active. It helps my movement to materialise via the 'intelligence' of my whole body and actively influences the physical shaping of the movement and my position moving in relation to the practice site. It helps me to create my language through movement. Hence, my ego serves as a tool facilitating transformation from 'story' to embodied message.

This technique is like trance in that it functions as a channel for receiving impulses from both inside and outside. This trance, however, is one where practitioners are fully aware of their own identity in the environment in an everyday sense. They practise with eyes open. So the term 'half-trance' seems appropriate. It is also like the condition of open receptiveness called *rasa* by the Javanese. In Amerta Movement, *rasa* includes the 'feeling' of the physical body, heart and head, i.e. the whole person, not just the 'feeling of the heart'. When we receive impulses from outside while in this state of 'half trance', we are functioning as a channel but in a state of awareness. We might also call it a kind of meditation in an awakened condition.[27] The ego's capacity for receiving and acting on internal and external material has been temporarily expanded. This condition of half-trance has nothing to do with religion. It is a way of using oneself for communication. It can be used in many contexts, one of which is religious practice. What is crucial in the present context is that the practitioner is able to act and thus is responsible for which 'story' is being channelled. It is like a pipe or tube that is conscious. This also influences the physical practice. The ego is not completely passive but active in the sense of being able to make choices and influence the form of the movements during the improvisation. Prapto saw this as adding a cultural approach based on human values to the practice and called it 'dressing' or 'design'.

Differences between *Pribadi* and Messenger Art

As well as the differences already noted between the 'sources' of *Pribadi* and Messenger Art, we should also note that in relation to the cultural sites, there is a difference in terms of empathy. Tuning oneself to the sites in Messenger Art happens on a deeper level than in *Pribadi* because students spend much more time at the site and already have more experience with the practice.

Both approaches entail responsibility. In *Pribadi*, this is honesty in my attitude to body and mind; in Messenger Art, this is honesty in relation to passing on the message and how it is passed on. I channel the 'story' with my whole body in a condition of awareness. So I can choose to pass on the message unchanged or, to some extent, change it by actively influencing form, gestures,

---

[27] According to Prapto, different forms of meditation or different techniques for entering into inner consciousness processes beyond the ego may lead to spiritual liberation. One of these is sound and voice, using mantra as a device for meditation. Another is through vision by creating pictures and another one again is through the physicality of the body as in Amerta Movement.

movements and attitudes. This could be a choice in relation to the condition of onlookers or spectators when communicating. Messengers can choose the manner in which to deliver the message and whether to pass on the message. Prapto draws a parallel to the way Javanese people in some mystical practices channel messages from spirits or from god. They just pass them on without taking any responsibility for the impact on the receiver, saying that they are only channels for the guidance (*tuntunan*) of god or a spirit. Nevertheless, Prapto also recognises that this way of channelling may represent the highest form of religious practice when done by an absolutely pure person.

According to Prapto:

> *Messenger is opposite Pribadi, but the result can be the same.*
> *Pribadi has to do with 'home', with containing one's own feelings.*

> *Messenger is more, I need to say something to you, but you, you as*
> *an objective not as an object. It's not me, [it's] like channelling*
> *more, like pamong sense [meditation guide sense], messenger sense.*

> *Pribadi is more expression. Messenger is more communication.*

In his 1996 programme, Prapto describes the approaches as follows:

Individual Art [Pribadi Art]

> *Starting from sense of personal development, reality, gravity,*
> *character, personality, … Element becomes language.*

Messenger Art

> *Starting from sense of performer, stage, channelling, dream*
> *world, non-gravity, no-character, impersonality. Language*
> *becomes embodied.*

The retreat sites, through their architecture, history, myths and most importantly atmosphere, constitute a reference frame within which students practise. For the students, these sites often involve expressions of the sacred. However, Prapto does not teach religion and does not relate to the retreat sites from the traditional mystical approach of Javanese culture.

Prapto teaches physical movement including body-consciousness, attitude-consciousness and space-consciousness. For him, the cultural sites embody specific aspects of Javanese culture and different attitudes to life. Students on the Messenger Art programme are intensely exposed to the attitudes to life they represent. Sukuh's apparent roughness and its *wayang* atmosphere, for example, point to a very different approach from that embodied by the monumental elegance of Candi Borobudur. Both contrast with the open space and changing nature of Parangtritis Beach. The differences of framework and atmosphere influence students' practice. The sites help to make them space-conscious, as well as attitude-conscious by making them aware of the specific qualities of each site as well as aware that life can be approached from different perspectives.

Art and Amerta Movement

Ellin Krinsley sees Prapto's work with Amerta Movement as art, not a high art, but nevertheless art, a non-mainstream art in contrast to mainstream intercultural performance art like that of Grotowski and Peter Brook, for example. She also stresses Amerta Movement's quality of practice, saying that,

> *Prapto has chosen to create experimental intercultural performance practice that comes from Javanese cultural beliefs of the interconnectedness of human identity, God and nature and Amerta Movement touches ritual, rather than the traditional 'high' or classic forms of Javanese performance. Amerta Movement is not built on Western 'fantasies' of traditional culture and offers new techniques for intercultural dialogue and collaboration in performance.* (2001: 29)

The Messenger Art Programme

'Messenger Art' consisted in the late 1990s of three courses: 'The Way of Going to the Ocean', 'Liberation of Sukuh Pyramid' and 'Borobudur Circulation'.

COURSE	1. The Way going to the Ocean	2. Liberation of Sukuh Pyramid	3. Borobudur Circulation
SITE	Candi Sukuh, Borobudur, Parangtritis	Candi Sukuh	Candi Borobudur
THEME	Purification	Liberation	'Enlightenment'/Knowledge of Life/Consciousness of attitudes

Messenger Art's three sub-courses, sites and themes

Course 1: The Way going to the Ocean

Through its theme of purification, this course was primarily linked to Parangtritis Beach (described in Chapter 7).

Prapto took great care to tell students that when they started the practice they had to remember their background. They were coming from different countries with different cultural approaches to life than the Javanese and they were only in Java for one month. They would meet Javanese cultural and traditional values concerning what it means to be human within a community, and what is meant by harmonious relationships. Moreover, on the course, they would also meet the different values of other participants. So it was important for practitioners to keep their own cultural background in mind. On a physical practice level, this also meant being aware of their back, which, in a physical sense, represents their own past, and where the cells of the muscles sometimes contain memories of a person's past, memories that might be released through a process of awareness and of relaxation of those muscles by the student. Prapto also reminded us of previous students who had applied their experience with Amerta Movement in their home countries by starting movement groups or other activities related to their personal experience with Amerta Movement. It was important that students went on to create something in their own country, not in the sense of promulgating Amerta Movement but for their own sake.

The journey to the ocean for each practitioner constituted a process of increasing awareness. At Parangtritis, we let all the impressions of the journey flow through our body and being, purifying these, as they returned to the ocean, the origin of all life. This flow constituted the 'language' of students' bodily movements. It constituted our expressions or delivery of the 'story' as message.

Course 2: Liberation of Sukuh Pyramid

In Prapto's annual programme, 1993-1994, the 'Liberation of Sukuh Pyramid' sub-course was offered with the following text: "This … works in the situation of puppet shadow of Sukuh Temple". Although the course presented a new approach to Amerta practice [at the time], many themes were similar to the ones in the *Pribadi Art* 'Vocabulary' course. Others were new.

On a physical level, the Messenger programme was quite new and very different from *Pribadi's* individual art approach. It was inspired by Prapto's experience with creating a new kind of shadow puppet theatre, combining the traditional way with Amerta movement. With his performance entitled *Wayang Budha,* Prapto applied his new concept and created a new style of puppet (*wayang)* performance. In *Wayang Budha,* Prapto moved with the puppets, which was unusual as the puppets' shadows are normally only projected onto a screen. Prapto also used very large puppets in contrast to the ones used in other shadow puppet performances. Finally, he used cloths as moving screens, torches, and a combination of traditional and contemporary music, instead of the traditional *gamelan* accompaniment.

Wayang Budha and the new practice concept with masks and cloths

Describing his *Wayang Budha* performance, Prapto introduced the new elements with which students were going to practise during the course. These took the form of props, masks, textiles and music. As part of the movement, students were also going to practise how to make sound. Prapto added these new elements to create a framework or a kind of scenography. Hence *Wayang Budha* was mainly used on a physical level in the practice by giving students instruments to help them become messengers and embody the 'story'.

Before 1994, students had been used to practising Amerta movement without props and music except in the crystallisations. Movement devoid of any kind of props or sound was considered one of the hallmarks of Amerta Movement. Although sound had been part of earlier practice, it had not been explored. Prapto had insisted that practitioners' movement expressions should be translated within the body and expressed via the contours of the body and through all the cells of the skin. In the introduction Prapto defined this new approach as a kind of modern animism. It was intended to create a contemporary style of improvised and new ritualistic event or an improvised, spiritually-based 'happening'.

Masks were used to contact the ancestors as the source of the spirits. By going far enough back in the line of ancestors one would reach the first ancestor. Prapto had developed the concept by using the mask to contact god (Tuhan), as the first ancestor. He added half joking that he hoped that on their way to reaching god as the first ancestor, students would not be caught by ghosts or devils. Prapto meant that he did not want to start working with an ancestor-cult in the traditional sense with its world of spirits and ghosts. His intention was for students to directly contact the Supreme Being in the modern sense.

> *.....with the screen, with the torch, with the movement, music, with something like meditation combined, and then somehow the idea is like modern animism and then I try to apply in this programme.*

> *It is like a kind of ritual that uses the mask for contacting the source of the spirit[s], maybe the ancestors (leluhur). I hope you can develop not only the first ancestor, (leluhur bapa), but the first ancestor as god. Then you're not being caught by any devil or by ghosts. Please really contact of god as an ancestor of the ancestors.*

The group did not use exactly the same props in the course as Prapto did in his *Wayang Budha,* nor were they used in the same way. But the point was to encourage or to inspire the group to use theatrical effects while moving, in this case masks and cloths because these would add 'a sense of fairy-tale' and theatre to the practice. Furthermore, Prapto had chosen Candi Sukuh as the site for the course because Sukuh for him is connected to history in terms of an atmosphere of fairy-tale. It evokes the visionary, the dream and myth. The props, which he called fairy-tale elements, were to stimulate the group to create its own 'story' and to get it into Sukuh's 'story'. This was a way for the group as modern human beings to relate to the ancient atmosphere of Candi Sukuh.

We might conclude that, for a Western participant observer, it is not easy to integrate one's personal story into that of Candi Sukuh – which was our main task during the course. We cannot easily draw parallels between ourselves and the ancient reliefs, the statues or stories. The dilemma also applies to the way to liberation as illustrated by the Dewaruci story, even though we may perfectly well understand the story's message in terms of spiritual liberation, as well as the need to transcend physicality and one's own being. The issue is that students do not deal with this in an abstract way, but in a way that is based on the body, bodily movement and an awareness and heightened sensitivity of one's whole body in the present moment, as is characteristic of Amerta Movement.

So Western students have to translate Candi Sukuh's animist atmosphere (its 'story') into a message for modern times. This process has to take place via physical movement and means incorporating collective symbols and behavioural patterns, different from our own, into our personal life, body, gender, sexuality, sense of the sacred, and so on. The student has to reach this insight through direct contact with the site and its 'story' and by processing it through the body in movement practice. So, this insight is reached only via a consciousness process based on a wholeness of body, mind and spirit, i.e. beyond the ego's control, since the ego only controls the conscious mind. In short, the Sukuh 'story' makes itself known via impulses from outside the participant's conscious mind. These impulses come from the unknown space of the subconscious since we read the 'story' with the whole body. This implies that the insight we achieve is not primarily intellectual but based on our whole being. It stays in the body and might form the basis for making choices or taking new steps in life. So our experience parallels Bima's liberation. We are liberated via insights gained on the course through an experience felt in our bodies.

Bima is liberated and transformed when he finds god in himself.[28] He is not the same after his journey. The realisation that he is not the old Bima is liberating. The message is that humans are spiritual beings and come from a spiritual source to which they return again. Essential in relation to Amerta Movement is that this existence as a spiritual being, a part of nature and of god, proceeds within a framework of ordinary human beings going about their everyday lives.

---

[28] For Bima having found 'God' in himself, see Stange (1977: 109-122)

Course 3: Borobudur Circulation

The last course in Messenger Art was 'Borobudur Circulation', which took place at Candi Borobudur. Its theme was 'enlightenment' or knowledge about life through a consciousness of attitudes via viewing life from the Borobudur 'story'. In 1996, it took place in the month of the Buddhist *Waisak* festival, which inspired the course's atmosphere but was not part of the schedule. Prapto defined 'circulation' as a 'dynamic stream of life within an organism of wholeness'. [29] One may compare it with the bloodstream that gives life to the human being by circulating in the body. So the term circulation may be seen both in relation to Candi Borobudur itself and in relation to the student.

First, the circulation in relation to the temple: Candi Borobudur embodies a doctrine of completeness. Borobudur is an 'organism', whole and alive in the present. In this sense, circulation refers to the temple's architecture of an ascending spiral embodying Buddhist doctrine, a doctrine of wholeness. The temple makes the visitor circulate upwards when studying Buddhism by following the reliefs, which lead to enlightenment. Circulation in relation to the course may be interpreted to mean that students are studying the way to enlightenment by circulating in Candi Borobudur. As we have seen, however, it is not enlightenment in the conventional Buddhist sense, but rather self-knowledge and clarity on a higher level inspired by Borobudur. By studying the universe of wholeness or cyclic completeness as represented at Borobudur, students study the attitude to life embodied there. They study by 'circulating' or moving in the temple and exploring its reliefs, Buddhas and mudras. They do not, however, follow Buddhist doctrine, as Buddhists traditionally would do at Borobudur. By reading the temple with their whole body and being, students are said to be channelling its 'story' into the message of their movements there.

There are several differences between practice with the *mudras* in *Pribadi Art* and Messenger Art. The first is that Messenger Art takes place almost entirely in the atmosphere and life of Borobudur Temple. This cannot help but influence the practitioners in a more fundamental manner than practising there for just a few days. The second difference is one of source. Focus has shifted away from the practitioner's self to the 'story'. *Pribadi* is based on the reading source. Through it, practitioners become aware of and express their own being through movement with the aim of personal development. In Borobudur Circulation, the conceptual starting point, or the source, is the 'story' which is external to the practitioner.

---

[29] Prapto also talked about his students as his 'circulation'. We could say that the practitioners of Amerta Movement animate the concept of Amerta Movement by practising it.

This means that Borobudur with its form, reliefs, statues, *mudras*, doctrine, atmosphere and life stream (circulation) is at the course's centre. Borobudur, not the individual student, is the 'starter of the practice'. The temple inspires or imposes a certain conduct and attitude upon the practitioner. Prapto expressed the 'story' approach when he said "We try to understand the humanity and nature … looked at from Borobudur." In practice, the tool that students use is reading with their whole body as in *Pribadi Art*. The difference in Messenger Art is consciousness of attitude and channelling, in the Amerta manner of being aware of one's inside and outside world, rather than individual expression being the focus.

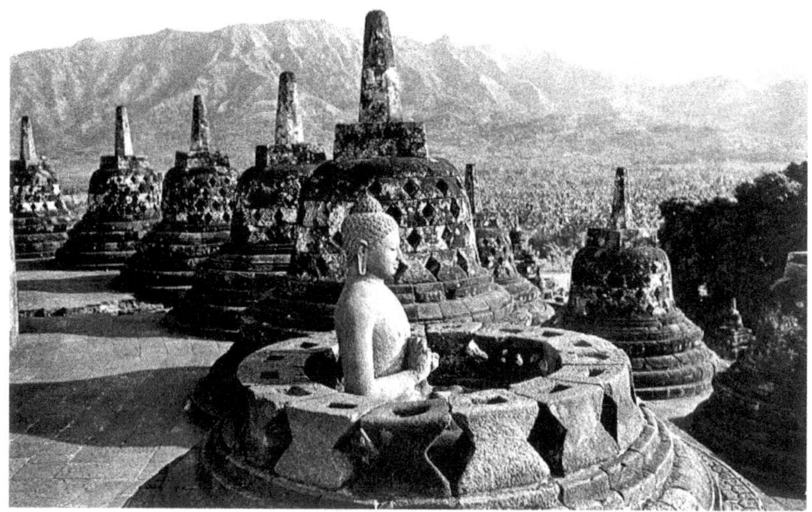

Buddha, Candi Borobudur

Practice

The same is true of practising with the mudras. The point of departure is that the mudras are looked at from the point of view of Borobudur. Through their physical forms and attitudes to life, the mudras constitute a 'story' that is external to the practitioner's being. In contrast to *Pribadi Art*, Prapto seems to leave it up to the individual practitioner to decide how to practise with the mudras. Each mudra is the expression of an inner attitude. Practising in order to embody inner attitudes is called 'making costume' by Prapto. This is similar to using masks and cloths for embodying the 'story' in Candi Sukuh. This technique was anticipated in the Vocabulary course in *Pribadi Art*. Prapto added that it was characteristic for Messenger Art to use 'costume' in the practice in order to embody an attitude, a feeling or a vision.

'Costume' is as an attitude with mudra[s] like 'clothes' and the mudra[s] like clothes are materialisations of the attitude.

The 'story' channelled by the practitioner forms the message. But the 'story' and the message are two different things. The 'story' is related to the site of practice, in this case Borobudur, and the message is related to transformation of the 'story' by the practitioner. This is a language personally formed by the practitioner's body. The more the practitioner translates the 'story' and the attitudes connected to it without influencing it by personal bias, the more this language and its message will be understood. One may also see the movements as comprising a kind of crystallisation within the practice itself, specifically at moments where the message of the 'story' becomes clear and speaks out. This relationship between process and crystallisation may be compared to dreams. Amidst a long 'tale'– which often makes no sense even to people experienced in dealing with dreams – a clear picture or message can emerge, often in very short form. This can be compared to a crystallisation in Amerta Movement.

Mudra as 'story'

Students at Borobudur practised with the mudras as a source of inspiration for their movements. The emphasis was now on exploring the mudras in terms of communicative gesture for message giving. When practising with a mudra in Messenger Art, practitioners might start by copying the mudra directly. In this way, they sense it with their own body as form. They also might use it as a communicative gesture in their practice because it is a well-known gesture. But they might just as easily be inspired by the mudra. If so, they practise with it as an example of a gesture or of an embodied message and improvise on it. They might use it as a 'starter', a physical expression from outside, to get into the flow of movement, or they might choose the attitude connected to the mudra for the starting concept of their practice. In this way, they start their practice while still applying the usual Amerta methods through walking, sitting, standing, etc. At the same time they will have in mind the attitude conveyed by the mudra and the aim of building their practice around communicating that attitude as a message.

The 'story' as gesture

I explore the 'story' as gesture both horizontally between myself and the spectator and vertically between myself and the spiritual or sacred dimension. My movement has both secular and sacred energies. What does exploring a gesture involve? In theory, any movement can be chosen. It is not a matter of what the movement looks like, but of the attitude it represents. Often the gestures explored this way are based on spontaneously arising finger, hand

and arm gestures during practice or based on walking gaits. One might see all the practitioners' movements as gestures embodying or channelling the Borobudur 'story'.

The following example illustrates the point. A student happens to make a spiral movement with her arm. Then she consciously decides to explore that movement, by following the path or the 'line' of the spiral in Prapto's terms and improvising on it, exploring the spiral gesture itself. She does not explore the spiral because of its connection to Nirvana. The gesture itself, independently of its meaning and origin, has become the 'story'. From the spiral as the 'story', she initiates the movement practice and goes on to create new gestures with new forms. In this way she creates a new movement language, which is personally formed. These gestures may or may not speak to others as the mudras do. So whether the student's new gestures communicate something depends on the situation, on her skill and the spectator's receptivity.

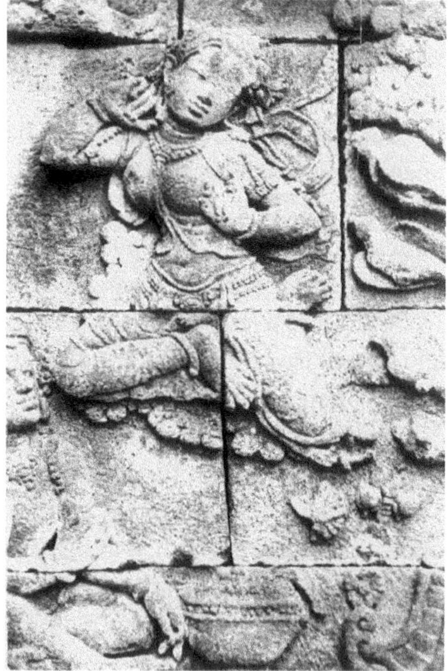

Dancer, Candi Borobudur

Making new gestures in this way does not mean practising movement for movement's sake. The aim is to explore movement and gesture as tools for communicating the 'story' and for translating it into a message. The movement expression is no longer seen as an expression of the practitioner's being or self, but is an embodiment of the immaterial flux of life. The body becomes the instrument through which this stream flows as channelled by the practitioner.

And because it is based on the non-material, this bodily message is said to come from the 'Dream World'. The gesture is, however, personally formed by the individual. So it may constitute a new non-standardised form, or language through movement, different from the usual one connected to Borobudur and Buddhism. The freedom within Amerta Movement as to outer form gives freedom of choice in the practice's embodied expression, rhythm and so on, in the outside world. This is what Prapto meant by 'practising movement as happenings'[30] without identifying with them. Students practise with the principle of change itself, thereby freeing themselves from identifying with any outer form in any definitive way. By doing so students learn to develop an attitude of being flexible and able to adapt to changes in life: "Human beings are basically in constant movement, aren't they?"[31] This freedom points to the Messenger Art approach as one of receptivity from one moment to the next. The attitude is not defined by the practitioner's ego. Rather, the attitude is one of passing on a message, which demands the active responsibility of the practitioner, who thus contributes to forming the message by actively choosing a gesture. This choice depends on the energy accompanying the specific movement expression chosen, in relation to time and place, and the practitioner's honesty and integrity.

Prapto's definition of liberation is based on the Javanese term *pamudaran.* He translates this as 'making less the binding, the boundary'. This implies that, spiritually, people are free as birds and that recognition of this permits the retrieval of the spiritual dimension and the loosening of the strings tying identity to material existence.[32] So, we are not identified with our material existence. Movements can be seen as our physical expression of liberation. They set free our inner essence or spiritual dimension of life. At the same time, these movements constitute our message.

---

[30] In the Amerta Movement programme Prapto says that "The main idea is how to make less of identification by moving in art happenings". (Lavelle, 2006: 10). He is trying to find a way to practise movement in 'art happenings' without identifying himself with his movements. By 'art happenings' he means spontaneous performance events both in practice and in nature.

[31] *"Manusia itu pada dasarnya kan bergerak terus"* – Frans Sartono (1996: 61).

[32] By 'making less the binding' Prapto means to lessen his identification with a material existence and with his physical body. 'Making less the boundary' is another way of saying it. It means to reduce the boundary between the material and spiritual aspects of life on earth incarnated in a body.

A lesson

In relation to Amerta Movement, Borobudur functions as a place of education. In the Borobudur Circulation course, as we have just seen, this education is aimed at 'enlightenment' or knowledge of life via consciousness of attitudes. This is meant in the sense that practitioners thereby achieve knowledge of life beyond their personal universe. We become conscious of our attitudes to life, when these are mirrored in the larger life frame or 'book of wisdom', constituted by Borobudur. Questions arise. Sometimes a kind of 'enlightenment' occurs. One day after lunch, the group with Prapto was seated around a large table. They were speaking about human relations in Javanese and Western culture, according to one Western woman present:[33]

> "[We were talking] especially about the dualism struggle within us. I had been feeling this (Western dualism) intensely in my practice so I asked Prapto about my own struggles in daily behaviour, seeing it so magnified through the movement practice. *'How can I deal with this? How can I fully 'enter' a situation?'* I asked.

> Prapto: *'Please put this flower in front of you on the table.'*

> He pointed to some hibiscus blossoms at the centre of the table … (a Javanese custom for hospitality). I picked up a red blossom…and put it right down in front of me. Oh … I realised immediately that I had not included my seeing, my feeling or mindfulness in the action. I had simply operated on automatic.

> Prapto: *'Yes you see. Do again, please.'*

> I tried again. This time I was very tentative, heavy-handed, about what might be a good place and position for the flower.

> Prapto: *'Not like this. You have one last chance'*, he said jokingly.

> This time, my awareness opened suddenly. I could see the space, the table, the group, the faces, the general atmosphere and my hand went to the blossom and it found the right position for the flower on the table. It felt more like offering the flower to the space and to all present, more like sharing, and I felt a tremendous warmth and aliveness.

> Prapto: *'Yes. Maybe you can practise like this?'"*

---

[33] Andrea Morein (1994)

We might look at this as a 'lesson' in Buddhism, at least in practising mindfulness. But above all it may be a lesson in how to live and how to be awake to the present. The lesson arose spontaneously out of circumstances accompanying the practice in the middle of everyday activities. This way of imparting knowledge is characteristic of Prapto. It just happens and comes about naturally in an everyday context with students free to interpret such lessons as they like.

Prapto's concept of art and Messenger Art

Messenger Art centres on modern society and culture in tune with time, nature, the sacred and social life. Performance as art in the usual sense was not important to Prapto. What was important was the technique, i.e. the tool of the Amerta Movement practice itself whereby one communicates i.e. in a conscious, interconnection between the performer and the surroundings.[34] Moreover, Prapto's focus with Amerta Movement, especially during this early period of Amerta Movement, was life rather than art. He was interested in aliveness. *Amerta* means life in the sense of the nectar of life or, literally 'eternal life'/ 'immortality', in contrast to death. So, if Amerta Movement is used as a language for creating professional performance, the most important element is that it generates life. For Prapto personally being on stage was a success if he created a dialogue with those experiencing his movement, especially if he generated new creativity, new rituals and thereby new impulses for life. Prapto's performances were not performances in the finished sense.[35] They were ongoing – as is life. As one of his students expresses it: "They are a theatre piece under construction".

---

[34] Frans Sartono (1996: 61)

[35] Ardus M. Sawega (1994)

Conclusion

Prapto managed to create a genuine interest in, and respect for, his movement work based on improvisation in the present moment, context and our attitudes to life – something that is not easy with an avant-garde art like Amerta Movement. This may be, first, because he patiently and persistently moved forward, and, second, because he used a modern, multi-cultural, multi-spiritual and multi-artistic approach not only to life and society, but also to his movement, an approach characteristic of *kejawen*.

Moreover, instead of being a traditional guru he saw himself as a gardener or a pedagogue who was a colleague and a sparring-partner to his students. He also embraced diversity, i.e. different cultures, nationalities, ethnic groups and expressions of the sacred: within Amerta Movement, there is ample room for individual differences as to religion, the sacred, background, culture and society. Prapto also favoured a democratic approach, where the students were his equals in a society of equals. In the *wayang* figure of Yudistira, the eldest of the five Pandawa-brothers in the Mahabharata Epic, he found a symbol of democracy: the second name of Yudistira is Samiaji, which means 'equal value' in Javanese, i.e. democracy, according to Prapto.

Amerta Movement was also influenced, especially during the early period treated in this book, by Prapto's students from abroad, coming from all walks of life to study with him in Java and by Prapto visiting the West, sharing his movement teaching with students in their own environment, thereby encouraging them to move at heritage sites in their own cultures, just as they did with him in Java, thus applying Amerta Movement techniques in their culture, their own professions and their own lives. Outside Indonesia Amerta Movement is also called Sharing Movement.

In conclusion we can say that Amerta Movement is a flexible tool, which patiently includes and accepts differences based on an open and tolerant mind capable of comprising diversity. But is that not exactly a continuation of the traditional Indonesian spirit of patience, of trying to include rather than exclude and of trying to accept rather than to reject? Such attitudes are a hallmark of Java's high civilisation, long history and long experience in having to accommodate new influences. As the American anthropologist Clifford Geertz says:

> *Java – which has been civilised longer than England; which*
> *over a period of more than fifteen hundred years has seen*
> *Indians, Arabs, Chinese, Portuguese, and Dutch come and go;*

> *and which has today one of the world's densest populations,*
> *highest development of the arts … – is not easily characterised*
> *under a single label or easily pictured in terms of a dominant*
> *theme.* (Geertz, 1976: 7)

So we can say, perhaps, that Prapto, through his faith in and promotion of traditional Javanese culture adjusted to a modern world, allowed the roots of that culture to embrace changes into a transformation towards the future, communicated via dance and movement.

While incorporating global developments and changes Prapto carefully guarded his cultural, *kejawen* roots. This flexible bridging between ancient and modern constitutes a key to Prapto's success not least overseas and to the fact that Amerta Movement can be applied to multiple fields, such as pedagogy, therapy, spirituality and performing art. As a result, more and more young Indonesians found their way to Prapto's teaching, curious to discover and learn from the movement work of their internationally known compatriot. They were modern Muslims, not being well versed in the *kejawen* tradition. They were open to the world and this is maybe why they chose Prapto, among others, as a mentor and a constructive link between Java, Indonesia and the wider world.

We may also say that Prapto and his work with Amerta Movement have contributed to opening up an understanding of praxis, as a way of learning and of understanding life, for mute, non-verbal and 'practice-based knowledge' that complements intellectual knowledge. Amerta Movement has contributed to opening a way in contemporary societies not only for what is 'practice-based research' and 'practice-based knowledge' through the moving body in the here and now. But, in the arts, Amerta Movement has also contributed to the practice of what is termed, 'artistic research' and 'artistic knowledge', again an inspiration from Javanese ways, filtered through the body-mind-spirit of Prapto, in a manner of a Messenger, passing on life, allowing life to unfold and blossom.

Amerta Movement is still blossoming not only in Java but also in other places around the world as,

> *A practice which is not only a language for communication but*
> *also an expression of being.*

Epilogue

Amerta on the Road in the 21ˢᵗ century

Since the the turn of the century, the pace of Amerta Movement became very rapid. Prapto and Amerta Movement were widely recognised and moved closer to art than before. This art is not necessarily high art, but it is still art, not least in terms of spiritually-based art and new rituals. Prapto himself saw his practice in terms of process rather than performance.

New courses with new movement programmes were created at home and at abroad with titles like, 'Art in Amerta Movement', 'Growing in Indonesia', 'Awakening in Australia', 'Blossoming in Europe', 'Remembering in America'.

Striking features of Prapto's teaching programmes in the 21ˢᵗ century, as compared to the 1986-1997 period treated in this book, were:

- Courses had new names and were shortened.

- Courses were often related to art and new rituals and also conducted a dialogue with established art forms and rituals with the aim of purification and renewal.

- The same course happened in several places within Indonesia.

- Amerta practice was clearly not only for personal growth and development; it stressed sharing, communication and renewal via purification and via giving something to society.

Prapto was invited to share his work not only in Central Java, but also in art centres in Sulawesi, Sumatra and Bali as well as overseas. Part of his work moved to Tejakula in north Bali. In some ways he became more of a Messenger sharing Amerta with the world, being invited by Amerta movers to visit their countries, leaving his movement school, his Padepokan Lemah Putih at home to his children. He still taught courses in Indonesia but Amerta Movement was on the road.

Prapto's work with Amerta Movement became a success at home, as well as in Europe and worldwide. It brought Westerners as well as people from other parts of Asia to Indonesia to study with him. He continued to teach courses in Indonesia, not least at cultural sites like Candi Sukuh, Candi Borobudur and Parangtritis Beach. Amerta Movement as taught by Prapto, contributed to propagating Indonesian culture. This was due to enthusiastic foreigners who fell in love with the Amerta practice and also with Java and Bali as these places were revealed to them through Prapto's teaching during Amerta courses. Subsequently they invested much energy in spreading the word at home and applying their experiences there. Moreover, many of Prapto's students are highly educated professionals such as teachers, doctors, psychologists, architects, therapists, movement instructors, social workers or trained artists in dance, acting, music, song and so on. This enables them to communicate and sometimes initiate projects based on their experiences in Java and Bali, thus further promoting not only Amerta Movement, their application of Amerta Movement and thereby creating new movement arts, but also Indonesian culture and art, as they have experienced them. Moreover, through Prapto and Amerta Movement, several artists from Java and Bali were able to study in Europe and perform there.

Prapto himself saw his practice in terms of process rather than performance. He left specialisation to his applicants and students. They can explore free Amerta movement for a specific use, discipline, product or trademark, based on their personal background and profession. Thus they can apply it to healing, to a specific art genre or a specific performance or they can create new rituals related to events in their own culture… or whatever they like. Prapto's tool was the broad general language of the Amerta practice.

Glossary

Amerta (Old Jav from Skr 'Amrit') ~ The nectar of life; immortality.[36]

Artistic Research ~ Research conducted with artistic practice as its base and artistic practice as its object.

Arupadhatu (Jav) ~ The world of non-form; at Candi Borobudur, the third, top level, representing one of the three cosmic worlds (see also ***Kamadhatu*** and ***Rupadhatu***).

Bapak, Bapa Abbr, **Pak** (Indo) ~ Father, (spiritual) founder, form of address to (older) men, e.g. Pak Prapto; in Javanese, Mbah, e.g. Mbah Prapto.

Batara (Indo); *Bathara* (Jav/Old Jav) ~ Male god; title of male god; messenger.

Bathara Guru (Jav) ~ Title of the god Shiva.

Batin (Indo) ~ relates to an inner, subtle, spiritual dimension in contrast to the material dimension of outer perception, called *lahir* (Indo). Within Amerta Movement these two aspects have fluid borders and can be viewed as a continuum within the wholeness of the practitioner's body-mind-spirit; *Kebatinan* [Indo], mysticism; movements of, see ***Sumarah***.

Bayu (Jav/ Old Jav) ~ Power/wind, the god of the wind; 'life's energy'; a neutral, non-emotional energy, like Chinese **Chi**.

Being ~ relates to, *ada* (Indo) and, *hana* (Jav); connected to place and time. One's self, one's existence in the world, one's 'inner being', 'true being', 'genuine being'/'true self'.

Bergerak (Indo) ~ To move; from *gerak,* movement.

Bodhi tree (Jav) ~ The type of tree (*Ficus religiosa*) the Buddha sat under when he received enlightenment.

Bodhisattva (Skr) ~ Future Buddha.

Body and mind ~ Prapto used the expressions 'landscape' and 'skyscape' as metaphors for the practitioner's body and mind:

---

[36] Abbreviations (Abbr) in this Glossary are as follows: Indonesian (Indo); Javanese (Jav); Latin (Lat.); Old Javanese (Old Jav); Sanskrit (Skr).

'Landscape' is equivalent to the earth (also in Java termed *Ibu Bumi* [Mother Earth]), and to the practitioner's body;

'Skyscape' is equivalent to the sky (also in Java termed *Bapa Angkasa* [Father Sky]) and to the practitioner's mind.

Body as a diagnostic tool ~ 'Using the body as a diagnostic tool', is a term first coined by Alice Kemp-Welch (a.k.a. Alice Pitty):

Prapto, through using his body as a diagnostic tool, entered into a state of enhanced sensitivity and of a heightened awareness of himself, body, mind and feelings, as well as of the person(s) he was guiding in the movement. In that manner, he managed to detect movement patterns within the individual student which were still unconscious to the latter. Prapto's ability in using his body as a diagnostic tool was a trained ability, based on his long experience with meditation and physical movement, thereby training in the sharpness of his intuition and the sensitivity of his senses.

Body-light ~ Body-light has two aspects. One is the material dimension of outer perception, the other an inner, non-material, subtler spiritual dimension used in meditation.

Body-light refers to movement linked to my head/mind in terms of light, thinking, eyesight, the perception of seeing and hence to clarity, vision and creativity. The body is perceived in terms of light and the mind. It includes paying attention to light/shadow and calligraphy. *Body-light* is also understood as insight in the sense of higher, visionary aspects, including higher consciousness and inner dimensions of vision and *aura*, possibly related to the Javanese concept of receiving divine revelation or blessing (*wahyu* [Jav]).

Body-light is linked to movement in an oval shaped space/practice area, to the field of 'nature' and the overall theme of 'purification' through awareness of nature's circulation inside outside us and, facilitates the specific movement quality of 'purification in circulation'.

Body-nature ~ Body-nature has two aspects: One is the material dimension of outer perception, the other an inner, non-material, subtler spiritual dimension as used in meditation.

Body-nature (also termed 'body-body') refers to movement purposefully based on my own, individual, organic nature or physicality and on my 'genuine being', from one moment to the next. It includes paying attention to 'texture' and 'sculpturing' in the outside world. Thereby I create my own individual, 'person-specific' movement vocabulary and movement language.

Body-nature is connected to instinct, reflexes, muscles, sensations and the five senses. It is linked to movement in a square/rectangular shaped space/practice area. It relates, moreover, to the field of, 'human', to the overall theme of, 'physical/bodily expression', and facilitates the specific movement quality of, 'creation in reflection'.

Body-sound ~ Body-sound has two aspects: One is the material dimension of outer perception, the other an inner, non-material, subtler spiritual dimension as used in meditation.

Body-sound is movement based on perceiving my body from my heart in terms of sound and hearing, including echo, resonance, inner dimensions of vibration and inner feeling as the feeling of heart/intuition and the emotional.

Inner feeling may also mean scanning my inner and outer world for input at the level of the heart in a non-attached way. Body-sound, furthermore, includes paying attention to colour and painting in the outside world.

Body-sound is linked to movement in a circular shaped space/practice area, to the field of the 'sacred' and the overall theme of 'prayer, the spiritual, the 'source of life', and facilitates the specific movement quality of 'bowing in praying'.

Candi (Indo); *Candhi* (Jav) ~ Hindu or Buddhist temple or shrine; in Javanese also (ancient) stone structure used as a temple and/or burial place.

Chakra (Indo); *Cakra* ([Jav] lit. 'wheel') ~ Any of several points of physical or spiritual energy in the human body according to *yoga* philosophy; alternatively, psychic organ, occult centre of perception.

Classical Danish Relaxation and Movement, see Prahm, Ingrid.

Dagaba (Skr), see *Stupa*

Dalang (Indo); *Dhalang* (Jav) ~ [Puppeteer and narrator of traditional Javanese shadow puppet plays (*wayang kulit*)].

Dari mana ke mana (Indo) ~ Lit 'from where to where'; is a popular, daily-life greeting in Java, e.g. '*Dari mana?*' [Hello/How are you? – Literally: 'where do you come from?'] and '*Ke mana?*' [Hello/How are you? – Literally: 'where are you going?']

In Java, *Dari mana ke mana* also indicates the philosophy of 'Origin and Destination'; see below, *Sangkan paraning dumadi/Sangkan-paran* (Jav).

Darma (Indo); *Dharma* (Jav) ~ Duty, obligation.

Deva (Skr + Pali) ~ God or spirit

Dhyani **Buddhas** (Skr) ~ Meditation Buddhas.

Dialogue with life ~ Paying attention not only to our own condition and feelings but also to what is going on in other people around us, as well as in the wider environment and in life in general, thereby entering an exchange [a dialogue] between ourselves and our environment. Also, we need to pay attention to the others in the practice space, in order not to bump into each other, just as we also need to be sensitive to the form, material and atmosphere of a place. This is because the movement is improvised in the here and now and anything can happen. Furthermore, I need to see my own movement as taking place within the frame of life in general, not just in terms of my personal life but also that of others, because we are all inter-connected.

Dukun (Indo); ***dhukun*** (Jav) ~ Shaman, native healer, medical practitioner, clairvoyant.

Ethics ~ Traditionally in Java, and in keeping with the Hindu-Buddhist philosophy of life that permeates Javanese thinking, dancing as an art form expresses philosophical concepts (***mataya*** [Jav]), and considers the performance of dance movement as a yogic practice, a kind of an education in the 'art of living'.

For many Javanese, dancing is a means of identification with heroes and heroines embodying their cultural ideals. The highly stylised dances result from the ritual context in which dancing is traditionally practised in Java. Hence, many dances are context-bound; examples are the female ritual court dances named ***Bedhaya,*** the most famous being the ***Bedaya Ketawang,*** see Brakel-Papenhuyzen (1995) and Suharto (1990).

Gamelan (Indo) ~ Traditional Javanese music and orchestra consisting mainly of percussion instruments.

Garden ~ Prapto, [especially during the late 1990s, i.e. after this book], talked about the garden as a mixture of nature and human design or culture, a place for meeting and socialising with a quality of religiosity, joy and freshness, (as Zen gardens) as well, as a place for practising movement in terms of process and instant improvisation, sometimes termed 'garden art'.

Garuda (Indo) ~ The mythical eagle and emblem of the Republic of Indonesia.

Gerak (Indo & Jav) ~ Movement (see also ***bergerak*** to move).

Gerak bebas (Indo) ~ Free movement.

Gerak ngolet [Jav] ~ Stretch movement.

Gerak meditasi (Indo) ~ Movement meditation.

Gerak penyembuhan (Indo) ~ Healing movement.

Gerak tari (Indo) ~ Movement dance.

God ~ In Java, according to the sociologist, N. Mulder (1994, 5-9), god refers both to the more transcendental conceptions of the Middle-Eastern monotheistic religions, such as Islam and Christianity (= Allah or *Tuhan* in Indonesian), and also, as part of Javanese mysticism (**kejawen**), is omnipresent, immanent, non-personal, can be felt in one's inner being and is synonymous with the essence of life; in this sense, god is 'Life Itself', the 'Totality of Existence'' 'The All-Soul' or 'The Numinous'.

Within Amerta Movement, god is the modern god of Islam and Christianity or, for Prapto, the Buddha or also Life, the Totality of Existence as a divine principle, Nature and Reality.

Guru (Indo & Jav) ~ Teacher.

Hasta brata (Jav) The eight ancient virtues or principles for development and for receiving divine blessing (often adapted today to be the key attributes of statesmanship or leadership). See also **wahyu** below:

1) Indra Brata: Indra is God's nature which takes care of everything. With Indra, one tries to meet one's own and other people's basic needs.

2) Yama Brata: Lord Yama is God's power. Brata will punish those who have made mistakes, but helping to teach and repair in the process.

3) Surya Brata: Surya is the sun. Surya motivates and gives strength and makes people aware of their responsibilities.

4) Casi Brata: Casi is the moon. With Casi, one learns to feel comfortable and safe and helps others to do the same.

5) Bayu Brata: Bayu is the wind. Bayu is present, brings freshness and will understand the problems that people face.

6) Dhanaba Brata: Dhanaba relates to wealth and requires us to pay attention to prosperity of all sorts.

7) Paça Brata: Paça refers to Lord Baruna, the Lord of Sea. With Paça comes power from having wide knowledge, wisdom and insight.

8) Agni Brata: with Agni, one is always motivated and can motivate others.

Human evolution ~ With **Messenger Art**, Prapto envisaged an art which is, "… not just for entertainment or aesthetics", but an art which has an impact on society, as well as on the evolution of the human being. This art is not for personal but for collective development, whereby the positive potential of a society may take form and transcend the old one.

For Prapto, **human evolution** was about how society handles nature, the sacred, the planet and ecology, and about how our relations, attitudes to life, ethical values and behaviour, as well as cultural roots, are managed. (Lavelle, 2006: 217).

Jalan-jalan (Indo) ~ 'Walking-walking', Free movement, within Amerta Movement.

Jati diri (Indo) ~ True self.

Joged (Jav) ~ Dance; *Joged Amerta* was Prapto's personal movement work based on Amerta Movement (Lavelle, 2006: 260); *Joged* Mataram is the inner or esoteric aspects of Mataram court dance of Central Java, (Suharto, 1990).

Kinaesthetic sense, see **Proprioception**

Kamadhatu (Jav) ~ The world of desire; at Candi Borobudur, the ground level (most of it is hidden by a wall, except in the south-east corner); *Kamadhatu is* one of the three cosmic worlds (with *Arupadhatu & Rupadhatu*).

Karma (Old Jav) ~ *Karma* in the sense of actions done, relates to how good deeds are rewarded and bad ones punished.

Kejawen (Jav) and *kejawaan* [Indo] ~ derived from traditional Javanese culture based on mystic philosophy and practices. It is linked geographically to the area of the court city of Solo.

For *kejawen* in modern Javanese society, see N. Mulder who describes *kejawen* as, "a cosmology, a mythology, an anthropology, and a mysticism" (1994, xi). Furthermore, he defines it as basically a, "characteristic culturally induced attitude toward life that transcends religious diversity" (1994, 3). This means that people in Central Java might practise both a modern religion like Islam, Christianity or Buddhism and also *kejawen* mysticism where god is a non-personal part of nature. For *Kejawen, see* also online Suryo S. Negoro (1999).

Ketoprak (Indo); *Kethoprak* (Jav) ~ Javanese operatic drama depicting historical or pseudo-historical events; See also *Lesung ketoprak.*

Ketuhanan (Indo & Jav) ~ God, divinity, spirituality, religiosity. See *Tuhan.*

Kinaesthetic sense, ~ see **Proprioception.**

Kraton (Jav) ~ Palace, court.

Lahir (Indo) ~ Material, dimension of outer perception in contrast to the inner, subtler, spiritual dimension (see *batin*).

Laku (Indo *&* Jav, [Lit. 'to walk']) ~ "Ascetic practices for development, such as *kungkum* (submersion in the river), fasting, solitude in sacred places, in caves and on the road without sleeping throughout the night. *Laku* pratices for youths, in general, are actually training for adulthood and a way that an adolescent can be close to and learn from nature." (Prayitno, 1994: 147).

According to Prapto, *laku,* in Javanese, means 'to walk' or to make spiritual retreat. This is because traditional retreats often included walks as pilgrimages in the mountains. The term also implies 'to walk' symbolically i.e. transformation into new developments as when one makes a new step in life. (Prapto found that these transformations in his time must be seen as changes within traditional society itself. They are not transformations as when tradition changes into modernity.) See also **Purification.**

Lemah Putih (Jav) ~ The School of Amerta Movement in the village of Plesungan, Mojosongo district; See also, *Padepokan Lemah Putih.*

Lesung ketoprak (Indo) ~ Popular Javanese operatic drama involving dance and rhythmic music using rice pounders (*lesung*) and dance/movement improvisation.

Lingga-yoni (Old Jav) ~ Symbol of male and female genitalia, as in Candi Sukuh.

'Looking' ~ *see 'Reading'.*

Mahayana ~ A form of Buddhism based on Sanskrit texts which emphasizes the role of the compassionate *Bodhisattva,* (Candi Borobudur is an example)

Mandala (Skr) ~ 'Circle', a Hindu or Buddhist graphic symbol of the Universe; an octagon formed practice platform in the open landscape of the *Lemah Putih* School.

Mantra (Skr) ~ Sacred utterance in Hinduism and Buddhism considered to possess mystical or spiritual efficacy; device for meditation.

Messenger Art ~ Aimed at professional performance art, installations and new ritual art, **Messenger Art,** the second approach to Amerta Movement, also termed The **Dream World** approach, was officially introduced in 1997. The first, approach is *Pribadi Art* or Individual Art or The **Reality** approach,

1986, centred on personal development and expression based on the courses, 'Basic', 'Vocabulary' and 'Communication'. ***Pribadi Art*** is the focus of this book; See **New Rituals** and ***Pribadi Art*** below.

Mudra (Skr) ~ Hand- and finger-gestures indicating different attitudes.

New rituals ~ Rituals based on, or containing, new ingredients in contrast to traditional rituals: examples are,

1. when Prapto applied non-stylised, improvisational Amerta Movement to the traditional shadow puppet theatre (*wayang kulit*). He often used large and unusual sized puppets compared to the traditional ones and took them away from their traditional, fixed place and moved physically with them, i.e. in new areas of the space, as compared to the traditional *wayang kulit*.

2. when Prapto used music not only from the traditional Javanese *gamelan*, as is usual for a *wayang kulit* performance, but also modern Indonesian or other international music, as he did for his Buddhist centred *wayang* creation, *Wayang Budha* (Lavelle et al. 2006).

Overtones An overtone is "any frequency greater than the fundamental frequency of a sound. … When a resonant system such as a blown pipe or plucked string is excited, a number of overtones may be produced along with the fundamental tone." (*Wikipedia*).

Padepokan (Jav) ~ Private art centre/school; (Centre for spirituality, *asram*/residence of a holy man).

Padepokan Lemah Putih (Jav); Abbr, ***PLP*** ~ The Amerta Movement School, lit: The 'White Land School': *lemah* (Jav) [earth]; *putih* (Jav) [white]; *padepokan* (Jav) [art centre/school]. The ***PLP*** was Prapto's movement art school in the northern part of Solo.

Pali ~ [The earliest, holy Buddhist language]. - Buddha lived in the Northern part of India. Buddha's learning in its oral form came to Sri Lanka in the 4th century BCE and was written down a few centuries later. The first version of the holy writing in Theravada Buddhism was written down in *Pali*.

Pamong (Jav) ~ Meditation-guide in **Sumarah** meditation movement; (government official).

Pamudaran (Jav) ~ Liberation; in Prapto's terms: 'no boundary' / 'no binding'; (see Lavelle, 2006).

Pencak silat (Indo) ~ Indonesian martial arts.

Pendopo (Indo); ***Pendhapa*** (Jav) ~ Open, square formed hall/structure of Javanese architectural design; practice hall. (In the village it is for public use, for ceremonies and the performing arts; attached to a private home, it serves as a private room for the reception of guests).

Person-specific ~ I coined this term to complement the well-known term and concept, **'site-specific'.** It indicates free, non-stylised, improvised movement expression, characteristic of, related to, and determined by the individual Amerta Movement practitioner's specific body (structure and functions), mind and spirit from one moment to the next in a dialogue with co-practitioners, the site of practice and whole environment the in the present moment.

Prahm, Ingrid, ~ former Royal Danish ballet dancer (d. 1995), one of the pioneers of 'Classical Danish Relaxation and Movement pedagogy', as this arose in Denmark from the 1930s onwards. At her school, 'the Ingrid Prahm Seminarium of Relaxation and Movement', her techniques of relaxation and movement were taught in a 3-year training programme. She collaborated with other experts in the field, including Moshe Feldenkrais, Gerda Alexander, founder of *Eutony,* and the Norwegian pioneer, Lillemor Johnsen.

Pribadi (Indo & Jav) ~ In Indonesian ***pribadi*** translates as 'individual' or 'personal', and in Javanese as, 'alone' in the sense of standing on one's own/on one's own feet. The latter definition is the one especially stressed within Amerta Movement, though it is always seen in relation to, nature, the Almighty/the Sacred, and society.

This book focuses particularly on ***Pribadi Art***, which is not a therapy, but a contemporary art of life, an ongoing practice for human development through enhanced awareness and sensitivity, as well as through the practitioner relating and communicating with co-practitioners, the site and the whole environment; (See also **Messenger Art** above).

Programming ~ Earlier learnt patterns of movement running as an automatic program in our body, when we move freely. An example is the sitting posture in the Chinese movement art of *tai chi,* or in martial arts, where practitioners also tend to move with legs bent – unconsciously reproduced when moving 'freely'. These forms of programming can be released by 'de-coding' or 'de-programming' oneself, through awareness.

Proprioception ~ The kinaesthetic sense is also termed *proprioception,* which is the Latin term for one's own sensory perceptions from muscles and joints. Proprioceptive information tells the brain when and how muscles contract and are stretched. Moreover, it tells the brain when and how the joints bend, are straightened, stretched or pressed together. This information enables the brain, i.e. the practitioner, to know where each part of the body is situated and how it moves in a space. Hence, **proprioception** (the kinaesthetic sense) helps people to move in a space, yes is necessary for this to happen smoothly.

Purification ~ According to Prapto, in order to express ourselves and to create a vocabulary, based on our life and nature in the present moment, purification of self is needed. This means students' movement should originate from what he called their 'genuine being' or 'true self'. Prapto said the human body, at the outset of movement practice, is normally dominated by desire so that our 'readings', our perceptions of ourselves and of the environment, are unclear. So it is essential, as part of the process of physical practice, that my body (body-mind-spirit) be purified, turning it into a clear mirror to reflect my physical, emotional, mental and spiritual condition. This is achieved through awareness and sensitivity. Prapto compared this purification process of the individual mover to the Javanese tradition of undertaking spiritual retreats in the wild. Also see, **Tapa brata** below.

Rasa (Indo and Jav) ~ Feeling, sensing, intuition, essence; *Rasa* is the tool whereby one receives or experiences all aspects of life, including those beyond one's conscious mind and five senses, i.e. also mystical experience; *Rasa* is the reception function and the essence of the whole human body and, in Amerta Movement, is seen as constantly moving within the whole body.

Ritual & Rite de passage ~ "His, [Prapto's] expression of ritual is not a pre-determined sequence of events, but more like a continuous improvisation in response to the subtle flows of the 'movement of life' " … "Prapto simply remains open and attentive to the essence of ritual itself, the conscious awareness of the rite de passage as it evolves from moment to moment." (Kemp-Welsh, 2001).

'Reading' ~ For acquiring consciousness, Prapto used a technique he called **'reading'** which is unique to Amerta Movement. It is inspired by Borobudur Temple. The monks of former times, by circulating in the aisles of the temple, were studying ('reading') its reliefs. By so doing they were brought to higher insights and knowledge of the Buddhist religion as they advanced towards the temple's top. In Amerta Movement, **reading** means using the whole body as a neutral instrument for receiving and giving information about oneself and one's surroundings. The term 'reading' was introduced in the early 1990s. The technique itself had, however, existed from the practice's beginning and was sometimes termed **'looking'** (i.e. 'looking' with the body, mind and feelings').

Rupadhatu (Jav) ~ 'The world of form'; at Candi Borobudur ***Rupadhatu*** is today the lowest level to which the visitor has access. It represents one of the three cosmic worlds (see also, ***Arupadhatu*** and ***Kamadhatu***).

Sakti (Indo & Jav / Skr) ~ Powerful, supernatural, holy.

Sangkan paraning dumadi/Sangkan paran (Jav) ~ The philosophy of 'Origin and Destination' in Java: that we all come from and return to a common spiritual source of life; See also, ***Dari mana ke mana.***

Seni (Indo) ~ Art.

Srawung (Old Jav / Jav) ~ Together/Socialise, as in, *Srawung Seni,* Sharing Art.

Stupa (Skr), (also called a ***dagaba***[37]) ~ Reliquary, a usually dome-shaped structure or mound serving as a Buddhist shrine.

Sudarno Ong ~ ***Pamong,*** meditation guide, within the **Sumarah** meditation movement; teacher of Prapto

Sufi, Sufism ~ Islamic mystic, mysticism.

Suhu (Chinese) ~ Master of self-defence, healer.

Sumarah (Jav) ~ The verb literally means, 'to surrender', or 'to accept' in the sense of recognising reality, i.e. recognising the state of affairs of a situation, whether pleasant or unpleasant;

The noun Sumarah, in this book, refers to the Sumarah meditation movement, where people from different religious backgrounds practise meditation together, based on a relaxed attitude to body and mind. Formerly, Prapto practised Sumarah, especially with the ***pamong,*** Sudarmo Ong. Several Amerta Movement practitioners in the 21st century are Sumarah practitioners.

Tapa (Indo & Jav) ~ Spiritual retreat with ascetic practice and meditation, especially in order to acquire power and blessing.

Tapa brata (Skr) ~ Spiritual retreat with ascetic practice and meditation (a higher form than ***tapa***); to live as an ascetic; to meditate to acquire power and blessing. There are no ascetic exercises in Amerta Movement.

---

[37] The word *dagaba* is a combination of the Sanskrit *dhatu* (relic) and *garba* (womb, chamber, receptable). The implication is that the relics, planted in the womb of the structure like a quickening seed, exert an animating influence on this seemingly dead mass of masonry, generating and perpetuating for all time and for all men the spiritual power of the Buddha. (Hoadley, 1998)

Tari (Indo) ~ Dance.

Theravada (Pali*)* ~ *Theravada* is a name for *Hinayana,* a 'low church' form of Buddhism based on texts in the *Pali* language. This group stresses the role of the individual in seeking liberation, (Rawson, 1995: 285).

Tuhan (Indo & Jav) ~ God, Allah / (***Tuhan Yang Maha Esa*** (Old Jav), [god who is all in one]; or god as a divine being in the modern personalised sense. See also **God**.

Vajra *(*Skr*)* ~ symbolises the highest truth as a diamond, thunderbolt or phallus.

Vajrayana (Skr) ~ The Diamond way in Buddhist teachings, focused on the cult of the *Vajra,* - best understood as an evolution of Mahayana Buddhism.

Vihara (Pali) ~ Buddhist monastery or nunnery.

Waisak* (Wesak)* (Pali; Skr) ~ Festival, holiday commemorating the Buddha's birth, enlightenment and passing.

Wayang (Jav) ~ Traditional drama, referring to the Javanese shadow puppet theatre, *wayang kulit*, with flat leather puppets.

Wahyu (Jav) ~ Divine revelation, blessing of cosmic power descending from 'God'. In former times, in Java, it was only the king, queen or statesmen who could receive divine blessing ['***wahyu***'] directly from god. Peasants or common people had to go via the king's palace (**kraton**) to receive divine blessing. In some ways this mechanism still plays a role in Central Java [at the end of the 20th century], according to Prapto, who wanted to create a kind of democracy within spirituality, so that everyone can receive divine blessing directly from the Supreme Being. To the eight nature-elements or rules and principles for development and for receiving divine blessing, (see **hasta brata** above), Prapto added a ninth, **ndaru** (Jav), which indicates a divine blessing on nature from a power superior to the natural order. This ninth element (**nawa brata** [Jav]) is crucial, because it adds to nature philosophy as practised traditionally in Java a divine principle like the Holy Spirit or God in a Western sense. Unlike the **hasta brata**, the eight rules, this new element is not part of nature. Rather, it comes to nature from outside or from above. In this way, Prapto's nature-view differed from the traditional Javanese one where the divine principle is part of nature and is seen as being both inside and outside a human being at the same time.

Bibliography

Alisjahbana, T. (1980) *Perempuan di Persimpangan Zaman: Kumpulan sajak [Woman at The Crossroads: A collection of poems]*, Dian Rakyat

Amerta Movement in Lemah Putih 1995-1996 (1995) Padepokan Lemah Putih. [Programme of the 'Vocabulary, Nature and Life' course 1995-1996]

Anderson, B.R. O'G. (1965) *Mythology and the Tolerance of the Javanese*, Cornell University Press

Asma, T. (1978) 'The Megalithic Tradition', in H. Soebadio and C. du Marchie Sarvaas (eds), *Dynamics of Indonesian history*, North-Holland

Barba, E. (1999) 'Tacit Knowledge: Heritage and Waste', Working-paper for the symposium on occasion of the 35th anniversary of Odin Teatret, J. Barba, (transl.), Nordisk Teaterlaboratorium, (xeroxed)

Barba, E. and Savarese, N. (1995) *A Dictionary of Theatre Anthropology: The secret art of the performer*, Routledge

Barlow, W. (1979 [1973]) *The Alexander Principle: The revolutionary technique that has helped thousands*, Anchor Press

Becker, J. (1980) *Traditional Music in Modern Java: Gamelan in a changing society*, University Press of Hawaii

Bentsen, B.S. (1991) *Børnemotorik: Udvikling og sammenhæng* [Childrens' Motorics: Development and coherence], 6th ed, Gyldendal

Bloom, K, Galanter, M. and Reeve, S. (eds) (2014) *Embodied Lives: Reflections on the influence of Suprapto Suryodarmo and Amerta Movement*, Triarchy Press

Bloom, K. (2006) *The Embodied Self: Movement and psychoanalysis*, Karnac Books

Blossoming in Europe (1998) Padepokan Lemah Putih, [Programme of Amerta Movement in Europe 1998]

Bodrogi, T. (1972) *L'Art de l'Indonésie* [*The Art of Indonesia*], Editions Cercle d'Art

Borobudur Archaeological Park Indonesia (1991) Taman Wisata Candi Borobudur, Prambanan and Ratu Boko, (pamphlet)

Brakel-Papenhuyzen, C. (1995) *Classical Javanese Dance: The Surakarta tradition and its terminology*, KITLV Press

Brakel-Papenhuyzen, C. and Ngaliman, S. (1991) *Seni Tari Jawa: Tradisi Surakarta dan peristilihannya* [Javanese Dance, The Surakarta tradition and its terminology], Jakarta: ILDEP-RUL [Series, Indonesian publications]

Brieghel-Müller, G. (1979 [1972]) *Eutonie et Relaxation: détente corporelle et mentale*, 2nd ed, Delachaux et Niestlé

Buckwalter, M. (2010) *Composing while Dancing: An improviser's companion*, University of Wisconsin Press

Carey, P. (2007) *The power of Prophecy: Prince Dipanagara and the end of an old order in Java, 1785-1855*, KITLV Press

Cornu, P. (2001) *Dictionnaire Encyclopédique du Bouddhisme*, Éditions du Seuil

Cribb, R. (2000) *Historical Atlas of Indonesia*, Curzon Press

______ (1992) *Historical Dictionary of Indonesia*, Scarecrow Press

Csordas, T.J. (1993) 'Somatic Modes of Attention', *Cultural Anthropology* 8(2): 135-156, American Anthropological Society

Echols, J.M, and Shadily, H. (1996 [1976]) *Kamus Inggris-Indonesia, An English-Indonesian dictionary*, Cornell University Press; Gramedia Pustaka Utama

Echols, J.M, Shadily, H., Collins, J.T. and Wolff, J.U. (1994 [1961]) *Kamus Indonesia-Inggris: An Indonesian-English dictionary*, 3rd ed, Cornell University Press; Gramedia Pustaka Utama

Endraningsih, D. (1995) *Tinjauan Konsep Gerak Meditasi Suprapto* [Observations of Suprapto's Movement-Meditation Concept], [B.A. essay], STSI Indonesian National Arts Institute Surakarta in Solo, (xeroxed)

Geertz, C. (1976 [1960]) *The Religion of Java*, Free Press of Glencoe

Ghulam-Sarwar, Y. (1994) *Dictionary of Traditional South-East Asian Theatre*, Oxford University Press

Haerdter, M. and Kawai, S. (eds) (1988) *Butoh: Die Rebellion des Körpers: Ein Tanz aus Japan*, Alexander Verlag

Hahn, T. (2007) *Sensational Knowledge: Embodying culture through Japanese dance*, Wesleyan University Press

Hamilton-Merritt, J. (2012 [1976]) *A Meditator's Diary: A western woman's unique experiences in Thailand monasteries*, Souvenir Press

Hanna, T. (1988 [1928]) *Somatics: Reawakening the mind's control of movement, flexibility, and health*, Perseus Books

Hausgjerd, S. (1975) 'Preface', in (L. Johnsen 1975)

Heine-Geldern, R. (1993, [1956]) *Conceptions of State and Kingship in Southeast Asia*, Cornell University, Southeast Asia Program, (Data Paper, 18)

Helgesen, G, and Thomsen, S.R. (eds) (2006) *Politics, Culture and Self: East Asian and North European attitudes*, NIAS Press

Hellman, J. (2004) *Performing the Nation: Cultural politics in New Order Indonesia*, RoutledgeCurson (Monograph series, Nordic Institute of Asian Studies, 89)

Hoadley, A.-G. N. (2005) *Indonesian Literature vs New Order Orthodoxy: The aftermath of 1965-1966*, NIAS Press

Hoadley, M.C. and A.-G. N. Hoadley (1996) 'Developing Indonesia's Village Co-operative', in M.C. Hoadley and C. Gunnarsson (eds), *The Village Concept in the Transformation of Rural Southeast Asia*, pp. 183-201, Curzon Press

Hoadley, M.C. (1998) *Southeast Asian History 800-1800: Parochial v. cosmopolitan*, Mega, Southeast Asia

Holt, C. (1967) *Art in Indonesia: Continuities and change*, Cornell University Press

Howe, D.G. (1980) *Sumarah: A study of the art of living*, PhD dissertation, University of North Carolina at Chapel Hill, (unpublished), (ebook 1980)

Howell, J.D. (1987) 'Origins of the Hindu Renaissance in Java: Monism in the early writings of W. Hardjanto Pradjapangarsa', in *Religious Traditions: A New Journal in the Study of Religion* 10: 107-133

Iyer, A. (a.k.a. Lopez y Royo, A.) (2004) 'Choreographing Heritage, Performing the Site' [online], pp. 1-12, http://bit.ly/TProots10

______ (1996a) 'South Asian and Southeast Asian performing arts: reassessing convergence, divergence and continuities', *Aditi News*, November, pp. 8-9

______ (1996b) 'Dance Review, Javanese dance at SOAS', *Aditi News*, Nov, p. 12

Jodjana (1981) *A Book of Self Re-Education: The structure and functions of the human body as an instrument of expression*, Camelot Press

Johnsen, L (1975) *Integrert Respirasjonsterapi, En Nøkkel til Livsgledens Skjulte Kilde: Om Menneskets Psykofysiske Utvikling - åndedrettet- respirasjon - kropp og psyke* [*Integrated Respiration Therapy: A key to the hidden source of the joy of life: About the human being's psycho-physical development - breath - respiration - body and psyche*], Universitetsforlaget

Jung, C.G. and Jaffé, A. (ed.) (1993 [1967]) *Memories, Dreams, Reflections*, (transl. from German), Fontana Press

Kartini and Geertz, H. (ed.) (1976) *Letters of a Javanese Princess*, (transl. from Dutch), Heinemann Educational Books

Kemp-Welsh, A. (a.k.a. Pitty, A.) (2001) 'Rituals of Chaos: The movement work of Suprapto Suryodarmo', in A. Iyer (ed.), *Contemporary Theatre Review* 11 (2): 55-68

Koentjaraningrat (1985) *Javanese Culture*, Oxford University Press

Krinsley, E. (2001) *A Selected Overview of Intercultural Performance Practitioners, Mainstream and Non-Mainstream, East and West*, M.A. thesis, University of Woolongong, Australia, (xeroxed)

Kumar, A. (1997) *Java and Modern Europe: Ambiguous encounters*, Curzon Press

Kussudiarjo, B. (1995). 'Gerak Ngolet Soeprapto' [Suprapto's Stretch Movement], *Gatra*, [Indonesian magazine], 23rd Sept., p. 76

König, M. (1997) *Theater als Lebensweise - Theater als Ethnologie: Der indonesische Regisseur Boedi S. Otong*, Gunter Narr (Forum Modernes Theater. Schriftenreihe, Band 23)

Lavelle, L. (2017) 'Embodied Encounters: Identities in Experiential, Informal Dance and Movement in Central Java' [online], in C. Svendler Nielsen and S.R. Koff (eds), *Exploring Identities in Dance: Proceedings from the 13th World Congress of Dance and the Child International, University of Copenhagen*, http://bit.ly/TProots01

______ (2015) 'An Approach to an Improvised, Practice-based Healing Performance as a Rite de passage' [online], in *Expanding Notions: Dance/Practice/Research/Method: [Proceedings] 12th International NOFOD Conference, Reykjavik, 2015*, pp. 42-44 http://bit.ly/TProots03

______ (2014) 'Crystallization-Performance: A new expression in its own right', in K. Bloom, M. Galanter and S. Reeve (eds), *Embodied Lives: Reflections on the influence of Suprapto Suryodarmo and Amerta Movement*, pp. 127-136, Triarchy Press

______ (2013) 'Successfully coping with change without losing roots: Suprapto Suryodarmo and Joged Amerta Movement' [online], in C.A. Woodrich, F. Dhont (eds), *International Indonesia Forum, 2013, Working Paper Series, Vol. 3.* (Proceedings of the 6th IIF Conference) http://bit.ly/TProots04

______ (2011) [workshop] 'Reading Inner and Outer Space in Amerta Movement Improvisation: A technique for composing while moving', [online], in S. Ravn (ed.), *Spacing Dance(s) - Dancing Space(s): Proceedings, 10th Int. NOFOD Conference, Odense, 2011*, pp. 276-283 http://bit.ly/TProots05

______ (2009) 'Embodying the present moment: Basic features of an Asian movement improvisation', in L. Rouhiainen (ed.), *Dance - Movement - Mobility: Proceedings, 9th Int. NOFOD Conference, Tampere, 2009*, pp. 106-113. Abstract [online] http://bit.ly/TProots06 {accessed 27th Nov. 2018]

_____ (2006) *Amerta Movement of Java 1986-1997: An Asian Movement Improvisation*, PhD dissertation, Centre for Languages and Literature, Lund University. Abstract [online] http://bit.ly/TProots07

_____ (2001) 'Bevægelse: En praksis i nuet' [Movement: A practice in the present], in J.R. Schomacker (ed.), *5. Nordiske Danseforskerkonference: Rapport: afholdt 27-30. Jan 2000 på Københavns Universitet Amager*, NOFOD, pp. 92-97

_____ (2000) 'My Encounter with Odin Teatret', in K. Kowalewicz (ed.), *Meetings with the Odin Teatret*, University of Lodz, Chair of Sociology of Culture, pp. 57–65 (Anthropology, Sociology, Theatre Series)

Lilja, E. (2015) *Art, Research, Empowerment: On the artist as researcher*, Regeringskansliet, Ministry of Education and Research

Magnis-Suseno, F. (1996) *Etika Jawa: Sebuah analisa falsafi tentang kebijaksanaan hidup Jawa* [The Ethics of Java: An analysis of the philosophy of the wisdom of life in Java], Gramedia Pustaka Utama

Moertono, S. (1968) *State and Statecraft in Old Java: A study of the Later Mataram Period, 16th to 19th Century*, Southeast Asia Program, Cornell University (Modern Indonesia Project)

Morein, A. (1994) 'A Practice Called 'Road': 'Movement in Meditation' with Suprapto Suryodarmo in Central Java, Indonesia', *Contact Quarterly* 19 (1): 29-31

Mulder, N. (1994 [1989]) *Individual and Society in Java: A cultural analysis*, 2nd rev. edn, Gadjah Mada University Press

Negoro, S. S. 'Padepokan Lemah Putih' [online], in *Joglosemar, Sangga Sarana Persada*, 1997-2000 http://bit.ly/TProots08

_____ 'Kejawen, a Javanese traditional spiritual teaching' [online], in *Joglosemar, Sangga Sarana Persada*, http://bit.ly/TProots09

Nyanavajiro, A. (1977) *Buddhism in Theory and Practice*, Young Buddhist Association of Malaysia

_____ (n.d). *Meditation: The Buddha's Way and other talks*, Malaysian Buddhist Meditation Centre

_____ (n.d). *What is Buddhism? A brief introduction to the teachings of the Lord Buddha*, Hudson Enterprises

Pemberton, J. (1994) *On the Subject of 'Java'*, Cornell University Press

Perlez, J. (2003) 'Mall would desecrate Buddhist site, critics say', *New York Times*, 9 March

Pitty, A. (a.k.a. Kemp-Welsh, A.) (1994) 'Embodiment: The Shadow and Spiritual Emergence in the Moving Body', Essay, Core Process Psychotherapy studies, Great Britain, March, (xeroxed)

Prawiroatmodjo. S. (1989–1992) *Bausastra Jawa-Indonesia* [Javanese-Indonesian Dictionary], 2 Vols, Haji Masagung

Prayitno, A.B. (2014), 'Mantra Gerak' in (Bloom et al. 2014) pp. 147-156

______ (1989) *Sketsa Penelitian Gerak Pamudaran Ki Suprapto Suryodarmo, Padepokan Lemah Putih di Surakarta, Pereode Juni–Juli–Augustus 1989,* [Research Draft of the Movement of Liberation of Master Suprapto Suryodarmo, Padepokan Lemah Putih, Surakarta, Period, June-July-August, 1989, ed. and published by the author, (xeroxed)

Pujangga Surakarta [The Surakarta Literati], (1991) *Serat Dewaruci: Kidung dari bentuk kakawin* [The Dewaruci Epistle: A ballad from old Javanese poetry], Dahara Prize

Ramelan, K. (1995) 'Kejawen tanpa Hanacaraka' [Kejawen without the Javanese Alphabet], *Gatra* [Indonesian magazine], 23rd Sept., p. 76

Ravn, S. (2009) 'The pre-reflective performative body of dancers', in L. Rouhiainen (ed.), *Dance – Movement – Mobility: Proceedings, 9th International NOFOD Conference, Tampere, Finland, October 23-26 2008*, pp. 139-144. Abstract [online]: http://bit.ly/TProots06 [accessed 27th Nov 2018]

______ (2008) *Sensing Movement, Living Spaces: An investigation of movement based on the lived experience of 13 professional dancers*, PhD dissertation, Dept of Sports Science and Clinical Biomechanics, Faculty of Health Sciences, University of Southern Denmark

Rawson, P. (1995 [1967]) *The Art of Southeast Asia: Cambodia, Vietnam, Thailand, Laos, Burma, Java, Bali*, Thames and Hudson

Reeve, S. (ed.) (2021) *Body and Awareness (Ways of Being a Body, Vol. 3)*, Triarchy Press

______ (ed.) (2013) *Body and Performance (Ways of Being a Body, Vol. 2)*, Triarchy Press

______ (2011) *Nine Ways of Seeing a Body (Ways of Being a Body, Vol. 1)*, Triarchy Press

______ (2008) *The Ecological Body*, PhD dissertation, University of Exeter

______ (1997) *Cultural Movement: Response to the World Commission on Culture and Development, Our Creative Diversity*, published by the author, (xeroxed)

Ricklefs, M.C. (1998) *The Seen and the Unseen Worlds in Java 1726–1749: History, Literature and Islam in the Court of Pakubuwana II*, University of Hawai'i Press

______ (1990) *A History of Modern Indonesia; c. 1300*, Macmillan

Santoso, S. (1985) *Cerita sang Garuda: The Story of Garuda*, Citra Jaya Murti Surabaya in association with Surakarta Municipality Tourism Office

Sartono, F. (1996) *Suhu Padepokan Lemah Putih* [The Master of the Padepokan Lemah Putih], Interview with Suprapto Suryodarmo, *Jakarta-Jakarta*, 27 April-3 *May*, pp. 58-65

Sawega, A.M. (1994) 'Suprapto Suryodarmo', *Kompas* [Indonesian Newspaper] 17 April

Sbeghen, J.-A. M. (2004) *An analysis of the sculpture of Candi Sukuh in Central Java: its meanings and religious functions 1437-1443 C.E*, PhD dissertation, School of Languages and Comparative Cultural Studies, University of Queensland, Australia, (unpublished)

Soebadio, H. (1978) 'Indian Religions in Indonesia', in H. Soebadio and C.A. du Marchie Sarvaas, (eds), *Dynamics of Indonesian History*, North Holland Publishing

Soedarsono (1974) *Dances in Indonesia*, Gunung Agung

Soekmono (1976) *Candi Borobudur: A monument of mankind*. The UNESCO Press

Stange, P. (1994) 'Silences in Solonese Dance Production', *Southeast Asian Journal of Social Sciences* 22: 210-229

______ (1986) 'Legitimate Mysticism in Indonesia', *Review of Indonesian and Malayan Affairs* 20: 2:76-117

______ (1984) 'The logic of Rasa in Java', *Indonesia* 38 (Oct): 113-134

______ (1980) *The Sumarah Movement in Javanese Mysticism*, PhD dissertation, University of Wisconsin, (unpublished)

______ (1979) 'Configurations of Javanese Possession Experience', *Religious Traditions, A Journal in the Study of Religion* 2 (2): 39-54

______ (1977a) *Selected Sumarah Teachings*, (transl, ed, & introduced), Perth, Western Australian Institute of Technology, Dept of Asian Studies, (xeroxed)

______ (1977b) 'Mystical Symbolism in Javanese Wayang Mythology', *The South East Asian Review* 1(2): 109-122

Stelzer, C. (ed.) (1987a) *Talking about Walking*, Kemongo (xeroxed)

______ (ed.) (1987b) *A Small Group but Dynamic*, self-published (xeroxed)

Stempel-Thul, C. (1992) *Suprapto Suryodarmo: Portrait of a Javanese movement teacher*, Paper, Murdoch University, Australia (xeroxed)

Sudarko (1991) *Serat Pedhalangan. Lampahan Dewaruci* [Puppeteer's Manual of the Dewaruci Wayang Performance], Cendrawasih

Suharto, B. (1990) *Dance Power: The concept of Mataya in Yogyakarta dance*, M.A. thesis, University of California

Suryodarmo, S. (1998) 'An Idea', Enclosure, in 'Web Art Garden UK', by Sandra Reeve, circular letter, Web Art Garden UK ACE Project Office

Trungpa, C. and J. Baker, M. Casper (eds) (1988 [1976]) *The Myth of Freedom and the Way of Meditation*, Shambhala

______ (1987 [1973]) *Cutting Through Spiritual Materialism*, Shambala

Ulbricht, H. (1970) *Wayang Purwa: Shadows of the past*, Oxford University Press

Watters, Jo. (1994) 'Moving Mother', *Kindred Spirit* 3(6): 18-20

Wickert, J. D. (1988) *Borobudur*, Intermasa

Video-recordings (Off-Air)

Vocabulary, Nature and Life, Nov 14. 1995 - Jan 11, 1996, Legoretta, G, Solo, 1996, (private video). [video VHS]

Sharing Time, Cologne [Healing Theatre, Cologne], (1993), (3 tapes). 1. *Practice-Tape*, 2. *Performance-Tape* and 3. *Celebration-Tape*, mit Schlussworten [with commentaries] von Suprapto Suryodarmo, Hiltrud Cordes, Michael Dick [*und* Günther Heitzmann, Cologne, produced by Blume, R. [video VHS, Pal, Secam]

Pagelaran Dari Kelompok Lemah Putih (1988) [Informal Presentations by the Lemah Putih Group], Crystallizations entitled: 1. '*Hello Misterrr!*' 2. '*Can I Speak to you?* and 3. '*Hausgeiser* [Housespirits], *A Couple On The Road*, TBS (*Taman Budaya* Surakarta Art Centre) in Solo, [video VHS, Pal, Secam]

[*Movement Practice. Padepokan Lemah Putih*] (1987), TBS, (the Taman Budaya Surakarta Art Centre) Solo, [video VHS, Pal, Secam]

Video recordings illustrating Amerta Movement

The video tape of 1987, entitled *Movement Practice. Padepokan Lemah Putih*, recorded by the TBS in Solo, gives a good picture of the fundamentals of the free Amerta Movement as it started up in Lemah Putih. This is done without music and with just the natural sounds of life in the village according to practice at the time.

The 1988 tape *Pagelaran Dari Kelompok Lemah Putih* [Informal Presentation by the Lemah Putih Group] is also recorded by the TBS in Solo. It shows some of the first efforts to use Prapto's free movement as a language in improvised 'performance'. I consider the 1987 and the 1988 tapes as invaluable documents recording some of the first decisive steps in Amerta Movement.

In treating the Vocabulary Course 1995-1996, observations based on the video recording entitled *Vocabulary, Nature and Life,* Nov 14, 1995 - Jan 11, 1996, by García Legoretta, a dancer and a teacher/dialoguer of Amerta Movement – have also been included.

I have also used material from the three video recordings of Healing Theatre's Sharing Time art festival, Cologne, 1993, by Renée Blume. These recordings contain valuable information both on Amerta Movement and on what is a Sharing Time festival, showing the practice itself and the atmosphere in which it takes place. The three video recordings also include interviews with Prapto and some of the participants and relate nearly all of the activities inspired by Prapto's movement work at the time.

Unfortunately some of the recordings of the above mentioned tapes, especially the ones made in Indonesia, are poor quality.

All the video recordings were taken at events in which I took part, although not necessarily being present at every activity. These videos have been used to support my memory and to provide another look at the events. Some of the videos are privately produced and owned. They are kept in the possession of producers, such as García Legoretta in Mexico and Renée Blume in Cologne.

Amerta Movement courses and other programmes taking place at the Lemah Putih School have been recorded by the TBS in Solo, which holds the copyrights and they could/can be viewed at their video library. In addition there are video recordings which constitute part of Prapto's Private library. The Lemah Putih School, as far as is known, does not yet have a documentation library.

The Indonesian National Arts Institute in Solo (STSI) at the end of the 20th century, had its own library and documentation centre containing cassette tapes and video recordings of students' musical compositions and visual performances. Also TBS in Solo housed its own documentation centre, a video library with video recordings of performances.

Also available from Triarchy Press:

Suomenlinna | Gropius – Paula Kramer, a student of Prapto's Amerta Movement, offers two beautiful, evocative and touching 'contemplations' which take us on a double journey that starts with Site (one in Helsinki, one in Berlin), moves to Practice and concludes in Performance.

Based on a 3-year site-specific research project – a post-doc at Uniarts Helsinki's Centre for Artistic Research – the book explores Paula's embodied research into intermateriality. It reflects on the ways in which bodies, materials, sites, organisms, history, tuning, training, phenomena, events and the weather intermingle and speak, bringing forth what we later might call movement, dance or choreography.

RockSongs – Nick Sales, a student of Prapto's Amerta Movement, crystallises into book form a year-long writing/movement/performance project working with the river Sawdde above Rhydsaint in Wales.

Incorporating Dōgen's *Mountains and Waters Sūtra*, the journeys of George Borrow and the kites, otters, stones and flow of the riverscape, Nick explores the many ways in which land, history, legend, human and other animals permeate and shape one another – and shows graphically how that intermingling can be represented by the body, mind and spirit moving.

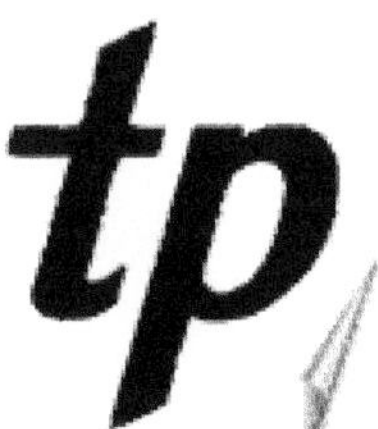

For more details of these and other titles, please visit:
www.triarchypress.net/movement

The Roots of Amerta Movement

The Javanese movement artist Suprapto Suryodarmo (universally known as Prapto) died in 2019. He had devoted his life to developing, embodying, teaching and sharing his practice of Amerta Movement / *Joged Amerta*, which, in his own words, is not only a language for communication but also an expression of being.

In the course of his life, Prapto worked with students and colleagues (people from all walks of life, including internationally-known artists, performers, practitioners and teachers, all of whom he treated equally as 'friends') in sacred, ancient and mundane sites around the world. He never attempted to write down his practice, although he encouraged many 'friends' to spread the word and the practice, sharing their own understandings of his work widely.

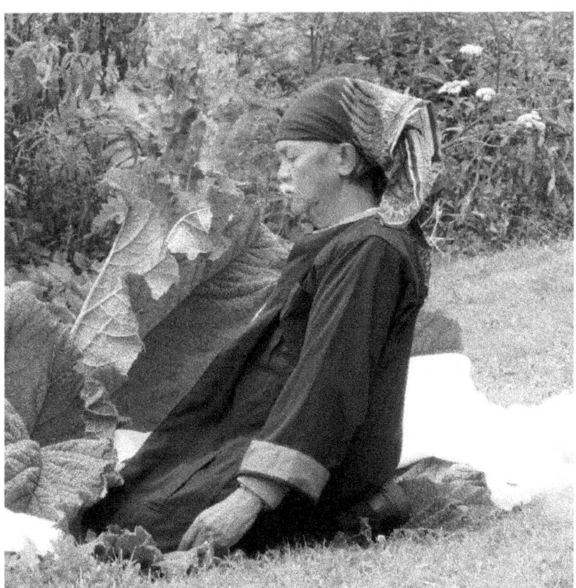

This book, covering the early years of Prapto's teaching, is the closest there is to a record of that period of his work in English. It is a radically revised, updated and edited version of Lise Lavelle's doctoral thesis and draws on her unrivalled knowledge of the culture, language, art, religion and traditions of Java – the pot in which Prapto's life, work and practice were cooked.

While *Amerta Movement* continued to evolve during this century, *The Roots of Amerta Movement* offers a clear and many-layered introduction. For anyone wanting to know more about Prapto and his work, it is a very good place to start.